3R+   1198

D0249140

Learn Faster &
Remember More

How New and Old Brains
Acquire & Recall Information

*There's rosemary, that's for remembrance; and
there is pansies, that's for thoughts.*
— Hamlet

Learn Faster &
Remember More

The Developing Brain, The Maturing Years
and The Experienced Mind

by

David Gamon, Ph.D.

and

Allen D. Bragdon

The Brainwaves Center
Cape Cod

Brainwaves Books, a division of
Allen D. Bragdon Publishers, Inc.
252 Great Western Road
South Yarmouth, MA 02664

Copyright © 2001 by Allen D. Bragdon Publishers, Inc.
All rights reserved. No part of this book may be reproduced in any
manner whatsoever without the written permission of the publisher

Design and editorial production: Carolyn Zellers
Editing: Wallace Exman and Carol M. Barker
Proofreading: Vida Morris
Graphics: David Zellers
Index: Michael Loo

Drawings by Malcolm Wells
Cover design by Carolyn Zellers.

Some images reproduced with permission of LifeArt Collection Images,
copyright © 1989-99 TechPOOL Studios, Cleveland, OH. Some images
copyright © 2001 www.arttoday.com. "The Little King" pages 22 and
27, copyright © 1933, 1961 by Otto Soglow. Reprinted by permission
of Henry Holt & Co., Inc. Photograph of *Aplysia Californica*, page 101,
printed with permission of Caroline Schooley, Fort Bragg, CA.

Library of Congress Catalog Number: 2001117821

ISBN 0-916410-79-X

Printed in the United States of America

01 02 03   10 9 8 7 6 5 4 3 2 1

ALSO BY THE AUTHORS

Building Mental Muscle
Conditioning Exercises for the Six Intelligence Zones

Building Left-Brain Power
Neuron-Strengthening Exercises and Tips
to Improve Mood and Develop Language and Math Skills

Brains That Work a Little Bit Differently
Recent Discoveries About Common Mental Diversities

Use It or Lose It!
How to Keep Your Brain Fit as It Ages

Brain-Building Games
Three Months to Sharper Skills

Exercises for the Whole Brain
Neuron-Builders to Stimulate and Entertain
Your Visual, Math and Executive-Planning Skills

How Sharp Is Your Pencil?
Can You Pass Any of These 45 Real-Life
Professional and Academic Exams?

Visit their Website at
www.brainwaves.com

TABLE OF CONTENTS

9 Introduction/Anatomy/Glossary The brain's basic tools for perceiving useful information, organizing it, committing it to memory and recalling it

I THE DEVELOPING BRAIN
The third trimester through high school

17 Learning in the Womb 🐛 Evolution has endowed human babies with an incredible ability to learn

22 The Eyes Have It 🐛 How children learn to read minds

28 Babies Are Self-Taught Linguists 🐛 Teach your baby grammar? Don't bother; brush up on your own

34 An Early Sign of Intelligence 🐛 Is my two-year-old a genius?

40 Language Learning 🐛 Reasons why a child may lag behind the normal timetable

48 Neglect 🐛 The worst form of abuse for learning

55 Self-Consciousness 🐛 The terrible twos

61 The Deceiving Brain 🐛 Very likely, a three-year-old really *does* remember seeing a reindeer on the roof

66 Temperamental Limitations 🐛 The poker hand an infant's genome deals it

72 Parenting 🐛 The three key ways to teach character

77 Music 🐛 The best whole-brain builder — Mozart notwithstanding

85 Strategies to Improve Memory 🐛 But children need time to catch onto them

92 Words at Play 🐛 The more words heard, from infancy on up, the higher the verbal test scores

100 Habituation 🐛 The virtues of *not* paying attention

II THE MATURING YEARS
From college to retirement

106 Focus on Focus ❦ Paying attention is the key to learning, especially under pressure

113 Learning the Easy Way ❦ A little emotion helps

118 Using Your Mind's Ear ❦ Executive function's versatile tool — the remarkable phonological loop

126 Long-Term Memory ❦ Why repetition, rehearsal and practice work so well

132 Memory is Plural ❦ Knowing how its systems interrelate improves coding into long-term memory

141 Mindlessness ❦ The brain on autopilot loses altitude

147 Stress ❦ A little bit too often kills memory cells

155 Make It Meaningful ❦ The three levels of remembering

161 Brain Nutrition ❦ What foods help you do your best work at different times of day

171 Caffeine ❦ In moderation, a smart drug

178 Learning Addiction ❦ The brain's reward for learning new skills

186 The Slighted Sense ❦ How smells influence memory

195 Dreams at Work ❦ The crucial role sleep plays in learning

203 False Testimony ❦ Memory for events is highly suggestible

209 Practice in the Mind ❦ Visualizing a motor skill sharpens performance

212 Learning Without Knowing It ❦ Why a bit of plagiarism is inevitable

III THE EXPERIENCED MIND
Maintaining treasured qualities of life

220   **Healthy Aging** ❦ Lessons from professors about outsmarting age-related memory loss

233   **The Trick to Remembering Names** ❦ "That's OK, I don't remember yours either"

240   **Making Memories** ❦ Techniques for getting around an imperfect memory

245   **Influence of Stress on Mood and Health** ❦ How moods influence the health of your brain and body

253   **Humor Therapy** ❦ When laughter becomes dead serious

259   **Performing Music** ❦ A mind-saving hobby for aging brains

269   **The Best Brain Workouts** ❦ Why Fill-in-the-Blank is better than Multiple-Choice

275   **Teaching to Stay Alive** ❦ A commitment to listening hard feeds neurons

279   **Full-Brain Engagement** ❦ How building a family tree puts into practice what the experts preach

284   **It's Usually Not Alzheimer's** ❦ Healthy aging versus dementia, and how to tell the difference

294   **Stroke!** ❦ Types, symptoms and a new treatment

301   **Rebuilding Brain Cells** ❦ How physical and mental exercise improve ability to learn and recall

308   **Coming Treatments** ❦ What the labs have discovered and what you can do in the meantime

314   **Index**

INTRODUCTION

Nine months after birth a normal human infant will surpass all adult, non-human primates, and by the time it is exposed to a formal curriculum it will have succeeded in teaching itself skills that few adults and no technologies could ever replicate — fluency in its native language and an amazing ability to recognize faces, to name only two.

The first third of this book describes what is happening in the brain as those learning years unfold, including the roles of parents as caregivers and examples, the signs of learning disabilities, how the various qualities of intelligence and of temperament reveal themselves. A child's motivation for this incredible achievement is governed by hard-wired survival instincts in the early months and, with the beginning of self-awareness in the second year, perhaps a sense of its vulnerability and need to learn. By the seventh year, the brain has developed enough to allow the child to play a responsible role in family tasks with future, not immediate, benefits.

The middle third of this book describes the activities and preoccupation of the mature brain from the mid-twenties, when it reaches the height of its powers, into the late fifties when the first signs of slowing down often begin to show, sometimes embarrassingly. This section describes the vectors that affect those years and offers insight into minimizing threats and maximizing skills with mental conditioning. People in their middle years commonly encounter and have to deal with causes and effects of stress, the importance of sleep for storing significant events, appropriate emotional responses, strategies for coding crucial data into memory and recalling it reliably, ways in which the brain's reward system encourages learning, exercises for sustaining concentration, even the effects of coffee, lunch and nutrition on brain function.

In later life, accumulated knowledge is the source of power, and memories are among the greatest delights. With retirement comes time for their cultivation, but also the easy routines that accelerate cognitive decline. The third section of this book addresses those opportunities and dangers. It includes current information and advice on remembering names, the long-term value of teaching, what kinds of mental exercise will slow down the slowing down, the power of humor to engage and to heal, how a positive mood sharpens thinking, rejuvenation from physical exercise, the truth about nutritional supplements and medications, what neuroscience is now learning about how to reverse the effects of dementia.

This is not just another book about how to double memory power in ten days. There are plenty such books out there, and they can be useful for learning tricks to get around the typical flaws and weaknesses of memory. In this book, we describe practical memory-improvement techniques of that kind, but we also provide an understanding of what recent brain research is revealing about the ways learning and memory work, how to steepen a normal learning curve and how memory can be maintained, even improved, on a deeper and more powerful level than that on which memory tricks operate.

For anyone interested in understanding how the human brain works, these are heady times. This book could not have been written even a single generation ago. New imaging technology — PET, fMRI, MEG, and more — reveals brain activity on a level of detail light years beyond the educated guesswork of most 20th-century psychologists and medical doctors. Advances in molecular biology have allowed neuroscientists to pin down the precise molecules involved in learning and memory formation, and to specify the exact structural changes that occur in the contact points between brain cells as memories are made. The mapping of the human genome has helped identify genes that code for specific facets of intelligence and temperament, as well as genes that can lead to brain diseases such as Alzheimer's. And sophisticated cell-tracking techniques have revealed that adult brains have stem cells that can manufacture new neurons without limit.

The implications of all this new-found knowledge are far-reaching, and sometimes scary. Brain researchers now know not just how the brain codes memories on a molecular and structural level, but also how one might manipulate that process to make memory formation automatic and effortless, or to block memories from forming, or even to erase memories once they're formed. PET scans illuminate not just the parts of the brain that become active while listening to *Raindrops Keep Falling on My Head,* but the parts that are active (and, equally important, inactive) during meditation or a religious epiphany. An Alzheimer's vaccine is in the offing that is designed to work by stimulating the body's own immune system to prevent or repair the damage wreaked by plaque-producing beta-amyloid proteins which damage neurons as they age. The hormones and even the stem cells responsible for maintaining mental acuity may now be taken in pill form or injected directly into the brain. And the Prozac revolution has stimulated our collective cultural imagination about how a pill that alters brain neurotransmitter systems not only can improve mood, but can manipulate ambition, self-esteem, temperament, and other aspects of personality that are uncomfortably close to the core of our identity.

As always, important new technology brings threats as well as promises, and may lead to some cures that are worse than the diseases. For both self-empowerment and self-defense, a basic grasp of brain science is important to every-one. An understanding of at least the general findings of the new brain research is becoming an increasingly crucial part of cultural literacy. General practitioners cannot be expected to keep abreast of it, much less apply it. The research findings are too crucially important to everyone's lives to rely on uninformed simplifications or anecdotal evidence.

Like all the titles produced by the Brainwaves Center for publication under the Brainwaves imprint, this one is intend-ed to help ordinary people understand and use research find-ings that may not be widely reported outside the world of corporate biotech labs and scientific journals. This is a time-sensitive goal because even though much of the technology upon which brain research depends is high-tech, arcane, and expensive, many of the research findings can be immediately applied cheaply and easily. Important knowledge about mind improvement and brain maintenance doesn't enjoy the bene-fits of commercial advertising and publicity because real-world applications of such findings are freely available to anyone so they cannot be exploited commercially as exclu-sive products. As in many other areas of public health and welfare, we must take steps on our own to become reliably informed about what's going on.

This is a sourcebook of current scientific information with practical advice on how to speed and consolidate learn-ing and recall, to build competence, confidence and mental productivity for oneself and for others. For that reason we dedicate it to students and to the parents, teachers and pro-fessional caregivers who empower and shape life's joys.

— THE AUTHORS

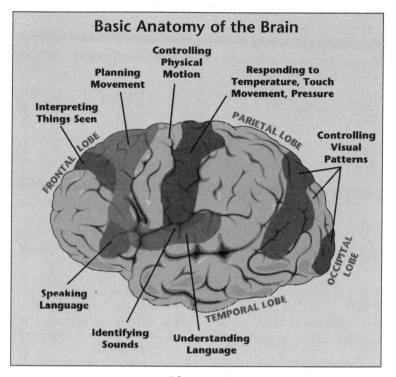

Basic Anatomy of the Brain

- Controlling Physical Motion
- Planning Movement
- Responding to Temperature, Touch Movement, Pressure
- Interpreting Things Seen
- PARIETAL LOBE
- Controlling Visual Patterns
- FRONTAL LOBE
- OCCIPITAL LOBE
- Speaking Language
- TEMPORAL LOBE
- Identifying Sounds
- Understanding Language

Glossary

Acetylcholine A neurotransmitter that plays an important role in attention, learning, and memory.

Amygdala Part of the limbic system always alert to threats.

Axon The long branch of a nerve cell that transmits information to other cells.

Conditioning A learned response to a stimulus that always precedes an event, as if the stimulus were the event itself.

Cortex The wrinkled layers of cells covering the surface of the brain, sometimes called *gray matter*.

Declarative memory The conscious recollection of facts and events; also called *explicit memory*.

Dendrite A branch of a nerve cell that receives information from other cells.

Dopamine A "pleasure" neurotransmitter that plays a central role in the brain's internal reward system.

Episodic memory Conscious memory for what happened, where. Sometimes called "autobiographical memory."

Frontal lobes The most recently evolved section of the brain, used for conscious planning, problem solving, and control of emotion.

Glutamate A neurotransmitter that plays a central role in creating learning and memory pathways between brain cells.

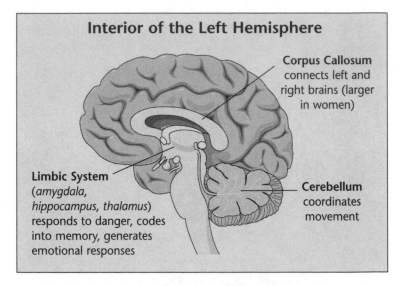

Interior of the Left Hemisphere

Corpus Callosum connects left and right brains (larger in women)

Limbic System (*amygdala, hippocampus, thalamus*) responds to danger, codes into memory, generates emotional responses

Cerebellum coordinates movement

Gray matter See *cortex*.

Habituation An unconscious form of learning by which our brain learns to ignore a repeatedly-applied stimulus once it has been categorized as non-threatening.

Hippocampus A part of the limbic system crucial for creating and accessing long-term memories.

Limbic system A collection of structures that play important roles in emotion, memory, and attention.

Long-term potentiation The process underlying learning and memory by which one brain cell becomes sensitive to stimulation from a neighbor cell.

Myelin The insulation surrounding a brain cell's axon.

Neurogenesis The production of new brain cells.

Neuron A nerve cell, or cell in the nervous system (which includes the brain). Often used interchangeably with *brain cell*.

Neurotransmitter A chemical messenger that brain cells use to communicate with one another.

Nondeclarative memory Unconscious forms of memory and learning that influence behavior without our being aware of it. Also called *implicit memory*.

Priming A form of subliminal memory in which one piece of information can cue recall of another.

Procedural memory Automatic memory for skills and habits, such as how to ride a bike or sign one's name; also "muscle memory."

Serotonin A "feel-good" neurotransmitter linked to mood, raised by antidepressants such as Prozac.

Subliminal Below the level of consciousness

Synapse The tiny gap between brain cells across which neurotransmitter chemicals convey messages.

White matter The part of the brain beneath the cortex that consists mostly of brain cell axons sheathed in myelin.

Working memory A short-term memory system for holding information "online" and manipulating it to solve problems.

THE DEVELOPING BRAIN

The third trimester through high school

Learning in the Womb

Evolution has endowed human babies with an incredible ability to learn

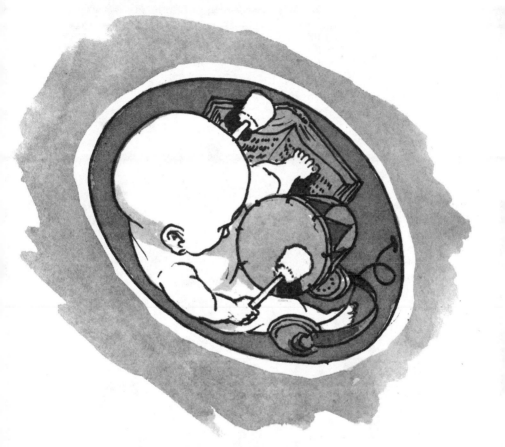

Human babies come helpless and dependent into the world, more so than the young of any other species. A baby elk can stand a few hours after birth, and run within a day. On the other hand, human babies, with their eager, adaptable brains, are able to learn far more in their first two years of life than an animal ever will. They can even master the basics of the miraculously complex, uniquely human skill — language.

Why Is the Human Brain Less Mature at Birth Than the Brains of Other Primates?

A leading theory is based on the fact that humans walked upright while their ancestors used their arms as forelegs, walking on their knuckles as the apes do. Perhaps the first humans stood upright so they could see above the grasses in the savannas in order to spot predators and game. (This may account for the weaker sense of smell in humans.) Upright posture may also have allowed their bodies to keep cool by venting heat through the head into the moving air above the grasses.

In the course of evolution the upright position must have shifted weight to the pelvis, which thickened to bear it, closing down the birth opening. As the pelvis was thickening, the head of the fetus continued to grow larger to accommodate the constantly enlarging brain. Whatever the reasons, the human fetus had to be born well before the brain and head had reached maturity so it would still be small enough to pass through the birth canal.

Are babies able to learn while still in the womb?

The powerful need that a baby has to learn is matched by an unusual ability which unfolds gradually in the infant brain. Its helplessness acts as a powerful motivator to figure out how to survive in its new environment when it can no longer depend on the peaceful, protected life in the womb where learning had already started. Investigators into the development of infant learning and memory have discovered that fetuses are not only listening to what's going on outside the womb, but are already capable of some basic kinds of learning and remembering. In other words, even before we're born, we're forming memories.

Memories formed in the womb

Any mother knows that her baby prefers her voice to that of any other person. That isn't just motherly conceit. Even before three days of age, newborns are capable of telling their mother's voice apart from other women's voices. Not only that, they're so fond of their own mother's voice they'll do whatever's in their power to hear it. Psychologists know this because of experiments in which a newborn infant is permitted to "produce" a voice — turn on a recording of a woman reading a story — by sucking on a specially-rigged pacifier. If it's their own mother's voice they turn on by sucking, they'll do so more vigorously and frequently than if it's the voice of some other woman. (New or prospective fathers might find it interesting to know that a fetus does not learn this kind of preference for its father's voice or, for that matter, for any voice coming from outside the body holding the womb. So don't feel hurt if your baby pays less attention to you.)

It takes a newborn a little longer to recognize its mother by her face. Since there's no way a baby can come into the world already armed with the knowledge of what its mother looks like, it has to learn this after birth — by matching the mother's voice to the face it's coming from. At one month, infants can match their mother's voice to her face. They prove it by looking at the mother's face, and ignoring the face of another woman sitting by her side, when a tape-recording of the mother's voice is played. After about three months, an infant can pick out its mother by sight alone.

One might think the newborn could have learned a preference for its mother's voice while bonding with the mother just after birth. But it goes deeper than that. In an experiment in which pregnant mothers read a certain story out loud once a week for the last six weeks of pregnancy, their newborns turned out to prefer that story to others. Another study showed that when pregnant women sing a certain melody once a day during the last two weeks of pregnancy, the babies prefer that melody to an unfamiliar one after they're born. So babies can not only hear their mother's voice while in the womb and recognize it after birth, they're even capable of attending to and remembering some of the finer details of what they hear, down to specific melodies and perhaps even the sounds of particular words.

How we know what a fetus learns
Other studies have even gone inside the womb to explore the capacity of third-trimester fetuses to learn. How can such an experiment be done? If you make a noise by placing a "vibroacoustic stimulator" against a pregnant mother's abdomen, the fetus will move. If this is done repeatedly the fetus will eventually stop moving in response to the noise. That shows that the fetus has *habituated* — it has learned to recognize the sound and tune it out. A fetus will show the effects of this simple kind of learning — responding less per-

sistently to the same stimulus reapplied in the future — not just after ten minutes, but even after 24 hours.

But don't rush out to buy a Latin Primer to tutor your unborn baby in the classics. Habituation is a kind of learning so basic that we share it with fruit flies and sea slugs. There is no evidence that newborns understand the *meaning* of what they have heard.

If, however, survival of a helpless newborn depends on bonding with the mother immediately after birth, presumably an infant's brain must be sufficiently developed to recognize matters essential for its post-natal well-being. Therefore, the bonding process must begin prior to birth. As we've seen, to conserve energy the fetus is able to learn *not* to react when a new event has proven that it is not a danger. To identify its food-source later on, the fetus acquires the life-preserving ability to recognize and crave the sound of its mother's voice. Research indicates that while still in the womb, the fetus acquires a preference for foods the mother eats, say carrots, and carries that preference with it into the world. Whether an infant inherits its mother's third-trimester cravings remains speculative.

References

Van Heteren, Cathelijne F., P. Focco Boekkooi, Henk W. Jongsma, and Jan G. Nijhuis (2000). Fetal learning and memory. The Lancet 356: 1169-70.

Ward, C.D. and R.P. Cooper (1999). A lack of evidence in 4-month-old human infants for paternal voice preference. Developmental Psychobiology 35(1): 49-59

an you reorder these panels into their proper sequence? This exercises executive planning skills and requires the ability to project oneself into the mind of the Little King, to see things from his point of view, to get the point. See p. 27 for the solution

From "The Little King" by Otto Soglow. Reprinted by permission of Henry Holt & Co., Inc.

THE EYES HAVE IT

How children learn to read minds

Humans are social animals. In our evolution, we've developed the ability to deduce what another person might be thinking, when they do or say something, and to predict their behavior based on that deduction. Communication that passes between two people goes beyond a simple understanding of the words that are exchanged. Infants begin to pick up non-verbal signals well before they have learned to speak.

From the age of about four months, babies learn to look at other people's eyes to figure out what their intentions might be. Even from the age of two months, infants look longer at the eyes than at any other part of a face. To most animals, direct eye contact is considered threatening; to humans, a look can also send a friendly, affectionate signal.

In an experiment with eight- and-nine-month-olds, the infants looked automatically at an adult's eyes if an action was ambiguous — for example, if the experimenter offered a toy but then pulled it back, or placed a toy in front of the infant but then placed a hand over it. Eyes communicate both by the direction in which they look and by revealing emotional states. Even pupil size is meaningful. We unconsciously tend to find another person more attractive if their pupils are dilated, perhaps because we infer that *they're* interested in *us* (see box, below).

From about the end of the first year of life, babies learn to infer from the direction of an adult's gaze what the adult is looking at or thinking about. This is something other animals, with the possible exception of some primates, do not do. Babies also learn, by about the same age, to direct the atten-

Eye-Talk Tricks

University of Chicago "eye language" researcher Eckhard Hess has pointed out that it became popular in the Middle Ages for women to take the pupil-dilating drug *belladonna* (literally, "beautiful woman") to enhance their beauty. He also reports that Chinese jade buyers wear dark glasses to hide their eyes from dealers, in the belief that their dilated pupils would otherwise betray their interest in a particular piece. Supposedly, Turkish rug dealers look for the same clue in their dealings with European buyers. And in experiments by Hess, heterosexual men show pupil enlargement when looking at pictures of women, but not of men or babies, while heterosexual women show pupil enlargement when looking at pictures of men or babies, but not of women.

A TEST

Inferring the Thoughts of Others

The term *theory of mind* refers to an ability to infer the mental states of others — their knowledge, beliefs, and desires. It's a uniquely human ability that develops during early to middle childhood, without which normal social interaction is impossible. It's also an indispensible skill for lying effectively and deceiving others.

By the age of four, most children have developed a theory of mind that lets them handle *first-order belief attributions,* the kind of skill that lets them infer, "He thinks that...." The first two stories below are designed to test that ability. By the age of six or seven, most children have moved to the stage of *second-order belief attributions,* allowing them to infer, "He thinks that she thinks that...." The third story on p. 27 is designed to test that ability.

First-order belief attribution (age four)

Joey's mother has given him a box of chocolates for his birthday. When he is alone, he takes the chocolates out of the box and hides them in the cookie jar. His friend Lisa has heard Joey got some chocolates as a birthday present. She comes over to visit him and sees the chocolate box and cookie jar. Where will Lisa look for the chocolates?

Sally and Ann both have little straw baskets. Sally also has a pretty glass marble that her aunt gave her, which she puts in her basket. Sally then goes out for a walk while Ann stays at home. As soon as Sally leaves, Ann takes the marble from Sally's basket and puts it in her own basket. When Sally comes home, where will she look for her marble?

Continued

tion of an adult to an object, by moving their eyes between the object and the adult's eyes, as well as by pointing.

A somewhat more sophisticated kind of mindreading falls under the heading *theory of mind,* which requires projecting one's own mind into the mind of another to size up their knowledge and beliefs. Lying and other forms of deception rest on this kind of ability. By about age four, most children can form an understanding along the lines of "I know that he knows...," and by about six they can handle another layer of mindreading along the lines of "I know that he knows that she knows..." (see box, p. 25).

References

Baron-Cohen, Simon (1994). How to build a baby that can read minds: cognitive mechanisms in mindreading. Cahiers de Psychologie Cognitive/Current Psychology of Cognition 13: 513-52.

Baron-Cohen, Simon, et al. (1997). Another advanced test of theory of mind: evidence from very high functioning adults with autism or Asperger's syndrome. Journal of Child Psychology and Psychiatry 38/7: 813-22.

Baron-Cohen, Simon, Alan M. Leslie, and Uta Frith (1985). Does the autistic child have a "theory of mind"? Cognition 21: 37-46.

Fletcher, P.C. et al. (1995). Other minds in the brain: a functional imaging study of "theory of mind" in story comprehension. Cognition 57: 109-28.

Hess, Eckhard, and S. Petrovich (1978). Pupillary behavior in communication. In A. Siegman and S. Feldstein (Eds.), Nonverbal Behavior and Communication. Hillsdale, NJ: Lawrence Erlbaum Associates.

Phillips, Wendy, Simon Baron-Cohen, and Michael Rutter (1992). The role of eye contact in goal detection: evidence from normal infants and children with autism or mental handicap. Development and Psychopathology 4: 375-83.

Second-order belief attribution (age six or seven)
During a war, the Red army captures a soldier from the
Blue army. The Red army wants to know where the Blue
army's tanks are. They know the tanks must be either by
the sea or in the mountains. They know that the soldier
they've captured will lie to save his army. The soldier is
very clever. The tanks are really in the mountains. The
soldier tells the Red army, "The tanks are in the mountains." Why did he say that?

(Based on Baron-Cohen et al. 1985 and Fletcher et al. 1995)

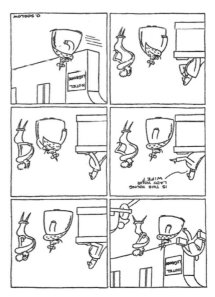

**Correct order of cartoon
panels,** p. 22

BABIES ARE SELF-TAUGHT LINGUISTS

**Teach your baby grammar? Don't bother;
brush up on your own**

Babies come into the world primed to learn language. They'll do it whether you want them to or not, without any instruction, in a sequence of stages that are the same for all children the world over, regardless of whether they're learning Swahili, Mandarin, or English. All they need is a little data — data supplied automatically by their environment, as long as there are people around them who are speaking. Then, they embark on a systematic analysis of their native-language-to-be that is so skilled it would put a linguistics graduate student to shame. They are, in effect, like little natural-born linguistic anthropologists, eagerly and instinctively performing phonological, morphological, semantic, and syntactic analyses of the language of the natives in their new-found world so they can figure out the rules of that language and become expert speakers themselves.

What's "normal" for a child?

Standard psychology textbooks will tell you that the stages of language acquisition go something like this. From about four to six months of age, infants produce brief, isolated consonant and vowel sounds as well as clicks, coos, grunts and sighs that bear little or no resemblance to speech sounds in any language. At about six months, they begin what's called the *babbling* stage, mouthing repetitive consonant-vowel sequences such as "KOO." (Interestingly, infants the world over almost never produce vowel-consonant sequences — such as "OOK" — during this stage.) Around the turn of the first year, the infant moves beyond babbling and begins to produce recognizable words in the language spoken around it. Within about six months after that, the average child has a vocabulary of about 50 words. From there, it moves on to the "two-word" stage, as in "Mommy go." The child progresses to syntactically more complex structures by age three. By age four or so, it has developed a grammar — *real* grammar, not artificial prescriptive rules of grammar such as "Never split an infinitive" — essentially the same as that of an adult speaker.

Toddlers probably learn language as fledgling birds learn to fly: They are born with the specialized tools

This rapid pace of language acquisition, which proceeds pretty much the same for all children except those with special deficits or children who are somehow isolated from human contact, is predictable and inevitable. That's one reason that language acquisition is sometimes claimed to be similar to other biologically-programmed behavior, such as developing binocular vision or learning to walk or fly, in both humans and other species. But careful studies have shown that a child's precociousness is even more impressive than the foregoing timetable indicates. Well before a baby can utter so much as a single word, it is already well on its way to figuring out the sound system of the mother tongue. This early stage of language learning doesn't stop at just recognizing which sounds are familiar and, therefore, belong to the native-language-to-be, and which ones are not. It's much trickier than that.

A baby's natural preference for its mother's voice

At birth, a baby already knows the difference between the sound of its mother's voice and that of a woman other than the mother (see *Learning in the Womb*). The baby also knows the difference between the sound of the language the mother speaks — i.e., "mother tongue" — and a foreign language. In fact, the baby doesn't just know the difference, it *prefers* the mother's voice and the mother tongue to any other. There's good evidence that infants learn initially to sort mother tongue from foreign language by paying attention to prosody, well before they've learned to pay attention to specific words.

The early preference for mother's voice presumably exists because it aids in the process of bonding the infant to the mother. Mother-baby bonding has obvious survival value for the infant. But what about mother-tongue preference? After all, when it comes to many other things in the baby's environment, it's *novelty* the baby prefers over familiarity. So why should language be different?

The newborn's preference for the mother tongue is just the first step in a single-minded focus on the sounds it needs to pay attention to in the process of language acquisition. One of the most striking things about this step is how quickly infants learn to narrow their focus, and *ignore* data that aren't relevant to the language-learning task.

All tongues, but what an infant hears, becomes foreign
Most of us have heard the claim that infants can produce the sounds of any language before they learn which small subset of that universal inventory their own language requires. Actually, this claim isn't quite true. All infants find some speech sounds easier to produce than others. Vowels are easy, as are consonant sounds such as "b," "n," or "d." Fricatives ("f," "th," etc.), affricates ("ch"), and liquids ("r," "l,") are universally harder to produce and are, therefore, relatively rare at this early stage.

On the other hand, a very young infant does have a remarkable ability to *hear* all the sounds, and differences in sounds, exploited by any of the world's 3,000 languages — despite the fact that most of those distinctions are ones their own mother tongue doesn't use. For example, a four-month-old Japanese infant can easily differentiate an "l" from an "r" sound, even if the parents can't. And an American four-month-old born into an English-language environment can discern differences between Chinese-language tones that are beyond the abilities of its parents.

What quickly begins to happen, though, is that the infant's ears become less acute. Of course, it's not literally the ears that are changing, but the brain, which is adjusting its phonetic-perception circuitry to the needs of just one language. Like so much else in early brain development, this learning process involves a *loss* of unnecessary synapses just as much as it involves the strengthening of relevant ones.

By around the age of six months, infants are already losing their ability to tell the difference between vowel sounds that they could easily tell apart just two months before. That's one of the things that makes the task of learning a second language harder the older you get: Your brain actually rewires itself to hear *only* the differences that your own native language uses, and to ignore everything else.

So an infant only a half-year old is already performing a sophisticated phonological analysis of language, sorting out the sound-differences that are meaningful from the ones that are not. Infants learn to do this earlier for vowels than for consonants. By about the age of 12 months, they've sorted out the consonant differences that are important to their language as well — which means they can no longer reliably hear the differences that only *other* languages consider important.

This sounds like an incredibly daunting task. However, many aspects of language-learning that are hard for a grown-up are much easier for an infant. The tools of analysis the infant is equipped with by nature are lost once they have done their job in the process of learning a native language. That is why infants can put almost any grown-up to shame in language-learning skill. A toddler can learn multiple languages with equal ease. An excellent argument for teaching another language in preschool classes lies in the following irony: Colleges need to impose foreign language *requirements* on paying students while parents couldn't *prevent* their infant from teaching itself language even if they tried.

References

Kuhl, Patricia K. (2000). A new view of language acquisition. Proceedings of the National Academy of Sciences USA 97/22: 11850-57.

Kuhl, Patricia K., et al. (1992). Linguistic experience alters phonetic perception in infants by 6 months of age. Science 255: 606-8.

Moon, Christine, Robin Panneton Cooper, and William P. Fifer (1993). Two-day-olds prefer their native language. Infant Behavior and Development 16: 495-500.

Polka, Linda, and Janet F. Werker (1994). Developmental changes in perception of nonnative vowel contrasts. Journal of Experimental Psychology 20/2: 421-35.

Calculus for Preschoolers?

In this age of preschool admission tests, some high-achieving parents think they can make their child smarter by pushing the developmental envelope. There are various tricks, some that cost money and others that don't, that some claim give a child an intellectual head start in life.

The problem is, the specific tricks used are often inappropriate to the age level and, therefore, the cognitive level of the child. For example, there is clear evidence that fetuses hear and even remember things in the womb (see *Learning in the Womb*). Why not, therefore, read passages out loud from a good book every evening, to start familiarizing the fetus with the classics? But the fetus doesn't understand what it hears, so there's no way an infant is going to get much out of Moby Dick. And there's evidence that six-month-olds have a grasp of the difference between quantities of one, two, and three — in other words, they have a grasp of some very basic math concepts. Why not start teaching with flash cards to jump-start the ability to master algebra? Again, though, the logical error lies in thinking that an instructional technique that works for older children will also work for much younger ones. Promoting age-appropriate stimulation and interaction is much more effective than quick-fix fads based loosely on stray bits of neuroscience research.

An Early Sign of Intelligence

Is my two-year-old a genius?

I like going places better than coming back. On the way there, every-thing is interesting to look at. On the way back, I can see the same mountains and stuff but it's nothing new.

Many parents are proud of their children if they learn how to do something — walk, talk, tie shoelaces — at a younger age than the neighbor's child. Is it true that more precocious development leads to greater ability or intelligence later in life? Are there other kinds of infant behavior that have this kind of predictive value? Can you tell how smart the ten-year-old is going to be by looking at the ten-month-old? And is there anything you can do about it?

Observers of child development, including mothers with more than one child, know that infants and children have their own timetable for learning and acquiring skills. Intelligence unfolds over years, sometimes in spurts that some researchers think correspond to rapid development of synapses between brain cells. The *order* of stages can't be changed, and most researchers believe that the developmental stages can't be accelerated. Different kinds of learning require different developmental stages to have been reached, and there's nothing parents can do about it. A child can't learn mathematical set theory, for example, before the ability to understand symbols and the concept of categorization have been installed in the developing brain.

The sorts of tests that propose to measure "intelligence" in infants include a variety of physical movement and coordination tasks ("rolls from back to stomach," "bangs spoon") as well as the cognitive kind that measure thinking skills. Overall, they won't tell you how smart your baby is going to end up to be, or even how it will score on IQ tests a few months or years down the road. But some researchers believe that a subset of the cognitive tasks do have some predictive value.

Mothers don't need a degree in psychology to know that babies like novelty. If you show them something they haven't seen before, they will pay attention to it. In fact, a way to tell if an infant remembers something is to notice whether the infant treats it as a novel item when you present it again.

Let's say a picture of a face is shown to a toddler who looks at it, becomes bored and looks away. After an interval of a few seconds the same face is shown again. The child may look at it again, but will become bored and turn away more quickly this time, even more quickly the next time the same face is shown and, eventually, may not pay attention to it at all. This kind of learning — tuning out a stimulus once it has become familiar and non-threatening — is called *habituation,* such a primitive kind of learning that fetuses do it in the womb (see *Learning in the Womb*).

Psychologists have found that some babies are more interested in new things than others, in the sense that they more clearly and quickly distinguish new from old and focus just on the former. That is, they become habituated more quickly. What's apparently happening is that they focus on novelty more readily, but then process it more quickly, and so are in a position to move on more rapidly to the next new thing.

In this sense, some infants respond more strongly to novelty than others. A stronger response to, say, a new doll comes to the same thing, in a way, as a weaker response to an old one. The infant must have processed the kind of visual information that defines the new doll as unique, and remembered the information well enough to recognize it as familiar the next time the infant sees the "new" doll. Only by being able to remember the unique qualities of a given object could the infant show heightened interest in something that is not familiar. So a strong response to novelty may mean the infant is quicker at this kind of processing, and better at remembering the results of it.

Is your baby a "short looker" or a "long looker"?
Psychologists have also found that some babies are "short lookers" and others are "long lookers." That is, some fix their attention for a longer period of time on a new object the first time they see it. You might think long lookers are taking in more. In fact, though, short lookers may have an advantage. Long lookers need more time to investigate the same amount of information as short lookers, and sometimes even take in less information overall than short lookers. Short lookers may be more adept, in other words, at taking in and processing new information.

Many neuropsychologists think this kind of speed of information processing might translate into better performance on an IQ test a few years down the road, assuming that information processing speed is something built into our brains from birth and, therefore, fairly stable throughout life. Some researchers even propose that a positive response to novelty defines intelligence. There does seem to be evidence that some brains operate relatively more quickly, in this way, than others. Researchers have found that infants who are quicker in the novelty tests also, on average, perform better on IQ tests in early and middle childhood. So some people may have an advantage over others from infancy.

There may be another way of understanding the difference between short lookers and long lookers. The difference may not lie only with speed of processing, but with *style* of processing. According to some studies, short lookers process a visual shape by quickly scanning the entire image. Long lookers focus more on the specific parts of the image. So the difference may lie in what is sometimes loosely referred to as "right brain" (short lookers) versus "left brain" (long lookers) information processing styles.

Other factors at work

Strategies for processing visual information also change as a child's brain develops. Tests of toddlers vs. preschool children show that the younger ones recognize people by picking out specific visual clues such as a moustache, hairline, glasses or skin color. That's why at Halloween, for example, a toddler might burst into screams when daddy puts on a funny nose. In the child's eyes that difference is enough to turn a familiar loving face into a complete stranger. Older children's brains have developed sufficiently to use the adult strategy for recognizing faces as being familiar or strange. They are able to scan quickly for an overall abstract pattern of lights, darks, hues and forms.

But, of course, there's only a correlation *to some degree* between information-processing speed in infancy and IQ later in life. Why only to some degree? Assuming processing speed is stable, there must be other factors that bear on a person's developing intelligence. What factors? You can see how an interest in novelty would do little good if the environment didn't provide enough new things to explore, while a richer environment might help an infant learn more skills even if the brain processes information a little more slowly. All children have a natural urge to learn and explore. The only thing that can really get in the way of that inborn predilection is a *lack* of things to explore. In this sense, environment always has the final say in the development of intelligence.

References

Colombo, J. (1993). Infant Cognition: Predicting later intellectual functioning. Newbury Park, CA: Sage Publications.

DiLalla, Lisabeth F., et al. (1990). Infant predictors of preschool and adult IQ: a study of infant twins and their parents. Developmental Psychology 26/5: 759-69.

McCall, Robert B., and Michael S. Carriger (1993). A meta-analysis of infant habituation and recognition memory performance as predictors of later IQ. Child Development 64: 57-79.

Stoecker, J.J., J. Colombo, J.E. Frick, and J.R. Allen (1998). Long- and short-looking infants' recognition of symmetrical and asymmetrical forms. Journal of Experimental Child Psychology 71/1: 63-78.

BIRTH ...just listening

1 year ...first word

1½ years ...50 words

2 years ...phrases...
...studying grammar

4 years ...speaks clearly
...learning new words

7 years ...10,000-word
vocabulary

LANGUAGE LEARNING

Reasons why a child may lag behind the normal timetable

Children all over the world have a natural urge to learn language built into their genes. Virtually any infant is genetically equipped to develop the motivation and brain circuits needed to learn the one or more languages it hears spoken around it, without any special help or instruction. Parents need never give lessons in how to change a verb into the past tense, or explain the significance of the difference in sound between *for* and *far*. A normal child learns such things just by listening.

By the age of four, a child will have become fluent through a sequence of stages that are pretty much the same for any child, and for any language, the world over. One-word utterances at age one lead to multi-word phrases a year later. A one-and-a-half-year-old's vocabulary of 50 words expands to 10,000 within five years. A two-year-old's baby talk matures by age seven into mastery of the full repertoire of all the sounds in the language. On average, as the language-learning systems within the brain unfold, girls have a tendency to be a little more precocious than boys.

There are, however, exceptions. Mental retardation or deafness can block a natural path to acquiring a language. Chemical influences or physical accidents suffered by a fetus, or genes that are activated in abnormal ways, can make normal language learning difficult for otherwise healthy, intelligent children. A number of these diversities have been lumped by psychologists under the general name of *Specific Language Impairment,* or SLI.

These SLI disorders relate only to language ability. They are not part of some general problem of cognitive development, intelligence, emotional trauma, or impoverished envi-

Typical Language Development Stages by Age

0-1 year: Babbles; learns to recognize own name.

1 year: Utters single words, such as *daddy, more, teddy*.

1½ years: Has active vocabulary of about 50 words; begins to combine words, such as *daddy cookie, all gone, hurt hand, all wet pants*.

2-3 years: Has productive vocabulary of about 500 words at 2½ years. Increases length of word combinations, such as *I sit down, here it comes, I watching kitty*. Begins to use grammatical morphemes, such as *-ing*, plurals, *the*, past tenses. Begins to use negative and question forms, such as *Will you help me?* and *I don't like you*.

3-4 years: Starts using more complex, multiclause utterances, such as *I show you how to do it, Watch me sit down, I want this one because it's big*.

ronment. The fact that some children are apparently born with brains that function well in all skills but language may mean that there are specific genes that code for language-processing regions of the brain and that may go awry. All the language disorders described below are more common among boys than girls, and all have a tendency to run in families.

The influence of inherited genes

Most types of SLI are caused by the failure of many genes to interact as intended. However, a recent study has identified a single gene responsible for a language disorder found in about half of the members of one family living in London. Though they are all normal in other ways, their speech disorder is so obvious that people outside the family can't understand them. It appears to result from the disruption of a single gene on chromosome 7, in the same area as a gene that has been linked to autism.

Sometimes the problem is with linking sounds and their meanings in proper sequence

Many researchers believe that some cases of SLI may not be specific to language at all. In their view, the disorder may sometimes result from a problem with *working memory,* a short-term memory system for storing information, manipulating it, and using it to solve a problem. Some SLI sufferers may have difficulty with their short-term memory for speech sounds. In other cases, the short-term memory problem may be more general. One experiment showed that some SLI children have difficulty remembering and repeating back any sequence of sounds that they hear, even if they are not speech sounds. A well-functioning working memory helps with performance on a variety of language- and reading-related skills, such as building a good vocabulary, learning a foreign language, and becoming a proficient reader.

All children develop their language abilities at different rates, so it can be hard to know at first if a child has a language-learning problem that needs to be addressed.

Example of Story Told by a Four-and-a-Half-Year-Old Child with SLI

The man got on the boat. He jump out the boat. He rocking the boat. He drop his thing. He drop his other thing. He tipping over. He fell off the boat.

(From Lindner and Johnston 1992)

A TEST: REPEATING BACK NON-WORDS
A Predictor of Vocabulary, Reading, and Foreign-Language-Learning Skills

Background

Several studies have found that a young child who can easily repeat back made-up "words" is likely to acquire a good vocabulary. The kind of short-term memory for sound that enables a child to repeat an unfamiliar sequence of syllables (the *phonological loop* component of working memory) is an important skill for learning new words. Researchers have also found that nonword repetition ability at age four is a good predictor of vocabulary and reading skills at age five. Conversely, difficulty in repeating non-words may predict future problems with acquiring vocabulary and learning foreign languages, and can even be used as a quick test for possible dyslexia.

Directions

Ask a child to repeat back each one of the non-words on the opposite page immediately after you say it. The "good scores," by age group, match the scores of relatively high-achieving children of high socioeconomic status from Cambridge, England.

Scoring

Good Scores:

Four-year-olds: At least five of the one-syllable non-words, five of the two-syllable non-words, four of the three-syllable non-words, and three of the four-syllable non-words.

Five-year-olds: At least seven of the one-syllable non-words, seven of the two-syllable non-words, six of the three-syllable non-words, and five of the four-syllable non-words.

Six-year-olds: At least eight of the one-syllable non-words, eight of the two-syllable non-words, seven of the three-syllable non-words, and six of the four-syllable non-words.

(A) One-syllable non-words

Sep	Grall
Hond	Fot
Bift	Nate
Smip	Thip
Clird	Tull

(B) Two-syllable non-words

Pennel	Ballop
Rubid	Diller
Bannow	Hampent
Glistow	Sladding
Tafflest	Prindle

(C) Three-syllable non-words

Doppelate	Bannifer
Barrazon	Commerine
Thickery	Glistering
Frescovent	Trumpertine
Brasterer	Skiticult

(D) Four-syllable non-words

Woogalamic	Fenneriser
Commeecitate	Loddenapish
Penneriful	Contramponist
Perplisteronk	Blonterstaping
Stopograttic	Empliforvent

Sometimes, worried parents are reassured with the story about Albert Einstein having been so slow to acquire language that his family thought he might be retarded. Normally, children will acquire language in predictable stages as shown in the schedule of the timetable on p. 42.

Symptoms of common language disorders

These are some of the most common types of SLI:

Phonological-syntactic deficit: These children have difficulty pronouncing words properly and decoding *syntax* — the rules for relating words to each other in a sentence. (*I like old people and cats*, for instance, is syntactically ambiguous, and so can be construed in two ways.) These children have a hard time comprehending long, complex sentences, may speak very little, and are hard to understand.

Semantic-pragmatic disorder: These children don't have pronunciation problems. They have difficulty with word meanings, as well as with the more subtle rules governing the use of words in social context (*pragmatics*). An example of the latter problem would be failing to understand "Do you like peppermints?" as a possible indirect offer, or "Your room is a mess" as a possible indirect request. Autistic children and adults typically have this kind of difficulty with pragmatics.

Lexical-semantic deficit: These children have difficulty understanding questions and messages out of context, and often have a hard time accessing the words they need to express themselves.

Developmental verbal dyspraxia: These children have problems moving their vocal apparatus in the appropriate way for normal speech, making themselves very hard to understand. The London family with a genetically-based language disorder has developmental dyspraxia. Their understanding of language isn't affected.

References

Fisher, Simon E., et al. (1998). Localization of a gene implicated in a severe speech and language disorder. Nature Genetics 18: 168-70.

Gathercole, Susan E., and Alan D. Baddeley (1989). Evaluation of the role of phonological STM in the development of vocabulary in children: a longitudinal study. Journal of Memory and Language 28: 200-13.

Gathercole, Susan E., et al. (1991). The influences of number of syllables and wordlikeness on children's repetition of nonwords. Applied Psycholinguistics 12: 349-67.

Lai, C.S., et al. (2000). The SPCH1 region on human 7q31: genomic characterization of the critical interval and localization of translocations associated with speech and language disorder. American Journal of Human Genetics 67/2: 357-68.

Montgomery, James W. (1998). Sentence comprehension and working memory in children with specific language impairment. In Memory and Language Impairment in Children and Adults: New Perspectives, Ronald B. Gillam (ed.). Gaithersburg, MD: Aspen Publishers.

Montgomery, James W. (1995). Examination of phonological working memory in specifically language-impaired children. Applied Psycholinguistics 16: 355-78.

Wijsman, E.M., et al. (2000). Segregation analysis of phenotypic components of learning disabilities. I. Nonword memory and digit span. American Journal of Human Genetics 67/3: 631-46.

THE EFFECTS OF NEGLECT ON THE DEVELOPING BRAIN
The Case of the Romanian Orphans

To learn about the effects of a bad environment on a developing human brain, researchers obviously can't conduct the same kinds of experiments they might perform on rats or monkeys. Instead, they have to rely on data gathered from "natural" experiments.

Recently, hundreds of Romanian orphans were adopted into good homes after having suffered unconscionable neglect in orphanages under the Ceaucescu regime. The conditions in those orphanages resembled the kind of "impoverished" environment that researchers impose on rats in biological experiments. The orphans were confined to cots, with few playthings and little attention from caregivers.

When they arrived in their adoptive countries, the orphans were severely impaired in their development. By following their progress, researchers have been able to gather data about what age, if any, is too late to fix brain-development problems caused by early deprivation.

The researchers have mostly good news to report. For most of the children, cognitive catch-up was essentially complete within a few years. At the same time — and here is where the encouraging findings need to be qualified — the older adoptees haven't caught up completely.

The encouraging conclusion is that the human brain is very resilient. Even severe deprivation during the first few years of life can be overcome to a remarkable degree. For the Romanian orphans, there was no point at any time during the first three and a half years of life when any developmental window slammed shut.

NEGLECT

The worst form of abuse for learning

There's been a lot of press lately about the importance of the first three years of life for a child's developing brain. This news carries with it a threat as well as a promise: If a child is denied the right amount and right kind of stimulation, critical windows of opportunity may slam shut and that child will forever be, in some way, limited.

The good news is that a young child's brain is so avidly searching for appropriate stimulation in its environment that the situation would have to be pretty extreme for it *not* to find what it needs to develop properly. Fortunately for us humans, most developmental windows of opportunity remain open a long time. If there is one message that recent brain science has to give us, it's that the human brain is a remarkably resilient organ that has the capacity to change and develop throughout life, not just during the first few years out of the womb.

Still, it is true that neglect can deprive a child's developing brain of the input it needs to grow to its full potential. Neglect may deprive a child of the self-confidence needed to take on new challenges. Abuse can guide a young brain along paths that may lead to mood, cognitive, and behavioral problems later in life. Only in the early 1990's did researchers have access to brain-scanning technology that could image exactly how early experiences can shape the brain abnormally. The growing body of insights into the process by which a bad early environment changes a young brain is useful also for the parents of children being raised in basically good environments.

The insecurity of neglect and abuse affects the developing brain in similar ways

In some ways, neglect and violent abuse can be very similar as far as an infant's brain is concerned. Neglect isn't just a matter of boredom or insufficient input for proper learning. Neglect is *stressful* for an infant. Animal studies have shown that separating a newborn from its mother instantly raises its stress hormone levels. Human infants need the attention of a loving caregiver, too. In nine-month-old babies, levels of stress hormones, measured in a simple saliva test, rise in response to a cold and distant caregiver, but not a friendly and playful one.

The importance of paying attention to an infant goes beyond momentary discomfort. Being paid attention to equals a sense of security in a helpless infant's mind. In fact, a wise teacher of child psychology once advised first-time parents that they can commit all the other mistakes of child rearing as long as they make the child sure of three things: That they love each other, that they want to pay attention to the child, and that food is always available. For an infant and young child, those three constants signal security.

Absence of security causes stress

In other animals, such as rats and monkeys, experiments
have shown that chronic stress triggers not just a rise in stress
hormones, but also the death of brain neurons and receptor
sites, and even cognitive impairment. On the other hand,
some experiments have also shown that adequate early physical contact and attention — licking and grooming by the
mother, for example — can help lower young animals' self-
destructive stress response *for the rest of their lives*. Their brain
system for modulating stress response works better, they lose
fewer neurons, and they even suffer less cognitive impairment when they get old.

How the brain causes and responds to stress

One of the best-studied areas in the brain and body's stress
response system is called the *hypothalamic-pituitary-adrenal*
(HPA) *axis*. The first two organs of the brain are directly
responsible for releasing the adrenaline hormone into the
blood (see *Stress*). In the HPA system, the perception of a
threat triggers the body's release of stress hormones that end
up acting on receptors in the brain. Stress hormones known as
glucocorticoids trigger the *amygdala*, the brain's threat-detecting
center, into high alert so it can tell the body to fight or flee.
But this is far from an optimal brain state for learning. Short-
term, stimulating the amygdala into a fight-or-flight response
also entails shutting down other brain systems, including
those responsible for learning and memory. Long-term, stress
hormones can do permanent damage to those systems.

Some researchers believe that childhood stress might lead
to learning problems in other ways as well. When the brain
attempts to cope with stress, it raises the levels of *dopamine,*
one of the brain's own natural chemicals for transmitting signals between cells that also imparts a feeling of satisfaction

INSECURE ATTACHMENT
When a Child Can't Find Comfort in His Mother

Proponents of a theory of child development known as *attachment* hold that the nature of the child's relationship with his primary caregiver early in life can have lasting effects on his brain and behavior. By this theory, the infant will be healthier if the caregiver (usually, the mother) habitually responds to signals of discomfort and distress with comforting behavior. This response creates "secure attachment" in the child's mind, which equips the child to form a permanently healthy and well-adjusted attitude toward life. Even in a child born with an anxious temperament, secure attachment protects its developing brain from the ravaging effects of glucocorticoid "stress" hormones. If, on the other hand, the mother habitually rejects the child's appeal for comfort, ignores the child, abuses it or even exhibits anxiety toward it, various kinds of insecure attachment can develop which may have a lasting impact on the child's brain and behavior.

and well-being. But high dopamine levels interfere with the proper function of the *prefrontal cortex*. This area in the very upper front of the brain is responsible for many of the kinds of behavior children are supposed to be in the process of trying to learn — planning, organizing, focusing, and tuning out distractions. Not coincidentally, perhaps, many researchers believe *Attention Deficit-Hyperactivity Disorder* (ADHD) is linked to an imbalance in the brain's dopamine system. Therefore, chronic stress early in life might lead, or at least contribute, to the development of a learning disability.

Psychologists use something called the "Strange Situations" test to gauge an infant's attachment status at 12 months of age. Basically, the test is designed to stress out the infant a little bit and then observe whether he finds comfort in his mother's presence. First, the infant and his mother are brought into an unfamiliar toy-filled room. Then, the mother leaves and returns twice. What the psychologists watch for is the infant's reaction to the departure and return of the mother each time. It's good if the infant is distressed or a little uncomfortable when his mother leaves, greets his mother when she returns, finds comfort, and then settles down to play. That's a sign of secure attachment. There are three scenarios that are a bad sign: If the infant shows no distress when the mother leaves and avoids her on her return; if the infant is extremely distressed when his mother leaves, approaches his mother on her return but can't be comforted; or if the infant seems confused or disoriented.

What caregivers can do to reduce the causes and effects of stress in the developing years

If the animal studies described above apply to humans, loving physical contact with an infant may help protect the brain from destructive effects of glucocorticoids even after the child has grown up. It may also help to protect against brain-based disorders — depression, anorexia nervosa, schizophrenia, and Alzheimer's — that some researchers believe to be linked to overactivity of the brain and body's stress-response system.

References

Arnsten, A. (1999). Development of the cerebral cortex: XIV. Stress impairs prefrontal cortical function. Journal of the American Academy of Child and Adolescent Psychiatry 38: 220-22.

Charney, D., et al. (1993). Psychobiological mechanisms of post-traumatic stress disorder. Archives of General Psychiatry 50: 294-305.

Glaser, Danya (2000). Child abuse and neglect and the brain — a review. Journal of Child Psychology and Psychiatry 41/1: 97-116.

Gunnar, M., et al. (1992). The stressfulness of separation among 9-month-old infants: effects of social context variables and infant temperament. Child Development 63: 290-303.

Liu, D., et al. (1997). Maternal care, hippocampal glucocorticoid receptors, and hypothalamic-pituitary-adrenal responses to stress. Science 277: 1659-62.

O'Brien, John T. (1997). The "glucocorticoid cascade" hypothesis in man: prolonged stress may cause permanent brain damage. British Journal of Psychiatry 170: 199-201.

O'Connor, T.G., et al. (2000). The effects of global severe deprivation on cognitive competence: extension and longitudinal follow-up. Child Development 71/2: 376-90.

Plotsky, P., and M. Meaney (1993). Early postnatal experience alters hypothalamic corticotropin-releasing factor (CRF) mRNA, median eminence CRF content and stress-induced release in adult rats. Molecular Brain Research 18: 195-2000.

Rutter, Michael et al. (1998). Developmental catch-up, and deficit, following adoption after severe global early privation. Journal of Child Psychology and Psychiatry 39/4: 465-76.

SELF-CONSCIOUSNESS

The terrible twos

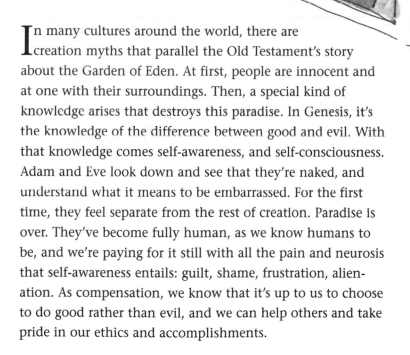

In many cultures around the world, there are creation myths that parallel the Old Testament's story about the Garden of Eden. At first, people are innocent and at one with their surroundings. Then, a special kind of knowledge arises that destroys this paradise. In Genesis, it's the knowledge of the difference between good and evil. With that knowledge comes self-awareness, and self-consciousness. Adam and Eve look down and see that they're naked, and understand what it means to be embarrassed. For the first time, they feel separate from the rest of creation. Paradise is over. They've become fully human, as we know humans to be, and we're paying for it still with all the pain and neurosis that self-awareness entails: guilt, shame, frustration, alien-ation. As compensation, we know that it's up to us to choose to do good rather than evil, and we can help others and take pride in our ethics and accomplishments.

An infant assumes everyone is just like he is

Why is that story so common around the world? Because it's
an allegory of a process of development that all infants in all
cultures experience early in life. Newborns have no awareness
of a boundary between themselves and the world around
them. At about age one, toddlers begin to recognize they can
do things that others can't, but they haven't yet grasped that
they are separate, independent agents. This is demonstrated
dramatically in the adult-child exchange of peek-a-boo.
When the mother covers her face with her hands, the toddler
imitates her; but when he uncovers his face, he's surprised
that his mother's face is still covered. Any two- or three-year-
old knows that a one-year-old little brother or sister is terrible
at hide-and-seek. The one-year-old will jump out from hiding
before being found because his brain has not developed
enough yet for him to have a clear sense of the difference
between "self" and "other."

Self-consciousness emerges in the minds of two-year-olds

By the age of two, a toddler begins to understand that other
people can have needs and feelings that are different from his
own. From that insight flows the awareness of possession or
ownership. Before this age, the concept of theft doesn't really
even have any meaning. (Did anybody own anything in the
Garden?) It isn't until about age two that a young child is
even capable of understanding the importance of respecting
the belongings of other children.

This is the age when self-awareness and self-consciousness arise. Around age two, children begin to experiment
with the difference between their own and their parents' will
and identity. They become conscious not just of the indepen-
dence of others, but of a sense of how things "should be,"

A Simple Test of Self-Awareness

If you want to test your toddler's self-awareness, put a little rouge on her nose or cheek and hold a mirror to her face. If she reaches up to touch the rouge on her *own* face (not the face in the reflection), she knows she's the person in the mirror. This kind of self-awareness begins to emerge between 18 and 25 months. Most children develop it between 24 and 28 months of age. With it comes the potential for embarrassment.

and they begin to feel frustration if something doesn't work right or if they can't do something they're told or expected to do. If you want to get a two-year-old upset, do something in front of him that you know he can't do, and watch what happens when he tries to imitate you. Along with self-awareness come the beginnings of empathy: Two-year-olds approach others who are in distress and try to comfort them, instead of just becoming distressed themselves as an infant will do.

Around the middle of the second year, the frontal lobe of the brain has developed sufficiently to give a child the awareness of social demands, and an understanding that some actions are "bad" or forbidden. This is the age when a toddler will begin to show tempestuous emotions in response to his own transgressions. He does not yet understand *why* his action is bad, but he is able to pick up the signals that he is responsible for the bad action.

How young children finally understand what seems obvious to adults

All these developments are accompanied by — indeed, depend on — structural and biochemical changes in the young child's brain during a period when new connections among the brain cells are growing by the hundreds of thousands every day. During the second year explosive growth of the brain's top surface of cells, often called "gray matter" is taking place in areas of the *prefrontal* part of the *cortex*, the very front part located just above the eyes. The prefrontal cortex is the most recently evolved part of the human brain, and it is the last part to develop fully in childhood. As its connections grow, little by little, it endows a child with the ability to imagine time before and after the present. As this miracle of consciousness becomes possible, so does the ability to plan ahead. Up to, and even well past, puberty, the cells in the cortex continue to expand their connections allowing the growing child to control emotional impulses, feel empathy and appreciate the value of performing even unpleasant duties in the present because of their future benefit. The brain cells in the cortex constantly extend their links to other parts of the brain, including deep down into the centers of emotion and across the *corpus callosum* connecting the two sides of the brain. As these *axon* nerve fibers lengthen, white *myelin* insulation grows around them to enhance the speed and strength of transmissions along them. According to Harvard developmental psychologist Jerome Kagan, as the child's brain more fully integrates information from different regions, it becomes capable of supporting language, a sense of right and wrong, self-awareness, and the ability to draw inferences.

Feelings of shame and pride are possible once a child becomes aware of himself as not being like others

The age of self-awareness and self-consciousness is also the age of the emergence of shame and pride. Parents have to be careful not to be too harsh in their punishment, since a two-

USE IT OR LOSE IT
From Tots to Teens

New imaging studies are revealing patterns of brain development in early childhood that extend into the teenage years. The new-found appreciation of the dynamic nature of the teen brain is emerging from MRI (magnetic resonance imaging) studies that scan a child's brain every two years, as he or she grows up.

In the first such longitudinal study of 145 children and adolescents, reported in 1999 by the National Institute of Mental Health (NIMH), the Institute's Dr. Judith Rapoport and colleagues were surprised to discover, just prior to puberty, a flurry of overproduction of *gray matter*, the thinking part of the brain. Possibly related to the influence of surging sex hormones, this thickening peaks at around age 11 in girls, 12 in boys, after which the gray matter actually thins some.

Prior to this study, research had shown that the brain overproduced gray matter for a brief period in early development — in the womb and for about the first 18 months of life — and then underwent just one bout of pruning. Researchers are now confronted with structural changes that occur much later. The gray matter growth-spurt just prior to puberty predominates in the frontal lobes, the seat of *executive* functions — planning, impulse control, and reasoning. It's tempting to interpret the new findings as empowering teens to protect and nurture their brain as a work in progress.

Citation
National Institute of Mental Health (NIMH) Office of
    Communications and Public Liaison

year-old's sense of self is still fragile: The child is likely to feel that the entire self is threatened, even if it's just a specific misdeed that's being punished.

It may be particularly important to exercise restraint with children who are temperamentally "difficult," since harsh discipline may evoke yet more difficult behavior in a self-reinforcing negative cycle. An overemphasis on negative control alone can lead to even more defiance. Most developmental psychologists believe a certain balance of encouragement and control is healthy. Encouragement helps a child take an active role in learning new skills, and helps to develop a healthy self-esteem. Common-sense control, or "setting limits," helps a young child avoid harsh reprimands from others. Like the confining rails of a playpen, setting limits may also allow the child to feel freer to explore his new capabilities without fear of straying too far into danger.

Reference
Herschkowitz, N., J. Kagan, and K. Zilles (1999). Neurobiological bases of behavioral development in the second year. Neuropediatrics 30/5: 221-30.

THE DECEIVING BRAIN

**Very likely, a three-year-old really *does*
remember seeing a reindeer on the roof**

When does a child learn to lie?
Three-year-olds don't seem to have
the ability to report their own past
belief states. In other words, if
they believe there's a monster
in the shed, and then learn
that's not true, they'll deny ever
having believed in the monster
at all. Is that lying? Not if
"lying" means knowing
that what you say
isn't true. Three-
year-olds haven't
developed the cog-
nitive ability to impute
false beliefs to others
(including a former self!)
when they themselves
know what the truth is. The
ability to understand alternate
mental representations, or other minds,
is sometimes called a *theory of mind* (see *The Eyes Have It*),
which children don't develop until about age four. Other
facts about the gradual development of memory and the
brain also shed light on why the concept of "lying" may just
not apply to a very young child.

Memory in infants

It's not until about the latter half of the first year of life that
infants begin to show what might be called explicit, or conscious, memory. During the first half year or so, and even in
the womb, infants have various kinds of memory, shared by

new animals. They display a primitive kind of learning known as *habituation*, in which they stop responding to a stimulus after they've encountered it a few times (see *Learning in the Womb*). Fruit flies and sea slugs can do this, too. Newborns can also be *conditioned* — as when the Russian scientist Pavlov taught dogs to salivate at the sound of a bell by ringing the bell every time he fed them. Even fruit flies can be conditioned.

Young infants also demonstrate a simple kind of *recognition* memory when they show interest in things they haven't seen or heard before, and when they recognize their mother's voice and even their mother tongue (see *Learning in the Womb*).

All these kinds of memory are automatic, and none are unique to humans. They correspond to what in an adult would be kinds of *implicit* memory, which means they happen independently of conscious awareness. (Implicit memory is different from *explicit* memory, also called *declarative* memory, which is the kind of memory — remembering a fact or having been someplace at a certain time — that we can talk about.)

Things begin to change in the second half of the first year. One of the most interesting things about the development of memory is that it doesn't involve a *switch* from implicit, unconscious memory to a more conscious kind. The conscious kind of memory is *added* to an array of unconscious, automatic memory abilities that remain with us for the rest of our lives. So the growing brain begins to accumulate different kinds of memory, and different kinds of learning, some of which are primitive and animal-like in nature, while others are more characteristically human.

In the second half of the first year, infants begin to develop the kinds of skills that we normally think of as depending on conscious memory. For example, by around 9 to 12 months, infants begin to be able to repeat a sequence of actions they've watched someone else perform, even after a considerable amount of time has passed. At around this time, infants also begin, very gradually, to develop some familiarity with skills that depend on *working memory*, a short-term memory system for storing and manipulating information. It's working memory that allows you to remember a phone number long enough to dial it, or multiply 9 by 12 in your head. This is a kind of memory that relates to problem-solving strategies, rather than simply recalling or recognizing something. Very gradually, through childhood and even past adolescence, people get better and better at devising problem-solving strategies that depend on working memory. One reason this development is slow is that it, in turn, depends on a part of the brain, the *prefrontal cortex*, that takes a long time to mature.

Memory of what happened when — or didn't really

An aspect of memory believed to depend on the prefrontal cortex is what's sometimes called *autobiographical,* or *episodic,* memory — the kind of memory that lets you consciously recall where you were and what you were doing while you were, say, on your last vacation. If a four-year-old sees you put a marble in a box, or hears you tell him you've put a marble in a box, he'll remember not just that there's a marble in the box but also *how* he knows — whether he saw it or was told. A three-year-old, on the other hand, may remember there's a marble in the box but not the circumstances of learning it, just as you probably don't remember how or when you learned that Paris is the capital of France. This kind of memory, called *source memory*, doesn't develop until about age four.

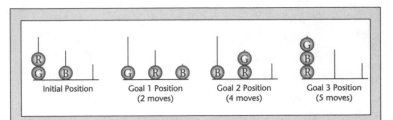

Initial Position   Goal 1 Position (2 moves)   Goal 2 Position (4 moves)   Goal 3 Position (5 moves)

Strategy Skills Develop Slowly as the Prefrontal Lobe Matures

The "Tower of Hanoi" puzzle is a good test of working memory abilities housed in the brain's prefrontal lobe. As the prefrontal lobe matures, a child gets better at planning the moves required to solve the puzzle efficiently. The first goal position (above) only requires two moves, and most four-year-olds can solve this one. The second one requires four moves. Only about 10 percent of four-year-olds can do this one without making extra moves. About 20 percent of eight-year-olds can do it, and 60 percent of teenagers. The final, five-move problem relies most heavily on the frontal lobe's ability to plan ahead. Hardly any four-year-olds can do it in five moves, while about 5 percent of five-year-olds can, 10 percent of seven-year-olds, a little under 20 percent of eight-year-olds, and 60 percent of teenagers.

That's why a three-year-old isn't lying if he says he saw Rudolf on the roof. He won't remember whether he actually saw something, or heard it in a story, or even just imagined it. All he'll remember is the fact of having gotten the idea in his head. It's no coincidence that it's also not until about age four that a child can explicitly relate the past to the present — to understand, say, that the reason the cat ran away is that he left the door open.

The slow development of these abilities may account for the fact that most people can't remember what happened during their first four years of life — something called *infantile amnesia*. Since the child's brain has not yet developed enough to create autobiographical memories, it won't later be able to recall being in a certain place and doing something at a certain time. That doesn't mean that other brain systems don't store data from that time of life, it's just that they cannot be accessed consciously.

Infantile amnesia also explains why judges have come to be very careful about relying on the testimony of very young children in court cases. A three-year-old may not be able to remember how he got the idea that a preschool worker molested him — whether because it actually happened or because somebody, perhaps a well-meaning social worker or police officer, suggested it to him.

References

Cowan, Nelson (Ed.) (1997). The Development of Memory in Childhood. Sussex UK: Psychology Press.

Luciana, Monica, and Charles A. Nelson (1998). The functional emergence of prefrontally-guided working memory systems in four- to eight-year-old children. Neuropsychologia 36/3: 273-93.

Nelson, Charles A. (1995). The ontogeny of human memory: a cognitive neuroscience perspective. Developmental Psychology 31/5: 723-38.

Nelson, Charles A., and Floyd E. Bloom (1997). Child development and neuroscience. Child Development 68/5: 970-87.

Van Petten, C., A.J. Sekfor, and W.M. Newberg (2000). Memory for drawings in locations: spatial source memory and event-related potentials. Psychophysiology 37/4: 551-64.

The Four Innate Traits of Temperament
as Defined by Robert Cloninger

Novelty Seeking
High
exploratory, impul-
sive, extravagant,
disorderly
Low
rigid, reflective,
reserved,
regimented

Persistence
High
eager, ambitious,
determined
Low
unambitious,
uninterested in
achievement

Harm Avoidance
High
worried, fearful, shy,
fatigable
Low
optimistic, confi-
dent, gregarious,
energetic

*Reward
Dependence*
High
sentimental,
attached, needful of
others' approval
Low
detached, cynical,
independent, social-
ly insensitive

Traditional European Model of Temperament
and Related Body Fluids

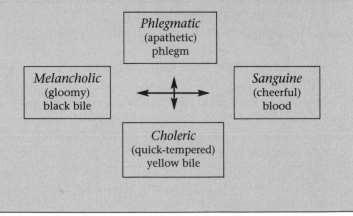

Phlegmatic
(apathetic)
phlegm

Melancholic
(gloomy)
black bile

Sanguine
(cheerful)
blood

Choleric
(quick-tempered)
yellow bile

TEMPERAMENTAL LIMITATIONS

The poker hand an infant's genome deals it

Any nursery school teacher knows that children have different temperaments from a very young age. One child may be shy, another highly outgoing, one even-tempered, another emotional. Midwives claim to be able to tell the temperament of a baby the moment it's born. There's even evidence that temperamental differences may already be present before birth: Children with a relatively rapid heartbeat in the womb are the ones that tend to end up being categorized as "shy" by their nursery school teachers.

Qualities that make up a child's innate temperament
Research into the development of personality suggests that there are some personality elements that are relatively stable,

innate, and at least partly genetically based, while other elements are more strongly molded by environment and upbringing. It's the former elements that are grouped under the heading *temperament,* while the latter are separated out under such terms as *character.*

The temperament that a child brings into the world with him has an influence on his style of learning, his patience and persistence, and even whether or not he thinks that achievement in school is important. But it's not deterministic. Temperament interacts with upbringing and life experiences to make the child what he is to become as an adult.

No two temperaments are identical. But we humans are avid categorizers. (As the joke goes: *There are two types of people: Those who divide the world into two types of people, and those who don't.*) In a long European tradition going back over 2,000 years, different temperament types used to be linked to the relative balance of four bodily *humors,* or fluids (see box, p. 66). In the 20th century, five-factor inventories became popular. Several have used variations on the theme of *extroversion, agreeableness, conscientiousness, emotional stability,* and *imagination.* Different traits can combine with one another so that, for example, one individual might be described as high in agreeableness and high in conscientiousness, while another is high in agreeableness and low in conscientiousness, and so on. With five traits, if we assume just three values (high, low, medium) for each trait, we get a system of 243 temperament types.

Four traits that are building blocks of temperament
Washington University psychologist Robert Cloninger proposes four temperament dimensions: *novelty seeking, harm avoidance, reward dependence,* and *persistence* (see box, p. 66). A person can have high, low, or average values for each dimen-

sion independently of the others. For example, people high in novelty seeking tend to be adventurous, impulsive, and quick to latch onto new ideas. Only if they also happen to be low in harm avoidance will they tend to indulge in dangerous and self-destructive behavior.

The logic of this kind of system is that, both intuitively and empirically, it does seem to be true that some personality traits are independent of others. If you're an extrovert, you might be either imaginative or unimaginative. So whatever gives rise to extroversion must be different from whatever it is that underlies imagination. What might those underlying factors be? Nobody believes in the bodily humor theory any longer. Modern neuroscientists believe that different systems in the brain, coded by different genes, might be responsible for different temperament traits.

Each temperament trait may be governed by one of the brain's neurotransmitters

Cloninger associates each of his temperament dimensions with a different *neurotransmitter*, chemicals naturally produced by the brain that transmit signals between brain cells and affect mood. He links novelty seeking to *dopamine*, and harm avoidance to *serotonin*, for example. One support for this theory is that antidepressants such as Prozac, which raise serotonin levels, tend to make people less anxious, pessimistic, depressed, and fatigable — all harm avoidance characteristics. The other factor is genetic. Researchers have actually found evidence that the *D4 dopamine receptor gene* may predispose a person to be high or low in novelty seeking, depending on whether that person has inherited the long or the short version of the gene.

Harvard temperament researcher Jerome Kagan cites evidence that certain fearless children might have genes that code for low levels of *norepinephrine*, a neurotransmitter that has, as one of its effects, the stimulation of the *amygdala*, a primitive "fear" center in the brain (see *Stress*). Those children also tend to have lower heart rates. A simple biological difference in a neurotransmitter system may, in effect, remove an obstacle to harmful, antisocial, violent behavior, in turn placing them at risk for criminality. A biological difference, therefore, would appear to influence morality, as temperament shades into character.

An important point for parents and teachers

Temperamental differences never determine anyone's personality as a whole. For example, someone low in Cloninger's dimension of reward dependence may be a nonconformist who is privately contemptuous of the opinions of others. But he may still be high in the character dimensions of cooperativeness and self-transcendence, and treat others with tolerance, respect, and compassion. In fact, temperamental differences in childhood don't even determine temperament in adulthood. A highly fearful baby isn't destined to develop an anxiety disorder in the process of growing up. Rather, a highly harm-avoidant temperament at birth simply makes it less likely that the child will end up becoming a temperamentally fearless, outgoing adult.

This brings up another point of importance to parents. According to studies by Kagan, about one third of children who are either highly or minimally fearful at four months — what Cloninger might call very high or low in harm avoidance — maintain this temperamental profile at 14 to 21 months of age. By contrast, virtually none of the highly fearful four-month-olds become minimally fearful later, or vice-versa. This shows how innate temperament places *constraints* on the way a child's temperament develops, but doesn't *determine* it.

But what accounts for the fact that two thirds of children change, while one third do not? Presumably, environment does. For example, if a child has an underactive amygdala due to low norepinephrine levels, as already explained, he's at risk for being minimally harm-avoidant and developing antisocial, violent behavior. Whether that risk becomes reality may be determined by environment: whether the child is or is not exposed to violent, antisocial behavior, and whether such behavior is punished or not. In this sense, environment and upbringing have the final say in the development of personality.

References

Benjamin, Jonathan, et al. (1996). Population and familial association between the D4 dopamine receptor gene and measures of novelty seeking. Nature Genetics 12: 81-4.

Cloninger, C. Robert. (1987). A systematic method for clinical description and classification of personality variants. Archives of General Psychiatry 44: 573-88.

Kagan, Jerome (1994). Galen's Prophecy. New York: Basic Books.

Kagan, Jerome (1997). Temperament and the reactions to unfamiliarity. Child Development 68/1: 139-43.

Parenting

The three key ways to teach character

Most psychologists agree that the personality that a child develops as he grows up is the product of a mix of factors, some innate and others learned. Washington University psychologist Robert Cloninger sums this up very simply in a model of personality that consists of two main elements, *temperament* and *character.*

Temperament versus character

Temperament, which has a genetic component and is relatively innate, refers to traits such as shyness or extroversion. To a great extent, temperament is what the child brings into the world with him, and while childhood temperament does not determine the adult temperament, it does stack the odds against certain outcomes by limiting future directions. Character, which is more a product of environment and upbringing, includes such traits as personal values, morality, ethics, and beliefs about the importance of education.

How children adopt their personality traits

In other words, a child's character is something parents (and, later, teachers and peers) can have a powerful influence on. Harvard psychologist Jerome Kagan views the ways that parents exert an influence on their child's development as falling into three main categories: *direct interactions, emotional identification,* and *family stories.* Here's a summary of what those categories mean, the ages at which they have the strongest effect on a child, and examples of how a parent, or other early caregiver, might use this knowledge to a child's benefit.

Direct interaction

Direct interaction includes such things as how often and for what reasons a young child encounters discipline. Discipline is absorbed by a child as another demonstration of protective

attention if it is experienced in the context of consistent support. On the other hand, lack of discipline for aggression or dis-
obedience can increase the risk of antisocial behavior, peer
rejection, and low self-esteem.

Significant early stimulants to later cognitive performance
include spending time reading or telling stories to a young
child, showing an interest in what a child enjoys, and taking
the time to point out the names of new objects and the meanings of new words. These are things that influence the child's
personality from infancy on and will bear fruit in higher levels
of achievement. Early reading and conversation of this kind
can build a larger working vocabulary. Language ability creates
a cascade of effects in the school years: good grades, high self-
esteem, intellectual curiosity and ambition.

From a toddler's point of view, receiving supportive attention in almost any way affects his health, both emotional and
physical, by reducing stress. Compared to other primates, a
human infant carries an unusually big brain in an unusually
tender, helpless body. An infant depends wholly on the reli-
able attention of a caregiver to fill its basic needs, and provide
security.

Emotional identification

By around age four or five, children start to develop an implicit
belief that they are like their parents. This is the age when the
concept of *role model* starts becoming particularly important. A
five-year-old absorbs what he perceives to be his caregivers'
fears, enjoyments, activities, and talents. At that age, the way a
parent behaves begins to become more important than what
the parent says. So from an early age, such things as an interest
in books or an interest in understanding, explaining, and talking about how the world works can start to have a big influence on a child's self-image in ways that may be indelible.

Scientists Link Early Learning with Preventing Alzheimer's

A new study suggests that a stimulating learning environment early in life might help ward off neurodegenerative diseases later on. The findings indicate that nurture may be more influential than nature when it comes to the brain's resilience to injury.

Researchers at Jefferson Medical College of Thomas Jefferson University in Philadelphia and at the University of Auckland in New Zealand raised one group of rats in an enriched learning environment with running wheels, tunnels, rubber balls, and a maze. Other rats were housed in standard conditions with no toys.

They found that laboratory rats raised in the cages offering a stimulating environment had 45 percent less age-related brain cell death than rats living in basic cages. What's more, when they fed a neurotoxin to the rats in both cages, the rats with the stimulating toys were nearly completely protected from brain cell loss, unlike those in the simpler environment.

Neuroscientist Matthew During, director of the Central Nervous System Gene Therapy Center at Jefferson University, was surprised how robust the enriched rat brains were. "We showed in this study that an enriched environment switched on the genes in the brain, and we believe by that mechanism the brain becomes super-resilient, resistant to aging and diseases, such as Alzheimer's, Parkinson's, and traumatic brain injury," he says.

(Excerpted from the April 1999 issue of the journal Nature Medicine)

Family stories

This third factor is one that, all too often, gets overlooked these days. For a child, and for the adult the child ends up to be, it's important to have a sense of family pride. Stories about the accomplishments and special talents of ancestors and relatives, perhaps told around the dinner table, help children to have confidence in their own talents, which can help to develop a belief in their abilities and prospects for success in life. In addition, children will begin to form a picture of what status or identity their family, and therefore the child himself, has in society. For example: "I am a black person." "My mom is a teacher and other people listen to what she says." "We are poorer than other people." "My dad is a really good cook and can fix cars." Perceptions such as these will have at least as much influence on the child's success later in life as whatever temperamental traits it was born with.

Neuroscientists studying child development believe that all three categories of parental influence interact with other influences, such as temperament, social class, birth order, ethnicity, and the salient characteristics of the historical period in which the child is brought up. This complex web of inherited and environmental forces acts on the development of a child's character. Though a parent may be powerless to control such influences, some of the controllable factors may compensate for bad luck in other domains. For example, family stories can help foster a sense of family pride that material poverty might otherwise undermine.

References

Cloninger, C. Robert (1987). A systematic method for clinical description and classification of personality variants. Archives of General Psychiatry 44: 573-88.

Kagan, Jerome (1999). The role of parents in children's psychological development. Pediatrics 104/1 Supplement: 164-7.

MUSIC

The best whole-brain builder —
Mozart notwithstanding

Some research reported since 1993 seems to show that listening to certain kinds of music can significantly boost IQ. Other research shows that preschool or grade school music education can have benefits for reasoning skills used in mathematics, engineering, and chess. On the other hand, some studies have shown no such effect, and one of the researchers who discovered what's been called the "Mozart effect" has criticized applications of that research as scientifically unfounded.

Mozart's genius as a composer turns out to be much more lasting that his "effect" as a quick fix
Perhaps no other brain research in the last decade has resonated throughout popular culture as the so-called "Mozart effect": the IQ-boosting effect of simply listening to a Mozart piano composition. And reporting about this phenomenon

hasn't just served to boost magazine sales. In early 1998, Governor Zell Miller of Georgia was so impressed by *Time* and *Newsweek* cover stories on infant brain plasticity that he proposed a state budget allocation of $105,000 for the purchase of Mozart CDs to be distributed to mothers of newborns. "No one questions," Miller explained to the state legislature, "that listening to music at a very early age affects the spatial-temporal reasoning that underlies math and engineering and even chess."

It may have surprised the governor to learn that such a claim would not only have invited skepticism from brain scientists, but would even have been rejected by the researchers who originally came up with the findings on which Miller's claim was apparently based. One of those researchers, University of California, Irvine (now University of Wisconsin) psychologist Frances Rauscher, when asked to comment on Miller's project, responded that "none of our studies show that listening casually has any effect at all for children."

What the original studies actually showed

The research that gave rise to the Mozart effect idea actually had nothing to do with newborns, or even children. In a 1993 letter printed in the prestigious journal *Nature*, Rauscher, Gordon L. Shaw, and Katherine N. Ky reported the results of an experiment in which a ten-minute session of listening to Mozart's sonata for two pianos in D major, K488, boosted college students' spatial IQ scores by an average of eight or nine points for a period of about ten to fifteen minutes. Listening to a relaxation tape for ten minutes, or simply sitting silently, had no effect at all. Also in 1993, an unpublished non-controlled pilot study (reported briefly in a 1994 issue of the journal *Science)* by Rauscher and Shaw showed beneficial effects of music education for preschoolers.

Out of an apparent blending of the results of these two different studies arose an understanding of the Mozart effect as the power of Mozart to make children smarter. Note that neither study actually investigated the effect of listening to Mozart on the spatial IQ of young children. But taken together, the results did seem to offer encouraging evidence that some kind of exposure to music, whether as a child or adult, might cross over into benefits for other kinds of intelligence. Since those early studies, some other experiments have provided further support for this view, while others have failed to. Here are some of the results that are important for any parent, or any person, trying to make sense of all this.

Just listening improved paper-folding visualization skills by a few points, and even that didn't last

The original study on the connection between Mozart and spatial IQ actually found improvement on only one very specific kind of task used in a standard IQ test, the Stanford-Binet. That task, known as Paper Folding, requires the test-taker to figure out, on the basis of visually-presented instructions for folding and cutting a sheet of paper in a certain sequence of steps, what the resulting pattern will turn out to be once the paper is unfolded (see box, p. 80).

The specific skill of Paper Folding tests is the *spatial-temporal reasoning* Governor Miller made reference to in his address to the Georgia legislature. Spatial-temporal reasoning differs from other kinds of spatial intelligence in that it specifically requires the visualization of a *succession* of patterns over time.

Tests of influence of other music on other skills

Other studies by other researchers have also supported the Mozart effect, as long as they used the right kind of music and tested the right kind of intelligence. Studies testing the

Spatial-Temporal Reasoning and the Mozart Effect

Researchers into the Mozart effect have found that listening to a Mozart sonata can improve a specific kind of spatial intelligence for a brief period of time. This type of intelligence, called "spatial-temporal," is illustrated by the test shown here. The idea is to imagine a piece of paper folded in a series of steps, as indicated by the dotted lines in the diagrams at right, and then cut with a scissors, as shown by the solid lines. Which of the shapes below the row showing the folding and cutting matches what the piece of paper would look like if you unfolded it? In the lower box, there's an added twist (so to speak): in addition to the folding and cutting, you have to imagine a rotation of 180 degrees. See p. 84 for the solutions.

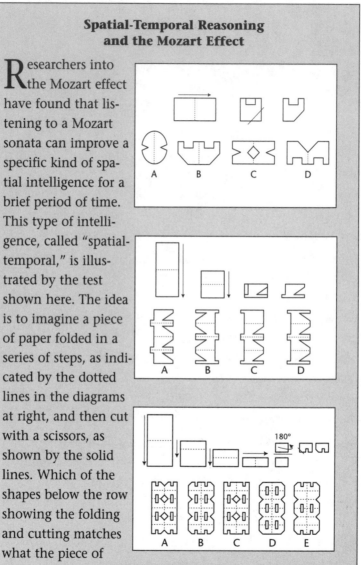

effect of Mozart on other skills failed to support the effect. And studies testing the effects of other musical pieces have had mixed results. Schubert's fantasia for piano, 4 hands in F minor, D940, Mozart's piano concerto No. 23 in A major, K488, and even a contemporary Yanni composition boosted spatial-temporal performance. Minimalist and contemporary "trance" music did not.

The way to boost intelligence is to learn to *play* music
As for the body of research findings pertaining to children, the 1993 pilot study suggested that piano lessons may improve three-year-olds' performance on one task used to test young children's spatial reasoning skills. That task, known technically as *object assembly,* requires the child to put a simple puzzle together; Rauscher and Shaw claimed that this was exactly the kind of skill they predicted music lessons might help to improve, since object assembly is spatial-temporal, requiring as it does the visualization of an evolving pattern.

Later, they tested this hypothesis in a controlled study of 78 preschoolers divided into four groups. One group received six months of piano lessons plus singing lessons, a second received just singing lessons, a third group received computer lessons, and a fourth received no lessons at all. Why piano lessons? Rauscher and Shaw theorized that the piano might help develop spatial-temporal skills because "the keyboard gives a visual linear representation of the spatial relationships between pitches," so playing a piano piece would involve conceptualizing a succession of spatial configurations over time.

In this controlled study, the researchers found that only the piano group made significant, and dramatic, improvements in the object assembly test. That group's performance on a spatial *recognition* task (matching similar-shaped objects to each other) didn't improve at all.

Cognitive skills developed by playing or singing music last longer because the brain physically changes

Significantly for parents, the improvement didn't fade as quickly as the ten-minute IQ boost of the Mozart effect. Children who were tested 24 hours after their last piano lesson showed the same improvement as children tested the same day of the last lesson. By definition, an improvement that lasts 24 hours depends on changes in long-term learning and memory, which in turn depend on physical changes in the structure of brain cells. The ten-minute improvement of the Mozart effect, by contrast, only showed that music could cause short-term changes by briefly altering brain wave patterns. Only the systematic, sustained piano lessons, then, really had the power to change the brain.

Other studies have yielded further information about both the Mozart effect and the effect of music training on the brain. Electroencephalogram (EEG) recordings have shown that the brain's response to listening to a Mozart sonata is similar, in both the location and type of activity, to the brain's activity while working to solve a temporal-spatial task. So it may be that the Mozart effect works by "priming" the brain through stimulation of the kind of firing patterns also required by spatial-temporal skills. Other EEG studies have shown that different kinds of music — Mozart, Schönberg, Bach, or jazz, for example — evoke different kinds of brain activity, which might explain why only one particular kind of music works to boost one particular kind of intelligence.

Of course, neither the Mozart effect nor the piano lesson effect would be very interesting if it only served to boost a kind of intelligence so rare and specific that it only came up on certain spatial IQ tests. The authors of these studies, as well as politicians, educators, and public policy advocates,

UNLEARNING SYNESTHESIA
An Infant's Brain Links Colors, Sounds and Smells

There's a rare ability, possessed by perhaps ten in a million adults, in which input from one sense (say, a musical tone) will trigger a vivid perception in another (say, a color). Known as *synesthesia*, this ability seems to be represented disproportionately among artists, including Rimski-Korsakov, the composer, and Nabokov, the writer.

Nabokov believed that synesthesia is a natural ability that most of us learn to "unlearn" early in life. Some researchers into infant sensory perception agree. For newborns, energy from different senses is relatively undifferentiated. For example, very young infants respond to spoken language not just in the "hearing" part of the brain, where an adult would process sounds and language, but in visual regions as well.

Babies may lose their synesthesia because they have *transient neural connections* that get pruned away during early brain development. So there might be communication links between, for example, visual and auditory regions that are lost during the first year of life.

It may be that the brain regions responsible for "normal" sensory perception haven't yet developed properly. In brain imaging studies of an adult with this rare artistic gift, an active synesthetic experience showed up as a dramatic shutdown of the cortex, the outer layer of the brain responsible for conscious thought. Some research suggests that, in adults, the cortex normally plays a role in inhibiting synesthesia, or at least blocking conscious awareness of it.

There is no way to increase a child's chances of becoming a gifted artist by retaining its synesthetic abilities. It's just one of those trade-offs that most of us have to accept as part of the process of growing up.

have always emphasized that music lessons would be worth spending public funds on if they crossed over into economically valued pursuits such as math and engineering. (For some reason, chess is usually mentioned in the same breath as these other skills as something worth getting our kids to be better at.) Another recent study by Shaw and other U.C., Irvine researchers provides evidence that piano lessons can steepen second graders' learning curves for fractions and proportional math. If interest in including music in school curricula is to be sustained, there will probably have to be a lot more evidence along these lines. Meanwhile, don't expect that just listening to Mozart will improve memory or sharpen learning skills over time, though it might create an atmosphere conducive to doing geometry homework.

Solution to Paper Folding Problem, p. 80
1=B
2=D
3=B You must turn the folded paper 180 degrees around a vertical axis

References
Graziano, Amy B., Matthew Peterson, and Gordon L. Shaw (1999). Enhanced learning of proportional math through music training and spatial-temporal training. Neurological Research 21/2: 139-52.

Rauscher, Frances H. et al. (1997). Music training causes long-term enhancement of preschool children's spatial-temporal reasoning. Neurological Research 19/1: 2-8.

Rauscher, Frances H. and Gordon L. Shaw (1998). Key components of the Mozart effect. Perceptual and Motor Skills 86: 835-41.

Sarnthein, Johannes et al. (1997). Persistent patterns of brain activity: an EEG coherence study of the positive effect of music on spatial-temporal reasoning. Neurological Research 19/2: 107-16.

STRATEGIES TO IMPROVE MEMORY

But children need time to catch onto them

PRE-SCHOOL 2ⁿᵈ GRADE 5ᵀᴴ GRADE COLLEGE
4 numbers 5 numbers 7 numbers 8 numbers

We all know that toddlers' brains have a prodigious learning capacity. For example, between the first and third birthdays, a child learns perhaps 2,500 words (that's three or four new words *a day*). And yet, younger children do worse on tests of memory than older children or adults. For example, in *digit span tests* — remembering and repeating back a string of numbers — preschoolers can remember about four digits, six- to eight-year-olds about five, nine- to-12-year-olds about seven, and college students about eight.

Often, young children perform worse on memory tasks because they're less likely to use memory *strategies*. For example, preschoolers don't rehearse information to remember it, a simple strategy that comes relatively naturally to an older child. They also have a hard time figuring out just what information is relevant to solving a problem, and difficulty tuning out distractions and focusing on just the task at hand.

Part of the reason has to do with the slow maturation of parts of the brain — in particular, the frontal lobes — that handle the tasks of strategy, organizing, and focusing. But Russian psychologist L.S. Vygotsky has pursued the idea that poorer memory performance among toddlers is more a matter of *inexperience* than limited brain capacity. According to his experiments, all it takes to help a young child learn and remember more efficiently is to give him ideas about strategies he might apply.

Using memory improvement strategies...

The kinds of strategies most often applied to memory improvement fall into three categories. *Rehearsal* means repeating or rehearsing the to-be-remembered information to help anchor it in memory until it needs to be used. *Organization* means grouping information into meaningful categories. If you're making a trip to the grocery store, it's easier to remember what you need to get if you break things down into smaller groups, such as breakfast, lunch, and dinner items. *Elaboration* is when you add extra information to help you remember something.

The strategy of elaboration works whether or not the extra information is factual or not. For example, if a child knows the meaning of *cow* and *coward*, it's reasonable to think that she might use that knowledge (perhaps uncon-

Memory and Organization

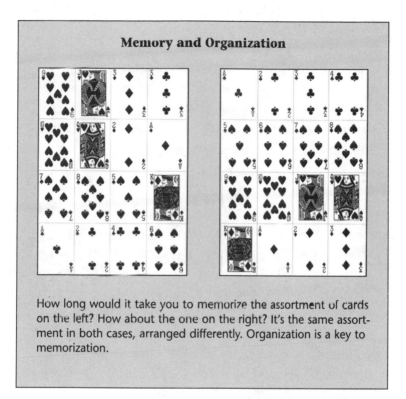

How long would it take you to memorize the assortment of cards on the left? How about the one on the right? It's the same assortment in both cases, arranged differently. Organization is a key to memorization.

sciously) to remember the meaning of the words *cower* and *cowed*. As it happens, there isn't really any relationship among those four words in their history. Believe it or not, they actually come from different ancestor words in different languages. But their fortuitous resemblance in both sound and meaning does still help to remember them.

...accelerates as a child's brain develops

Generally, an older child is more likely to have learned to apply a strategy to the task of remembering something. But young children do use some strategies spontaneously. Three- and four-year-olds, when asked to hide and remember the location of an object in one of 196 containers arranged in a 14 by 14 grid, try to hide the object in the same location in each

VISUAL 20 QUESTIONS
A Game to Help Develop Strategy Skills

Games such as 20 Questions help children develop strategy skills that can be generalized to solving real-world problems. Here's a visual version to make it more fun. One player silently selects one of the objects in the grid, opposite, and announces whether that object is "animal, vegetable, or mineral." The other player may ask up to 20 "yes-no" questions to figure out which object the first player has in mind. Then the players switch roles, and the one who needs fewer questions to get the answer wins. To be good at this game, you need the sorts of planning, strategy, and working memory skills your frontal lobes excel at.

Adults will naturally be better at this game than children, and older children better than younger children, because their frontal-lobe-based strategy skills will have developed farther. But you can help a child along by giving tips and hints the youngster might not think of. The youngest children will probably try to use the most simple-minded strategy, which would be to ask for each object in turn, "Is it the apple?" and so on. But with this type of strategy, there's only about a 50-50 chance of getting the answer in 20 questions, and as many as 41 questions might be needed.

A better approach would be to use what psychologists call *constraint-seeking questions* to narrow down the possibilities, and then ask more specific questions to test an emerging hypothesis. A good constraint-seeking question might be, "Is it bigger than my head?" or, "Is it

a man-made object?" A bad one (what psychologists call *pseudo-constraint-seeking*) would be, for example, "Does it have eight legs?" This question would be the same as asking, "Is it the spider?" and it wouldn't narrow down the possibilities at all. You might also help a child along by pointing out logical entailments, such as the fact that a "yes" answer to the question "Is it a tool?" eliminates the need to ask, "Is it a man-made object?"

of several successive attempts. Only children five years and older, however, use the trick of hiding the object in an easy-to-remember position, such as at one of the corners. Both are simple strategies that make the task of remembering easier.

Sometimes, older children do better because they've learned to ignore whether a memorization task makes sense. For all children and adults, anything is easier to remember if it's *meaningful,* as in the "cow" example above, especially if it's meaningful in real-life terms, and if there's a strong *motivation* to remember. Two-year-olds told to remember and repeat back a list of things to do that day, including fun things such as getting candy, as well as boring things such as chores, remember the fun things a lot better than the boring things.

Memorization strategies, like problem-solving strategies in general, are not built into our genes. That's why there's so much individual and cultural variation in the techniques that people apply to memorization tasks. It takes some effort to learn and practice strategies, but the initial expenditure of effort translates into greater long-term information-processing efficiency, especially as the strategies become more automatic.

The more knowledge the brain has to work with the easier it becomes to remember something because it can be associated with something else already known

As effective learning and remembering strategies yield better learning and remembering, a child builds up a more useful knowledge base which, in turn, stimulates further learning and remembering. This fundamental principle of memory improvement — that knowledge aids memory — is demonstrated by the fact that someone who knows how to play chess will have an easier time memorizing an arrangement of pieces on the board than someone who doesn't.

Of course, the way their brains are structured at birth makes learning and remembering easier for some children than others. Such built-in "bottom-up" differences as basic IQ and information-processing speed are largely outside a child's (or parent's) control. On the other hand, developing "top-down" skills such as effective learning and remembering strategies can influence the "bottom-up" ones. As learning and remembering strategies translate into a larger knowledge base, the larger knowledge base in turn translates into greater speed and efficiency of processing. That's why an experienced chess player can think of good moves more quickly than an inexperienced one.

Ready application of strategies not only separates an older child from a younger one, but also separates different children of the same age, and different adults from one another. Some "advanced" strategies are never learned even by many adults and, therefore, serve to differentiate high performers from low performers. For example, some people learn proficiency in organizing the knowledge in an article or book — underlining main points, summarizing arguments and findings — while others do not. The former have skills that help them understand and remember the information better, and that make them better readers than the ones who don't learn the technique. Whatever the learning situation, apply your mind actively by judging, questioning and comparing.

References

Bjorklund, David F., and Rhonda N. Douglas (1997). The development of memory strategies. In The Development of Memory in Childhood, ed. by Nelson Cowan. Sussex, UK: Psychology Press.

Pressley, M., J.G. Borkowski, and W. Schneider (1989). Good information processing: what it is and what education can do to promote it. International Journal of Educational Research 13: 857-67.

WORDS AT PLAY

The more words heard, from infancy on up, the higher the verbal test scores

Children the world over, regardless of culture, social class, or economic standing, are born primed to learn their mother tongue without any special help. The essentials of an adult-level proficiency are in place by about age four, preschool or no, and from then on it's mostly fine-tuning. And yet, it's the fine-tuning that separates people with good vocabularies from those with bad vocabularies, good from poor readers, William Shakespeare from the guy who can't pass Freshman English. Among the many factors that account for differences in academic performance, is there anything parents can do, early on, to equip their children with better language tools?

Higher socioeconomic status confers some advantages, at least as measured by IQ tests

Many studies have found that children from families with higher socioeconomic status perform, on average, better on intelligence tests. Why? There could be many reasons. Families with more money have more resources to finance better opportunities for formal education, which may translate into improved scores on measures of intelligence — assuming IQ is at least partly shaped by experience. Broadly speaking, people who enjoy higher socioeconomic status tend to achieve higher levels of formal education. If so, the influence of better-educated parents may help children develop stronger abilities of the sort that intelligence tests measure. Of course, given that IQ is believed to have a genetic component, it's also possible that well educated people are, on average, naturally more intelligent by these same measures, and that those "smart" genes are passed on. Any or all these factors may result in higher achievement by children of well-to-do parents.

Tools all parents can use to improve their children's performance in school

Harvard psychologist Jerome Kagan identifies three ways that parents can have an influence on their child's development: *direct interaction, emotional identification,* and *family stories* (see *Parenting*). Of these, the first two are especially relevant to building a child's verbal skills and require only an investment of time by parents or other caregivers.

Talk to your children. Researchers have identified talking to children as a tool that all parents, regardless of socioeconomic status, can use to increase their children's verbal intelligence, i.e., vocabulary size, reading ability, and other language-related skills. It has been shown, for example, that the more a parent speaks to a child the more rapidly the child's vocabulary will grow, which subsequently will be reflected in higher verbal test scores in school.

No matter how young the child, a proven path to good language skills is for parents to read to their children. Reading aloud to a child anytime, especially in a regular, private, unstressed "story time," also fills the child's need for reassurance and protection — an added benefit on top of helping the child develop future reading and vocabulary skills.

A simple way to make words important to a child is to explain what things are called and why

Point out the names of things when you're with your child. There's good evidence, on top of the self-evident nature of the idea, that children's vocabulary development benefits from parents who take time to point out the names for new things. Don't misunderstand this piece of advice. It has nothing to do with learning to be a fluent, fundamentally competent speaker. Any child will learn a native language without any special effort made on the part of the parent or caregiver

Latin Lesson

In the left-hand column are common English prefixes derived from Latin. In the right column are common Latin roots. By trying different combinations, you can come up with many words that have a meaning transparently composed of the meaning of the parts.

re- "back"
contra- "against"
male- "bad"
dis- "away, apart, not"
pre- "before, in front of"
e-, ex- "out of"
bene- "good"
de- "down (from)"
con-, com- "with, together"

mit "send"
ject "throw"
potent "powerful"
science "knowledge"
vene "come, arrive"
factor "maker, doer"
volent "willing, wishing"
diction "speech"
sonant "of sound"

Greek Lesson

Now see what combinations you can create from these Greek-derived prefixes and roots. You should be able to come up with some that have the same meaning as some of the Latin combinations, for example, *eulogy/benediction*. (Note: The *mis-* below is not the same prefix you find in *mistake, misplace*, etc., which is a native English prefix meaning "wrong.")

auto- "self"
poly- "many"
mis-, miso- "hatred"
demo- "people"
phil-, philo- "love"
syn-, sym- "with, together"
caco- "bad"
psych- "mind"
eu- "good"

logy, ology "speech, study of"
pathy "feeling"
anthropy "(of) people"
cracy "rule (by)"
chrony "time"
phony "sound"
gyny "of women"
sophy "wisdom"

to attach names to things in the child's environment. When a parent plays the naming game, the effect on the child's verbal skills is in the fine-tuning department. The effort will have a future effect on how big, or how advanced relative to that of age-mates, the child's vocabulary will be.

Talk about what a child already shows interest in
Another experimentally determined fact, and one that's a little less intuitive than the benefit of pointing out the names of things, is that a child is much more likely to learn the names of objects if the adult follows the child's focus of attention. A child will learn the names for objects faster if the parent or caregiver provides a label for what the child is looking at than if the adult tries to redirect the child's attention. Parents must resist the temptation to draw a child's attention to something the parent considers more interesting. By noticing what a child is paying attention to, an adult can participate in the child's own world by adjusting his or her conversation to address the child's interests.

As children mature, new approaches are required
When young children begin to identify with their parents, their language skills need to be nurtured from a less obvious, but no less important, point of view. Starting around age four or five, children begin to assume that they're like their parents. So if parents pay attention to their own vocabulary, and show an interest in words, the child is more likely to do so as well. Take the time to explain the meaning of new words, and suggest strategies for figuring out the meaning of words that the child may soon hear from other sources.

Strategies that good English teachers apply but parents may have to brush up on
From first to third grade, the average child's vocabulary grows by about 9,000 words. That's about eight words a day — an

awful lot, by an adult's standards. And from third to fifth grade, the rate goes up, to about 20,000 words. How could a child possibly learn so many new words so quickly?

To a great extent, a child learns how to *figure out* what a word means without having been told. This is something that's second nature to adults: Once you've learned the meaning of the term *day-trader,* nobody has to explain what the verb *day-trading* would mean. The knowledge that makes the meaning of the new word seem so self-evident to adults is something children learn a little later than they learn a lot of the other patterns of language.

Parents also have the power to teach somewhat more sophisticated strategies for figuring out new words, strategies of the sort that are obvious to adults. On the most basic level, this could mean explaining the meaning of common prefixes, suffixes, and roots. For example:

Prefixes	*Roots*
bene- "good"	*diction* "speech"
omni- "all"	*potent* "powerful"
col-, con-, com- "with"	*science* "knowledge"
pre- "before, in front of"	*mit* "send"
e-, ex- "out of"	*vene* "come"

Once a parent or teacher has pointed out the meanings of common prefixes and roots, a child can figure out the meaning of words he has never heard before — *benediction, omnipotent, prescience, emit,* and *convene,* for instance — by breaking the words down and looking at their component parts. This endows a child with an attitude toward words that goes well beyond the knowledge of a few roots and prefixes. By showing how to make a game of unraveling unfamiliar words, you'll help your child to be unintimidated by new words he may encounter in the future.

> ## VISUAL MNEMONICS
> ### How to Help Your Child Have a Good Vocabulary
>
> Visual *mnemonics* (from Greek *mnemosyne,* "memory") is the trick of using a visual image to help you remember something. Visual memory techniques can be used for more than just remembering people's names. If you want to help your child improve his vocabulary, try this: Let's say he has a hard time remembering what *pugnacious* means. Let's say you're not sure yourself. You look it up and see it means "quarrelsome, fond of fighting." Create a visual image of the "pug" face of a boxer, flattened from countless blows taken in the ring. For most people, this kind of visual association is remarkably stable, and quite effective for rescuing vocabulary from the dark "I-can-never-quite-remember-what-it-means" corner of their mind. Children tend to enjoy the technique, too.
>
> Try it yourself with these words:
> *saturnine* "gloomy" *prolix* "wordy" *nugatory* "worthless"
> *pusillanimous* "cowardly" *halcyon* "peaceful"

What parents choose to play with can determine their child's vocabulary

Any parent with a dictionary can unveil to a child the meanings of interesting words with Latin or Greek origins. Take *sympathy, malevolent,* and *benefactor* for starters. The strategy of breaking down an "opaque" piece of information into "transparent" components is one way of making things meaningful, and the trick of making things meaningful is a crucial step in the process of learning and remembering it. So a word such as *misanthropy,* instead of simply being an arbitrary sequence of four syllables to memorize as having a certain meaning, becomes more meaningful in terms of component parts that recur in other combinations as well.

When children see parents getting excited about the origin, current meaning and proper use of a word, as well as using the the dictionary, they begin to appreciate the value of words as interesting playthings. Few things a parent can do will affect a child's future verbal skills more than that.

References

Dunham, P.J., F. Dunham, and A. Curwin (1993). Joint-attentional states and lexical acquisition at 18 months. Developmental Psychology 29: 827-31.

Hart, B., and T.R. Risley (1995). Meaningful Differences in the Everyday Experience of Young American Children. Baltimore: Paul H. Brookes.

Hoff, Erika (2001). Language Development. Belmont, CA: Wadsworth/Thomson Learning.

Hoff-Ginsburg, Erika (1998). The relation of birth order and socioeconomic status to children's language experience and language development. Applied Psycholinguistics 19: 603-30.

Huttenlocher, J., et al. (1991). Early vocabulary growth: relation to language input and gender. Developmental Psychology 27: 236-48.

HABITUATION

The virtues of *not* paying attention

What does the lowly sea slug have in common with today's teenager? "Plenty," say neuroscientists. "No kidding," say mothers. Because from one intriguing perspective, there's very little difference between not cleaning up your messy room and not retracting

Aplysia Californica.
A sea slug widely used in neuroscience research

your water siphon out of harm's way when nudged. It all depends on how many times you're exposed to it.

Neuroscientists have long understood that figuring out how the human brain works often begins with this fundamental principle: If you want to solve a complex puzzle, solve a simple one first that shares its basic design features with the complex one. In this case, the complex puzzle is the human brain's mechanisms for learning and remembering. The simple puzzle is how the learning process works in a "mini-brain" (technically, it's a small mass of nerve tissue called a ganglion) of a marine gastropod mollusk called *Aplysia*, a California sea slug.

Mom: "Please clean up your room"
Teen: "I did already"

The human nervous system contains about 50 billion neurons. Each individual neuron is linked with many others, meaning that the number of communication points between all of them is exponentially very large indeed. Neuroscientist Robert Ornstein asserts there are more potential connections between the neurons in a single human brain than there are atoms in the universe.

Mom: "It looks exactly the same to me"
Teen: "Awww, Mom!"

By contrast, the California sea slug has only about 20,000 neurons in its nervous system. The simplicity of Aplysia wouldn't be of much help to neuroscientists if the organism didn't learn things the way we do, or if its nervous system didn't work the way ours does. But it turns out that this simple sea slug shares many types of learning behavior with us using a neural system that has many of the same structures, mechanisms, and chemicals that we have.

No one could be blamed for being skeptical that the ganglion of the California sea slug has much in common with a human brain, learning-wise, and it's certainly true that much of the learning we're proudest of is far beyond the abilities of Aplysia. But our brain's frontal lobes, which house conscious decision-making and strategic learning skills, are quite recent developments from an evolutionary standpoint. Other learning structures in the human brain are still much like those in the simplest organisms.

Mom: "Well? If not now, when?"
Teen: "Ummmuh"

Remember Pavlov's dog? About one hundred years ago, Russian physiologist Ivan Pavlov showed that if you rang a bell every time you fed a dog, just the ringing of the bell would

soon be enough to make the dog
salivate. This kind of learning, called *classical conditioning,* is outside the
control — and often
beneath the awareness
of — the conscious mind.
You might say it's the nervous system that's learned something, rather than the mind.

Mom: "Enough. Start cleaning it this minute!" (Silence)

Another simple form of learning is called *habituation.* This is
what happens when you stop reacting to, and soon become
unaware of, a stimulus that's repeatedly or constantly
applied. In the case of Aplysia, researchers have shown that
the sea slug will learn to stop withdrawing its siphon in
response to constant and repeated prodding, even though a
nudge is one of the ways the organism is warned of the presence of a hungry predator. An example of habituation in
human behavior is the tuning out of constant and repetitive
background noise, even though sound is one of the things
our brain reacts to as a warning of impending danger.

Mom: "Clean...up...your...room, NOW!" (Silence)

Evolution designed brains to ignore all passing data that is
not essential to survival. The slug responds to signs of a
predator (which repeated gentle prodding is not), of food,
and of an opportunity to reproduce. A teenager repeatedly
prodded with the same reprimand or command is just doing
what nature intended him to do. And, like the California sea
slug, he'll begin to respond only to novelty and learn to
ignore the overly familiar.

MOM: "I forgot to tell you, your friend Sally called. She'll be here any minute"

TEEN: "Mom, your communication skills are totally lame! Where did you put my clean torn jeans?"

(Silence)

References

Carew, Thomas J. (1996). Molecular enhancement of memory formation. Neuron 16: 5-8.

Mayford, Mark, and Eric R. Kandel (1999). Genetic approaches to memory storage. Trends in Genetics 15/11: 463-70.

Ruben, Peter, et al. (1981). What the marine mollusc Aplysia can tell the neurologist about behavioral neurophysiology. Canadian Journal of Neurological Sciences 8/4: 275-80.

THE MATURING YEARS

From college to retirement

SELF-TEST: Concentration

The exercise below was developed by the Royal Dutch Air Force to test and increase the ability of combat pilots to concentrate, and to lengthen their attention span. Prepare to time yourself before you look at the grid. When you are ready, start the timer. Allow yourself only 15 seconds to count how many 4's and how many g's there are in this grid of numbers and letters. If you are not able to find them within 15 seconds, try again. But this time look for c's and 5's, again allowing yourself 15 seconds. Repeat the exercise, looking each time for a different pair of numbers and letters. Allow yourself only 15 seconds each time. See p. 112 for the solution.

```
a 7 3 d g t p 9 6 2 x d e o
d g v c d w 3 6 7 9 w d z x
x c k l p o u t e e 4 c v b
p h 4 f d s a q w 6 r t y u
4 d e r g f r t y u i c s w
3 s w e d 3 5 h t c e 3 c d
e w q d c 5 6 o 1 r d w 2
j g e 2 3 7 b f d f g h y
n m s w e r u i o 5 3 4 4 d
i 7 o e r t y u i w s q x d
```

FOCUS ON FOCUS

Paying attention is the key to learning, especially under pressure

Some things will attract our attention because they're flashy and loud, like a streak of lightning across the dark summer sky or the thunderclap that follows. It would be reasonable to assume, therefore, that the things our brain decides to pay attention to are influenced by the nature of the input from our senses.

Locating the car keys

But the brain is by no means a passive recipient of what the eyes, ears, nose, tongue, and touch receptors may send to it. This is never more apparent than when we consciously make

a decision to pay attention to something that does not quali-
fy as crucial to survival — let's say, for example, the location
of the car keys that should be found right where they were
left, but aren't. The decision-making centers of the *prefrontal
cortex* and *parietal cortex* tell the primary sensory processing
parts of the brain what to pay attention to. This "what-to-be-
alert-for" message causes changes in the "downstream" brain
regions that process the *meaning* of visual data but, amazing-
ly, it also changes the raw data-processing areas that assemble
elemental visual inputs such as angles of lines, curves, edges,
colors. In its search for the keys, the visual cortex will alter its

The Eye-Brain Connection

The human eye doesn't really "see" anything at all.
The portions of the spectrum of electromagnetic
energy that pass through the eye stimulate the rod and
cone receptors in the back of the retina. Those receptors
relay information to the brain's *thalamus,* often called
"the gateway to the cortex," which in turn relays the
information to the primary visual cortex, which in turn
disseminates the information to other parts of the cortex
for more sophisticated processing and interpretation. It's
the cortex that interprets visual input as patterns of light-
ness, darkness, shape, color, and texture that make up
images. The cortex then recodes the data in ways that
carry meaning and the potential for memory. The eyes of
some people who suffer from color-blindness, or even
complete blindness, often function perfectly well. What
is not functioning are regions of the brain that normally
process and interpret data from their eyes.

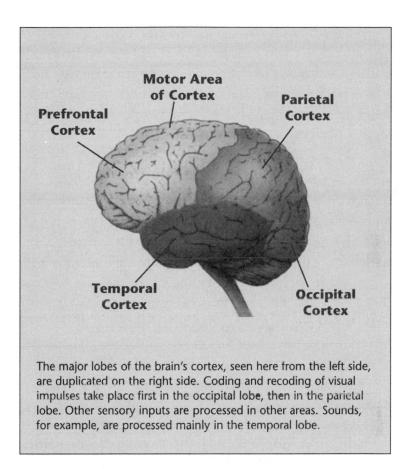

The major lobes of the brain's cortex, seen here from the left side, are duplicated on the right side. Coding and recoding of visual impulses take place first in the occipital lobe, then in the parietal lobe. Other sensory inputs are processed in other areas. Sounds, for example, are processed mainly in the temporal lobe.

interpretation of the raw impulses the eyes are sending to it by altering its neurons so they will fire in response to stimuli that match the physical characteristics of the bunch of keys. These changes occur in the visual cortex even before the eyes actually pick up the missing keys. In brief, neurons of just the right type fire in response to incoming information, matching what the decision-making part of the brain has told them to look for in a process that is literally mind over matter. (**Tip:** Be certain that you remember correctly what the bunch of missing keys looks like before starting to search for them.)

With the car keys found, and the process of selective attention successfully concluded, we're out the door and on our way. However, the process of selective attention may not always work perfectly, because a number of factors can interfere with its operation.

The power of distracting influences

What you just had to eat or whether or not you had enough sleep the night before are just two of the things that may impede the process of selective attention (see *Brain Nutrition* and *Dreams at Work*). But a much more common culprit is distraction. In a recent study that's bound to have repercussions in the debate over the use of cellular phones in cars, a group of British researchers found that it's difficult for the brain to focus on an important task when its working memory capacity is either full or overloaded with distracting stimuli.

Working memory is the brain's system for holding information online while it manipulates it to solve a problem (see *Mindlessness*). Many "higher" abilities — planning, decision-making, problem-solving, and language — depend upon working memory. And this wonderful mechanism can easily get filled up when we're solving a tricky problem in our head — say, multiplying 23 by 57 — or trying to do too many things at once.

In the British experiment, researchers asked the participants to perform a task requiring selective attention while, simultaneously, attempting to remember a sequence of five digits. The selective attention task was to identify the profession of a well-known person whose name was flashed on a screen along with a face. Sometimes, the face would match the name, while other times it wouldn't. So in order to make the proper match the participants had to ignore the face and focus just on the name.

When, at the same time, the participants were given a simple sequence of digits to remember — 0-1-2-3-4, for example — they could easily ignore the stimulus of the face and focus on the name. But when they had to remember a random series of digits — 4-0-1-3-2, for example, which placed a heavier burden on their working memory — they had a much more difficult time, often needing twice as long to match the profession with the name.

Where were the matching activities taking place?

A functional MRI imaging scan of the brains of the participants revealed that the more difficult working memory task engaged their prefrontal cortex, which was to be expected given that the prefrontal cortex houses brain regions most involved in working memory. But the scan also revealed that a face processing region in the parietal cortex became active when the participants were preoccupied with the harder working memory tasks — remembering the random order of digits. In other words, even though the participants were told explicitly to ignore the faces flashed on the screen, their brains couldn't follow those instructions when they were burdened by a tricky working memory task.

Paying attention to paying attention

All in all, research on working memory and selective attention shows that the conscious decision-making systems in the brain exercise crucial control over the parts of the brain that are receiving information from the senses. And since working memory can be a gatekeeper to long-term memory, all learning improves when the brain is forced to pay attention. In fact, one of the most common reasons for memory complaints is a failure to force the brain to become alert to the incoming data. In other words, if the brain doesn't notice something in the first place, it cannot recall it later. The rea-

son the brain needs to be *told* to be alert to things more subtle than a bolt of lightning is that it was designed *not* to pay
attention to everything on its own. Otherwise, the brain
would drain so much of the body's available energy that all
systems would be forced to shut down, much like a rolling
blackout.

Practical advice

During the process of performing tasks that require focus, it is
very important to keep the surroundings as free as possible
from distractions. Any speech or speech-like sounds will gain
automatic access to working memory, so it's important to
keep the TV off when concentrating on a task. If music is
playing in the background, instrumental music is less distracting than vocal music. Working memory begins to decline
early in adulthood, so these tips become more and more
important as time goes by.

Solution to Self-Test, p. 106
   There are five 4's and five g's
   There are seven c's and three 5's

References
De Fockert, Jan, et al. (2001). The role of working memory in visual
   selective attention. Science 291: 1803-6.
Somers, David C., et al. (1999). Functional MRI reveals spatially specif-
   ic attentional modulation in human primary visual cortex.
   Proceedings of the National Academy of Sciences USA 96: 1663-8.

LEARNING THE EASY WAY

A little emotion helps

Do you remember where you were when you heard that Lady Diana had been killed in a car crash? Or that the Federal Building in Oklahoma City had been bombed? Or that the space shuttle Challenger had blown up? Or, on a more personal level, do you know where you were when your mother died, when you first fell in love, or when you got your first speeding ticket?

Emotions at work

All of these experiences share a common factor that was crucially involved in searing them indelibly into long-term memory: *emotion*. Evolution designed the brain so that it identifies events perceived as essential to survival by creating a strong emotional reaction. Since survival is the brain's top priority, the event will trigger a built-in mechanism that ensures the brain will never forget it.

Neuroscientists have pinpointed the central component of this memory mechanism deep within the brain — a small almond-shaped structure called the *amygdala*. The amygdala is part of the evolutionarily ancient emotional center of the brain known as the *limbic system*. It's a key player in various forms of unconscious learning that we share with other animals.

Ouch, that hurts!

One form of unconscious learning is known as *conditioning*. This is the kind of learning done by lab rats when a neutral stimulus (say, a certain odor), is paired with an unpleasant stimulus (say, an electric shock). The rat quickly learns to fear the odor even when it isn't paired with the shock. This kind of learning is completely unconscious and automatic. In the human species it is very resistant to rational analysis because it has taken place independently of the "higher" thinking areas of the brain, and is therefore very hard for the conscious, rational mind to control. That's why phobias are so difficult to cure.

The amygdala seems to do all this by communicating with the hippocampus (also a crucial component of the more uniquely human declarative memory system) and the *basal ganglia* (a central part of the brain's system for learning new skills and habits), and encouraging them to take incoming data seriously. In some experiments, scientists have steepened the learning curve of rats just by injecting an amphetamine stimulant directly into the amygdala. Conversely, injections of lidocaine into the hippocampus or basal ganglia block the learning-enhancing effects of the amphetamine-injected amygdala.

It's not just bad vibes

The kinds of things the amygdala helps you learn aren't limited to unconscious, "primitive" knowledge such as fear, gut feelings, and the like. It can also help with explicit memory for facts and events. That's why the news about the Oklahoma

When the Brain Fears Danger, It Reacts Before You Know It — and Never Forgets It

How does the brain form memories of life's significant events — in particular, how are traumatic memories formed, stored, and retrieved? The brain has multiple memory systems, each devoted to a different kind of memory function (see *Memory Is Plural*). For traumatic memories, two systems are particularly important. If you return to the scene of an accident, you will be reminded of the accident and will recall where you were going, who you were with, and other details of the experience. These are *explicit* (conscious) memories. Also, your blood pressure and heart rate may rise, you may begin to sweat, and your muscles may tighten up. These are *implicit* (unconscious) memories.

The brain's response to threatening stimuli involves neural pathways that send information about the outside world to the amygdala. This system determines the significance of a potentially threatening stimulus and triggers emotional responses, like freezing or fleeing. Even before dinosaurs ruled the earth, evolution hit upon that way of wiring the brain to produce responses that are likely to keep the organism alive in dangerous situations. The solution was so effective that it has not changed since. (Of course, if this amygdala-driven system had *not* worked, the descendants of the creatures that had it wouldn't be around to discuss it.) It works pretty much the same in rats and people, birds and reptiles.

Citation
Ledoux, Joseph, Professor, Center of Neural Science, New York University. Adapted from a presentation at Learning and the Brain Conference, May 4, 2001, Washington, DC.

City bombing is better entrenched in most people's long-term memory than whatever else was in the news that day.

And it's not just memory for momentous events that's enhanced by emotion. Several studies have shown that people remember emotion-rousing stories better than stories of equal length and complexity but with little emotional content. The emotion doesn't even have to be particularly vivid or strong. PET scan studies have shown that the amygdala contributes to enhanced memory for emotionally-tinged data even if you aren't aware of any emotional arousal. (The exceptions to this rule are people with amygdala damage, who have no better memory for an emotional story than a neutral one.)

Practical applications for students

The role of emotion in helping to transfer experiences into long-term memory is the reason for the effectiveness of emotionally engaging teaching and studying styles. At the end of a class, for example, if you review the course material by debating it with classmates, you'll remember it for a longer time than if you cram. A debate tends to engage you emotionally, not just intellectually, so the class lessons are more likely to become firmly entrenched in your long-term memory. Incidentally, if you do cram, break up the sessions with 20 minute rest periods and, if at all possible, make sure you get a good night's sleep after your study session. This isn't just motherly advice — it's based on sound neuroscientific research (see *Dreams at Work*).

References

Adolphs, Ralph, et al. (1997). Impaired declarative memory for emotional material following bilateral amygdala damage in humans. Learning & Memory 4: 291-300.

Cahill, L. and J.L. McGaugh (1995). A novel demonstration of enhanced memory associated with emotional arousal. Consciousness and Cognition 4: 410-21.

Cahill, L., et al. (1996). Amygdala activity at encoding correlated with long-term, free recall of emotional information. Proceedings of the American Academy of Sciences USA 93: 8016-21.

McGaugh, J.L., L. Cahill, and B. Roozendaal (1996). Involvement of the amygdala in memory storage: interaction with other brain systems. Proceedings of the National Academy of Sciences USA 93: 13508-14.

Morris, J.S., A. Ohman, and R.J. Dolan (1998). Conscious and unconscious emotional learning in the human amygdala. Nature 393: 467-70.

What's the Capacity of Your Mind's Ear?

If you read these three numbers either out loud or to yourself, and then look away, chances are you can repeat them back accurately:

      3-7-6

      Next, try it with four numbers:
      3-7-6-8

      then five:
      3-7-6-8-5

      then six:
      3-7-6-8-5-2

      then seven:
      3-7-6-8-5-2-4

      then eight:
      3-7-6-8-5-2-4-6

Have you made a mistake yet?

USING YOUR MIND'S EAR

Executive function's versatile tool — the remarkable phonological loop

What was the name of that client my boss just introduced me to? Did the cop say to turn left or right at the first intersection? Did Aunt Martha ask for a dry sherry or a dry martini? In other words: Why do so many things seem to elude my short-term memory radar?

Psychologists refer to our short-term "mind's ear" mechanism as the *phonological loop*. This mechanism is one of the most important tools our brain has to keep track of and remember what we hear or read. Understanding how it works and what its limitations are can allow us to use it more effectively.

In an influential paper published over forty years ago, Princeton psychologist George A. Miller proposed that our short-term memory capacity is limited to about seven "bits" of information. These bits can be composed of either single digits and letters, or *chunks* of digits and letters, or combinations of both. Coincidentally (perhaps), telephone numbers contain seven digits. Whether or not it was planned this way, that means we're able to hold the number in our head long enough to dial it correctly after looking it up in the phone book.

If you think you might be able to handle more than seven information bits, try the test in the box opposite. (Psychologists refer to this as

an *immediate digit span* test.) On this kind of test, the top limit for most of us turns out to be six or seven numbers. But there are ways to increase the number of digits we can remember. One is by *chunking*, or grouping, single digits into a sequence of two-digit numbers. Most people find a sequence of four two-digit numbers — 37-68-52-46 — easier to repeat back than a string of eight one-digit numbers: 3-7-6-8-5-2-4-6. In fact, we do this kind of chunking routinely and automatically when we have to remember an area code along with a seven-digit phone number. Thus, (510) 434-9523 (5-1-0-4-3-4-9-5-2-3) becomes 5-10-4-3-4-95-23.

More recent work has shown that it's not just the *number* of chunks that limit the number of items humans can hold in their short-term acoustic memory store, but also *how long* the chunks take to pronounce. Thus, any familiar word will form a single chunk, but it's easier to remember a string of seven one-syllable words than a string of seven multi-syllable ones. The reason has to do with our dependence on the phonological loop's short-term store for this kind of memorization, and the fact that sounds exist in the phonological loop's store for only a brief period of time — about two to three seconds.

Of course, if information in your phonological loop really is extinguished after about two seconds or so, you'd expect the first items in a two-second-long sequence to have been forgotten by the time you start reciting it back. That doesn't happen. Why?

The answer is the same as the reason you can keep a phone number in your head if it takes you, say, ten seconds to get to the phone and dial it. Even though the temporary storage system for sound holds memory traces that fade away after about two seconds, those traces can be refreshed by repeating or *rehearsing* them out loud or in your head. This articulatory rehearsal system forms a second component of the phonological loop, along with the phonological store itself. The two components work together to manage information in an "online" manner, but are actually housed in different parts of the brain's left hemisphere.

Working memory and the mind's ear

The phonological loop is one of the tools used by working memory which is a component of what neuroscientists call the brain's "Executive" function. We often "play back" something we have just heard and automatically translated into sound in order to use that information to solve a problem or complete a task. Take the following sentence:

> *The bus driver motioned the red truck to continue, which turned left, stopped by the third driveway, and sounded its horn twice.*

In order to follow the meaning of a sentence such as this, let alone to answer a question based on the information it contains ("In which direction did the truck turn?"), we must

---

The Recency Effect

Read once through this list (or have someone read it aloud to you), and repeat back as many words as you can recall, in any order. Did you remember more words from the end of the list than the beginning?

wagon	zebra	bottle
ostrich	candle	painting
papaya	computer	lemon
motorcycle	tulip	pencil
pumpkin	shower	wristwatch

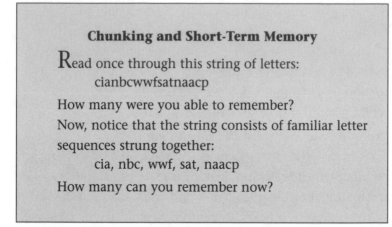

Chunking and Short-Term Memory

Read once through this string of letters:
    cianbcwwfsatnaacp
How many were you able to remember?
Now, notice that the string consists of familiar letter sequences strung together:
    cia, nbc, wwf, sat, naacp
How many can you remember now?

be able to hold each word in our short-term memory long enough to tie all the pieces together, go back over them if necessary, and decode them appropriately.

Dysfunctional phonological loops

Even with a poorly functioning phonological loop, everyday conversations can be managed without much difficulty because most of what people say in casual conversation is not structurally complex. Speakers tend to avoid difficult-to-parse structures not only because they're hard to decode, but because they're just as hard to construct, and place a burden on the speaker's language capacities as well as the listener's. On the other hand, a poorly functioning phonological loop may be the cause of other more serious difficulties.

It has been found that many children diagnosed with dyslexia also appear to suffer from a dysfunction in their phonological loop mechanism that renders them unable to break words down into their component sounds or learn the proper sound-to-letter translations. Young children who have difficulty repeating pseudowords such as "flimble" and "slex" also tend to have low vocabulary scores, and continue to have

New Treatment for Dyslexia

Recent studies have shown that the phonological loop deficit in dyslexia may be due to a more general difficulty than just segmenting the acoustic stream of speech into its component units. Children with language-learning impairments have an especially hard time detecting and keeping track of rapid changes not just in acoustic stimuli (such as speech) but also in visual stimuli (such as a series of visual symbols presented quickly on a computer screen). In other words, rather than having a cognitive deficit specific to language, they have a sensory processing deficit that affects their ability to learn language and language-based skills such as reading and writing.

What's the cause of the sensory processing deficit? Some very recent structural examinations and brain imaging studies indicate that dyslexics may have less *myelination* in the neurons of parts of their left hemisphere used for language processing. Myelin is the insulation on the axon, or message-transmitting component, of a brain cell. Less myelination means slower transmission of the electrical impulse along the axon and between brain cells, leading to difficulty in processing quickly-changing sensory signals, and in turn, leading to difficulty in processing language.

In a textbook example of the application of brain science to classroom learning and teaching, dyslexia researchers have discovered a way to improve the ability of language-learning-impaired children so dramatically that after only a few weeks of training, they're performing near, at, or above the level of other children their age on tests of auditory language comprehension. The technique involves first slowing down a synthetic speech stream to the point that the children have no difficulty segmenting it properly. Then, during multiple training sessions spread over a period of three to four weeks, the tape is very gradually increased to normal speed. In this way, using a method that may actually entail altering the wiring of the brain, the children's sensitivity to the incoming stream of sound is dramatically improved, opening the way to improvements in reading and writing as well.

poor vocabularies relative to their peers the older they grow. So pseudoword repetition difficulty can serve as an excellent indicator of trouble to come — in acquiring vocabulary and learning foreign languages, for example. It may also be used as a quick test for possible dyslexia.

Phonological loop capacity is not something that can be increased simply by practicing. If you keep repeating a string of numbers every day for a month, you won't get any better at it — at least, not if you're relying on your phonological loop alone. Even though the phonological loop plays a critical role in the working memory system, it has inherent limitations. Moreover, remembering or analyzing things by their sound is only the first step in a three-stage level of information processing. But without the phonological loop we would find the next levels of learning and remembering much more difficult, if not impossible, to attain.

References

Merzenich, Michael M., et al. (1996). Temporal processing deficits of language-learning impaired children ameliorated by training. Science 271: 77-81.

Tallal, Paula (2000). The science of literacy: from the laboratory to the classroom. Proceedings of the National Academy of Sciences USA 97/6:2402-4.

Tallal, Paula, et al. (1996). Language comprehension in language-learning impaired children improved with acoustically modified speech. Science 271: 81-4.

Temple, E., et al. (2000). Disruption in the neural response to rapid acoustic stimuli in dyslexia: evidence from functional MRI. Proceedings of the National Academy of Sciences USA 97/25: 13907-12.

Long-Term Memory

Why repetition, rehearsal and practice work so well

The problem with short-term memory is that it's, well, short-term. The phonological loop component of working memory can only hold something in our "mind's ear" for a few seconds. As soon as we dial the phone number, it's forgotten, because we stop repeating it in our mind. If you want to retain the number longer, you have to do something more.

One of the ways to transfer information (like a telephone number) from your mind's ear to your long-term memory is to return to it again and again (like the phone number of a close friend). Repetition's ability to consolidate knowledge in long-term memory works not just for *declarative* memory — memory of facts and events — but also for *procedural* knowledge of skills such as remembering how to use a computer mouse or (in countries and states where it's still legal to do so) how to dial a cell phone while driving.

Moreover, the most recent research indicates that these bits of information our brain pays special attention to during the day will also be rehearsed at night when we're asleep. So in addition to performing "live" repetitions of knowledge or a skill, our brain rehearses things offline as well — which is as good a reason as any to avoid skimping on sleep (see *Dreams at Work*).

Practice makes perfect

Neuroscientists have only recently figured out how the brain forgets most of the data flooding through our minds every second of every day, and yet allows us to remember those things that we practice and rehearse (see box, p. 129). But it's important to bear in mind that consolidation of knowledge in long-term memory does not guarantee it will stay there forever. If the same phone number is dialed every day, it will be memorized for the time being. But stop dialing it for any length of time and it's back to the phone book again. Cramming can work well if all you're worried about is passing the test. But it won't help much if you want to recall that knowledge a year later. In order to retain access to most factual knowledge, we must remind ourselves of the details, and use them, on an ongoing basis.

To sum up: Short-term memory traces fade quickly unless they are maintained by repetition, rehearsal, and practice. By coming back to information time after time, we can transfer it into our long-term memory banks even if it's as arbitrary as a PIN or combination lock number. But is there any way we can help the memory process along and steepen the learning curve? The answer is yes, but the important thing to remember in this connection is that memory does *not* work like a camera or tape recorder. We're making a mistake if we think of our brain as a passive recipient of information. As memory researcher Alan Baddeley puts it, the central feature of human learning is that it is dependent on *organization*.

Getting organized

Organization works on several levels. First, you can organize new information in a way that helps you remember just that information, without really integrating it into a larger knowledge base. Many mnemonic tricks work like that. If you try to remember the airport parking space number C-2 by picturing yourself returning from the baggage claim area with a friend and saying, "I *see* it, *too*," that's a situation-specific trick. It organizes the information into something meaningful so you can remember it long enough to get you to your car. Cramming for exams often works on this level, too.

But if you want to remember information permanently, it helps to relate it to what's *already* in your long-term memory.

MEMORY PILLS
Fact or Fiction

Recent research by Nobel Prize-winning neurobiologist Eric Kandel and others has identified a molecule called CREB as a key element in the chain of events leading from short-term to long-term memory. On a cellular level, a fundamental difference between short- and long-term memory is that long-term memory requires the growth of brand-new synapses — the communication points between brain cells. Short-term memory, by contrast, involves just a temporary change in the sensitivity of already-existing synapses. In order to grow new synapses, the brain must switch on genes that produce the proteins that build these new learning and memory pathways. CREB is the molecule that triggers those genes into action.

But what explains the fact that only some experiences prompt CREB to switch on this molecular chain of events? CREB has a counterpart, called CREB-2, that blocks the production of protein and new synapses. Normally, after just a single encounter with a new fact or experience, CREB-2 levels rise a little higher than levels of CREB and the production of new synapses is blocked.

The brain evolved this mechanism for two reasons. On the one hand, it wouldn't be advantageous to remember every detail that passed by your senses on a second-by-second basis, every minute, hour, and day of your life. Most of what your senses register is unimportant. You wouldn't want to remember for the rest of your life the fact that a garbage truck drove past your window just as you were reading this sentence. (The exceptions to this rule are isolated experiences that trigger strong emotional reactions. If the garbage truck happened to drive *through* the window and into your living room, the experience would undoubtedly trigger a strong emotional reaction, and in cases like this the CREB-2 memory-repressing mechanism seems to be bypassed.)

On the other hand, if something happens repeatedly, it must be important. If the phone rings and there's nothing but muted breathing at the other end of the line, it could be a random wrong number dialed by someone too embarrassed to admit his mistake. But if the same thing happens day after day, you need to remember the event in order to begin figuring out what to do about it. As James Bond creator Ian Fleming once put it, "Once is accident. Twice is coincidence. Three times is enemy action."

Research with fruit flies and sea slugs has yielded ways to manipulate learning and memory on the molecular level of CREB and CREB-2. If CREB is blocked or temporarily poisoned, the lab animals can't learn anything, regardless of how many training sessions they have. But if CREB-2 is blocked, the animals remember *after a single training session* what would normally take many training sessions to learn. The practical applications of this to helping people improve their memory (or, conversely, to prevent long-term memories of certain experiences from forming at all) are obvious. So is the Pandora's box of ethical and practical dilemmas that this kind of molecular memory manipulation would open.

So, instead of cramming on your own, get together with class-mates to discuss and debate the course material in greater depth. This experience will help you remember the material long after you've passed the test. The emotional component of the discussion will also improve your chances of remembering the material over the long term.

References

Baddeley, Alan (1999). Essentials of Human Memory. Hove, UK: Psychology Press.

Carew, Thomas J. (1996). Molecular enhancement of memory formation. Neuron 16: 5-8.

Dubnau, Josh, and Tim Tully (1998). Gene discovery in Drosophila: new insights for learning and memory. Annual Review of Neuroscience 21: 407-44.

Mayford, Mark, and Eric R. Kandel (1999). Genetic approaches to memory storage. Trends in Genetics 15/11: 463-70.

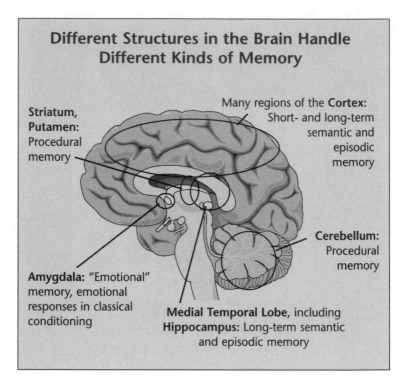

Different Structures in the Brain Handle Different Kinds of Memory

Striatum, Putamen: Procedural memory

Many regions of the **Cortex:** Short- and long-term semantic and episodic memory

Cerebellum: Procedural memory

Amygdala: "Emotional" memory, emotional responses in classical conditioning

Medial Temporal Lobe, including **Hippocampus:** Long-term semantic and episodic memory

MEMORY IS PLURAL

Knowing how its systems interrelate improves coding into long-term memory

A landmark case in the history of memory research is that of "H.M.," a man who developed amnesia after a part of his brain was removed in an operation to cure his epileptic seizures. H.M. had the kind of amnesia known as *anterograde,* meaning that he couldn't remember anything that happened after the amnesia began. For example, he would seem normal when being introduced to a new doctor, but if that doctor left the room and returned a few minutes later, he would have forgotten not only the doctor's name, but even the fact that they had met at all. In other words, he seemed unable to form any new memories. He also forgot everything that had happened in his adult life before the operation, retaining only memories from his childhood.

Why H.M.'s case fascinated neuroscientists

The psychologists who studied H.M. came to the startling realization that, even though he could form no new conscious memories, he could learn new things. For example, he showed a normal learning curve in acquiring expertise in mirror drawing, or tracing the outline of a shape while watching his hand in a mirror. For anyone, it's difficult at first, but after a few days' practice most people can learn to do it without making many mistakes. So could H.M. — even though, in each practice session, he had absolutely no recollection of ever having tried the task before.

H.M., then, was living proof that there are multiple memory systems that depend on different structures in the brain. What H.M. lost was his ability to form *conscious* memories of facts and events. But he retained an ability to learn new motor skills, along with other unconscious forms of memory.

For example, it's hard for anybody to tell what an object is when the image is broken into fragments, as shown here. But if you show most people a clearly outlined picture of the object, as it appears on page 136, they can much more easily identify the fragmented drawing if they see it again — even if they can't explicitly recall having seen the intact image before. So could H.M. This kind of memory, known as *priming*, doesn't rely on the explicit, conscious, kind of memory that we normally think of as memory — the kind that H.M. lost.

The conscious kind of memory for facts and events that was destroyed in H.M.'s brain has come to be called *declarative* — because it's the kind of memory you can talk about, as in, "Yesterday morning I spilled oatmeal on my cat." This is the "knowing *that*" kind of learning, as in knowing facts and events that may be true or false. It relies on structures in the *medial temporal lobe,* which include the hippocampus, that H.M.'s operation had destroyed.

Learning motor skills, on the other hand — "knowing *how*" — doesn't depend on the hippocampus, so H.M. had no problem with that. The same was true for priming and other types of unconscious, or *nondeclarative,* learning and memory that a variety of other brain systems control (see illustration, p. 132).

H.M.'s case showed that all these different memory systems are independent enough of one another that one can be destroyed while others remain intact. The different kinds of memory are operating parallel to one another all the time, influencing our behavior on multiple levels whether we're aware of it or not.

Tricking the amygdala for fun and profit

And yet, some researchers believe that the different memory systems, though distinct, are not *so* distinct as they have commonly come to be understood. The amygdala, for example, is a structure involved in "emotional" memories, including the kind that give rise to phobias, panic attacks, and post-traumatic stress disorder. These are all disorders that arise after an intensely frightening experience becomes seared into the brain. Since the brain system responsible for them operates independently of conscious, rational thought, they are all resistant to being cured by conscious, rational arguments. For somebody with a phobic fear of flying, it simply doesn't do

any good to say, *"Relax* — fewer people die in plane crashes each year than in bicycle accidents."

But the amygdala can also be tricked into tagging ordinary events and facts for permanent storage (see *Learning the Easy Way*). If the amygdala is damaged, it not only alters the brain's emotional response to things, but also impairs the acquisition of new, conscious knowledge. True, the amygdala specializes in the kind of emotional memory that results in a fear of flying after a terrifyingly turbulent flight. But that is why it can also be a powerful tool for committing ordinary data to memory when you dress up the plain data in dramatic, emotion-provoking clothing. Which will be easier to remember: "My phone number is 848-7465" or "My phone number spells out *VITRIOL*"?

How to use one memory system to pull up a fact lodged in another system

Memory of an experience at a certain time and in a certain place is usually visual; that's called an *episodic* memory. Such visual memories are often the first step in extracting information that adds to our *semantic* knowledge of facts about the world. For example, if a friend tells you how much his new Audi convertible cost, you may retain a visual image of the conversation. Later, you might forget the event and remember only the cost of an upmarket ragtop. *How* that fact was acquired is often forgotten forever. In that way, episodic and semantic memory interact.

The Science: How Researchers Use Sea Slugs and Fruit Flies to Study Human Memory

Since H.M.'s case taught researchers about multiple memory systems, a tremendous amount of detailed knowledge has been gathered about how different kinds and stages of memory work in the brain, on a fine-grained chemical and structural level.

Most of this work was done, believe it or not, by studying such creatures as sea slugs and fruit flies. Sea slugs have the advantage of possessing a small number of very large neurons that happen to work by the same principles as ours (see *Habituation*). So by studying very specific parts of very simple animal systems, scientists were able to learn a lot about much more complex human memory-creating and memory-storing systems.

Of course, there are some kinds of memory that humans have and sea slugs and fruit flies don't. Sea slugs can learn to stop reacting if you prod them repeatedly in the gill, a change in behavior relying on a simple type of learning and memory called *habituation*. Humans can handle this kind of learning while they're still in the womb (see *Learning in the Womb*). Fruit flies can learn to associate an odor with an unpleasant shock if the two occur repeatedly together, a form of learning and memory called *classical conditioning*. These kinds of memory have been around for hundreds of millions of years, far longer than humans have existed on this earth. They are useful enough that evolution doesn't dispense with them, it just builds on top of them as new species evolve.

But humans have other kinds of nondeclarative memory, such as skill and habit learning (*procedural memory*), as well as conscious forms of declarative memory for events (*episodic*) and facts (*semantic*). Some of these kinds of memory depend (as H.M. demonstrated) on the hippocampus and other nearby structures that sea slugs and fruit flies don't have. So how could you study these kinds of memory in an animal model?

Even though non-human species can't "declare" anything, some of them do have a hippocampus, and they display evidence of episodic memory when their behavior shows that they remember having been in a certain location before. Birds have a hippocampus and spatial memory, too. So researchers have been able to study these other, hippocampus-dependent forms of memory in animals such as monkeys and rodents. Using animals more complex than sea slugs, then, scientists have been able to study declarative memory on a detailed, molecular level as well. It turns out that, even though declarative memory uses different parts of the brain from nondeclarative memory, all kinds of learning share the same essential molecular mechanisms for converting experience into permanent structural changes in the brain.

It can also work the other way around: episodic memory can help access semantic memory. That is, recalling the location where something happened can also help you remember what you learned there. This fact has practical applications. Test scores tend to rise when the test is taken in the same room in which the material was learned and reviewed. Also, when people forget what they just walked into the room to get, it helps them to remember by picturing where they were and what they were doing when they made the decision to go get it. There are times, of course, that people may not *want* to remember or think about something. Insomniacs are often advised to use their bedroom only for sleep. If they also associate the room with work, for example, they may find themselves staring at the ceiling at 3 a.m. thinking about the presentation they prepared for the 8 a.m. meeting.

Memory of how to do one thing can help the brain access other knowledge

Procedural means the type of memory used to learn skills, such as riding a bike or driving a car, or acquiring the habit of taking the same route to work every day. Of all the nondeclarative memory systems, procedural memory is the most accessible to consciousness. After all, a skill like driving a car is something we devote conscious effort to, and we think of skills like that as part of our repertoire of knowledge along with the knowledge of facts and events that we have in our episodic and semantic memory systems. One type of knowledge may be knowing *how,* while the other is knowing *that,* but they both include types of knowledge that we're aware of.

On the other hand, the skills and habits in our procedural memory are much more stable than our memories of facts and events. The complex moves needed to ride a bike always come back. Once automatic routines like that get tucked away in the brain's procedural memory system they are hard to change — one reason both good and bad habits can be hard to break.

"Hooking"— a practical crutch that uses one kind of memory to remember something else

You can take advantage of the procedural memory system by "hooking" semantic knowledge to muscle memory. For example, if there's something you tend to forget (taking your pills in the morning), hook it to a habitual procedure (getting the coffee pot ready), so you can use one as a reminder to do the other.

You can also help to entrench new semantic knowledge in your mind by encoding new knowledge in your muscle memory so that it'll be more readily available when you need it. For a woman, it's one thing to know *in theory* what to do should you be attacked by a rapist; it's quite another to put it into practice when the adrenaline rush of fear overcomes you in the real situation. Probably, you'll panic. But if you act out and practice your response to an attack, in a "model mugging" class, for example, the chances are much better that you'll be able to use your knowledge when you really need it.

Another way to use procedural and episodic memory to bolster semantic memory is to act out scenes when you're learning a foreign language, rather than just studying alone in the privacy of your own room. That way, both the episodic memory of the scene and the procedural memory of using the newly-learned vocabulary and grammar help you to access that knowledge in the future.

References

Adolphs, Ralph, et al. (1997). Impaired declarative memory for emotional material following bilateral amygdala damage in humans. Learning & Memory 4: 291-300.

Milner, Brenda, Larry R. Squire, and Eric R. Kandel (1998). Cognitive neuroscience and the study of memory. Neuron 20: 445-68.

Squire, Larry R., and Stuart M. Zola (1996). Structure and function of declarative and nondeclarative memory systems. Proceedings of the National Academy of Sciences USA 93: 13515-22.

MINDLESSNESS

The brain on autopilot loses altitude

One day, a woman was paying for a purchase at a department store when the clerk noticed the woman had forgotten to sign the back of her credit card. He handed back the card for her to sign, which she did while the clerk looked on. The clerk ran the charge through and handed her the slip to sign. Then, he compared the signature on the slip with the one on the back of the card to make sure they matched. The final step was so routine that he didn't even think about the fact that the signatures couldn't possibly *fail* to match, given that he'd just watched the customer sign both the card and the slip in the space of a minute. The term *mindlessness* is used to refer to a mind-state that puts you at risk for making careless errors when you run through automatic routines. It's essentially the opposite of what we understand by the the concept of *paying attention*.

Exploring ways to reduce mindlessness and enhance learning performance begins with an understanding of *working memory* — that temporary, "online," short-term memory system that lets you hold information just long enough to use it. The working memory system includes three components: the *phonological loop*; the *visuospatial sketchpad*; and the *central executive* that controls the two others. Individual differences in phonological loop and visuospatial sketchpad capacity are largely fixed by genetic inheritance. But how well the central executive works depends a lot on practice and effort.

The phonological loop is the mechanism that lets you hold a string of digits — say, a telephone number—in your mind's ear long enough to punch it into a telephone keypad. The phonological loop also helps with language skills, such as acquiring new vocabulary and deciphering ambiguous or otherwise tricky-to-parse sentences (see box, opposite).

The visuospatial sketchpad is the mechanism that holds a group of numbers in the mind's eye, or allows visualization of the way a bicycle's gears move the chain. And it's the central executive that employs these short-term visual and auditory storehouses to solve a problem — to multiply numbers in our head if a piece of paper isn't handy, or to make a sketch of the way the bicycle's high gear makes the bike go faster if paper and pencil are at hand. All of these working memory skills require the focus and effort of the central executive. When the central executive isn't doing its work and careless errors ensue, that's mindlessness.

The upside of mindlessness

Let it be said that mindlessness is not always a bad thing. In fact, it may *improve* performance when you're doing something that relies on unconscious, nondeclarative kinds of

Going Down the Garden Path

Garden path sentences "lead you down the garden path" into a wrong interpretation of their structure and meaning. When you hear structurally ambiguous sentences like these, you have to rely on your phonological loop's short-term acoustic store to help you back out and reanalyze the sentence properly.

The dog walked through the park barked.

The man who whistles tunes pianos.

The cotton clothing is made of grows in Texas.

The old man the boat.

The horse raced past the barn fell.

The prime number few.

The man who hunts ducks into the bar after work.

Fat people eat can be unhealthy.

memory, such as hitting a baseball. When a baseball player is "in the zone," seeing a pitch as if the baseball were the size of a grapefruit and adjusting flawlessly to the movement of a curve ball, he's relying on unconscious memory systems. Indeed, if he were to think too much about what he was doing by bringing his conscious memory systems into play, it would *interfere* with his procedural knowledge of how to hit the ball. In sports, that's what's known as choking.

But in other circumstances, when the brain goes on autopilot, it's liable to make a mistake. The mistake can be as trivial as wearing a suit to work on casual Friday, or as serious as crashing a plane or sinking a supertanker.

From "A" for attention to "E" for effort

It's important to remember that the central executive component of working memory doesn't function automatically.
Focused attention requires *effort*. People have trouble remembering names, for example, because they aren't in the habit
of making the effort in the first place. Since working memory
functions as a gatekeeper to long-term memory, you won't
learn much unless you make that initial effort to focus on
what you're doing. Who hasn't had the experience of reading
several paragraphs of a book or newspaper article, only to
find they couldn't remember a single thing from the passage
because they'd been thinking about something else while
reading? A big part of what determines how effectively we
assimilate ideas from what we read is whether or not we're
giving our full attention to what's in front of our eyes.

Overloading the information highway

This brings up another point about the central executive in
particular, and about working memory in general. Even
though long-term memory is, for all intents and purposes,
infinite, working memory has a strictly finite capacity. And
the short-term memory storage components of working
memory are very limited indeed. In fact, they get "filled up"
by a fairly small amount of information — two seconds or so
of auditory information, for example, in the case of the
phonological loop. So there are two ways you can be sure to
flunk a short-term memory test. One is to fail to pay attention. The other is to try to handle too much data at once,
such as repeating twenty numbers in reverse order, or answering a hard question on an oral exam while mentally planning
the end-of-semester celebration party.

Often, short-term memory overload and poor focus may
be two sides of a single problem. Research on the phonologi-

cal loop has shown that this component of working memory can be disrupted by having any speech-like sounds in the background. If you're presented with several digits to remember and repeat back, your performance will be a lot worse if someone's talking in the background, even if the words being spoken are in a foreign language. Since we use the short-term phonological loop to hold numbers, letters, or words in our mind even if the numbers, letters, or words are presented visually, what seems to be happening is that speech or speech-like sounds gain automatic access to the phonological loop, reducing the amount of space available for what we're trying to focus our attention on.

Experiments with background music show the same results: If the music features a vocalist, working memory performance is poor; if the music is strictly instrumental, working memory is only slightly affected. It's this automatic, preconscious nature of the access of spoken words to the working memory's phonological store that makes it so hard to concentrate when people are talking in the background or the TV or radio is on. (On the other hand, some kinds of instrumental music may make it easier to focus — see *Music*.)

Making focused decisions

The importance of focus also applies to decision-making skills. How many good citizens wind up casting a poorly considered vote because they didn't pay attention to the details of what the candidates were saying in the televised debates? Intuitive judgments about the way the candidates "look" and "sound" require a lot less mental focus than attending to the response to a question about Social Security.

And how many relationships begin to falter when one or the other partner becomes too lazy and complacent to hear what the other is saying? When a relationship is young, its novelty, unpredictability, and emotional intensity make the task of paying attention automatic. But as infatuation subsides, and the relationship becomes more familiar, it requires conscious effort to really listen.

References

Baddeley, Alan (1998). Recent developments in working memory. Current Opinion in Neurobiology 8/2: 234-8.

Baddeley, A., S. Gathercole, and C. Papagno (1998). The phonological loop as a language learning device. Psychological Review 105/1: 158-73.

Stress

A little bit too often kills memory cells

Feeling stressed out? Can't think clearly? Is your memory not what it used to be? Are you getting sick more often than you used to? If the answer is yes to one of these questions, chances are good you'll answer yes to the others. Ample research now shows that, for many people, all of these complaints are linked by a network tying together hormones, the brain, and the immune system. Stress not only harms the body by interfering with the immune system, it harms brain cells, retards neuron growth, blocks memory, and may even hasten the onset of Alzheimer's.

Understanding the havoc stress inflicts on the brain

Is there anything you can do about it? Yes, there is. In fact, simply knowing that it is possible to control the situation may reduce the risk of suffering stress-induced brain deterioration. Here's how it works.

Imagine being confronted with a stressful event — say, a snake in the path or a curt comment from the boss. The brain immediately signals the adrenal glands to release the stress hormones *cortisol* (remember that word; it helps in small doses and harms in excess), *epinephrine* (adrenaline), and *norepinephrine.* In turn, extra blood rushes toward the brain, muscles, and heart. Extra fuel is pumped into the bloodstream as blood glucose levels jump. A threat-alerting structure in the primitive part of the brain, the *amygdala*, wakes up other systems. All the interlocking brain systems go on hyperalert to confront the possible threat. The nerves signal the muscles to freeze, fight hard or run fast. That reaction could save your life.

But if the stress is chronic, stress hormones actually harm the body and brain. Sustained high levels of cortisol can weaken the immune system, and can lead to ulcers, cardiovascular disease, and diabetes. Excess cortisol also kills brain cells.

Why panic blocks memory

The *hippocampus*, a brain structure centrally involved in learning and memory, is most sensitive to the harmful effects of cortisol. Evolution has designed the human brain so that it's hard for both the hippocampus and the amygdala to work well at the same time. To survive, the human brain must be able to respond instantly to an attacker, or die. (A favorite example among neuroscientists is: "If you could identify the type of dinosaur, it was too late.")

When the amygdala perceives a real or imagined threat, it takes over. It causes the hippocampus's memory-storage and retrieval systems to shut down (a reaction some researchers refer to as "downshifting"). A person primed for a fight-or-flight response may not remember all the details of the crisis very well after it's happened. When a panic reaction is in progress, the brain cannot access knowledge from memory,

Memory Problems? Can't Think? *Just Relax*

Tatiana Cooley, 28-year-old three-time U.S. Memoriad champion, has a word of advice for those who want to do well in exams, interviews, and other mentally stressful performances: *Relax*. Cooley, quoted in a recent Associated Press story, blames the chaos and stress of modern life for the fear so many people have that their memory is slipping. A crucial part of her own technique for acing the annual memory competition, she says, is to slow down, breathe deeply, and remind herself to take it easy.

Even though she clearly has a naturally excellent memory for some things — she discovered while taking an exam in college that she could recall all her class lecture notes verbatim — Cooley still has to rely on Post-it notes to remember many of the mundane details of life. And in at least some of the rounds of the Memoriad, she relies on mnemonic tricks that anybody can use. As she herself admits, "Anybody can train their mind to memorize."

Think you could win the Memoriad? Here are sample questions in several rounds from recent competitions, along with winning scores:

Names and Faces:
> Study 99 photographs of faces along with their names for 15 minutes. Then write down the first or last name matching each photograph (presented in random order). Winning score: 85.

Words:
> Study a list of 500 random words in columns of 25 words each, then write down as many as you can remember. Winning score: 78.

Poetry:

Memorize as much of a 50-line poem as you can. (For the Memoriad, a poet was enlisted to write one; if you try it, you should at least use a poem you don't know.) The first three lines of a poem used in a recent competition:

A Knight in armour falls pushed by his star
By the crow of a cock. A wedding ring
Bounced off a coffin by a finger caught it...
Winning score: 180.

Playing Cards:

Look through a randomly-shuffled deck of 52 cards, and remember the order of the cards as well as you can in five minutes. Hand the deck to the judge, who deals out the cards, one by one. You have to call out the name of each card before it's turned over.
Winning score: 22.

If you have a hard time matching these scores, take heart. None of the competitors — even Cooley — did well in all the rounds, even using special coding tricks. And you can certainly improve if you take one last lesson from her: "Every day, be it at home or at work, I make a conscious effort to do some kind of memorization of something."

since the hippocampus plays a role not just in making memories but also in retrieving knowledge from the brain's memory banks. That's why people often experience brain-lock when they try to recall the name of someone they know and just encountered. People who are not accustomed to public speaking can have their minds go blank. Students might do poorly on an exam if they lose self-confidence and begin to panic.

The upside and downside of cortisol's action

Once high cortisol levels start to harm the hippocampus, they may have a snowball effect that scientists call a "cascade" — a "domino effect" in the language of international relations. High levels of cortisol trigger chemical receptors in the hippocampus to reduce its production in the adrenal glands. When stress is short-lived, this feedback mechanism works well to restore cortisol levels to normal. Your heart and brain go on alert when a threat appears, but calm down once you've had a chance to flee, fight, or figure out that the snake in the path is just a stick.

But if stress is chronic, and cortisol starts to kill the neurons and receptors in the hippocampus that take part in the feedback process, the brain starts to lose its ability to modulate cortisol production. When cortisol levels peak repeatedly, they kill more brain cells, triggering a downward spiral, to the point where memory and cognition are impaired.

Stress plays a role in age-related mental decline

This "glucocorticoid cascade" process has been most extensively studied as a possible contributing factor in age-related cognitive decline and Alzheimer's disease. In fact, many researchers who subscribe to the glucocorticoid theory of aging believe that the very fact of getting older puts the human brain at greater risk for a cortisol-mediated downward spiral into dementia. New research has shown that the brains of very young rats are quick to restore glucocorticoids to normal levels after a stressful experience. Older rats, sadly, tend to have higher baseline levels of glucocorticoids, and are apt to release more of them in response to a mild stressor, thus making it more difficult to restore the balance.

A message for students

Stress can, literally, make a person sick. Even acute, short-lived stress in response to a single event can stimulate the stress-response system with effects that last well beyond the stressful event itself. Recent German studies with university students have shown that saliva levels of the antibody *immunoglobin A* (sIgA) fall during times of academic stress, such as during exams. The sIgA antibody is the body's first line of defense against viruses and other invading microorganisms. Levels of sIgA may remain depressed even for two or more weeks after an exam, well beyond the point that the students *perceive* themselves to feel stressed out.

Levels of the sIgA antibody are partly controlled by the cortisol stress hormone. So it's reasonable to assume that cortisol levels, too, may remain elevated for some time after a stressful experience. Given the destructive effect of cortisol on brain cells, even such stressors as college exams might harm the brain. (NB: The authors do not recommend citing this argument to try to get out of a midterm.)

Stress reducers under the individual's control

The branch of medicine that studies interactions between mental states (such as psychological stress) and physical body systems (such as the immune system) is relatively new to Western medicine. What research results are available confirm that the following well-tested methods help reduce psychological stress: Controlled breathing and visualization biofeedback techniques, and regular yoga or meditation. Some studies also indicate that regular exercise may help lower the body's "set point" of stress hormones, and help to modulate the body's reaction to stressors. Other studies have demonstrated that aerobic exercise can also boost the supply of oxygen and glucose to the brain, raise levels of brain growth hormones (which help to maintain and protect brain cells), and can even double the rate of *neurogenesis* (the growth of new brain cells) in the hippocampus of lab rats.

The executive-stressed monkey experiment

In addition to these relatively common-sense pieces of
advice, there's evidence that certain mental attitudes might
fend off destructive effects of stress. In an experiment cited in
many an introductory psychology textbook, Joseph Brady
once devised a cruel but clever way to assess the impact of
control on stress and health. Two monkeys were strapped side
by side into identical chairs, rigged so that an electric shock
could be applied to both monkeys simultaneously. But one
monkey had the power to control the shock — that is, turn it
off — by pressing a button in front of it. When that monkey
pressed the button to turn off the current, it also turned off
the current to the adjacent chair. So while both monkeys
received the exact same frequency and intensity of shocks,
only one had the responsibility of doing something about it.
The results? Only the monkey burdened with the task of
pushing the button to turn off the shock — the "executive
monkey" — got ulcers. The "flunky monkey" did not.

Frustration leading to apathy leads to disease

This was naturally interpreted to mean that the power to
make decisions in stressful situations would be more likely to
cause ulcers than a powerless role would. But there's more to
it. Later attempts to replicate the findings under various conditions showed that it was the animal with no control over
the shocks that more frequently got sick. Caged animals sub-
jected to shock would search frantically to find a way to turn
off the shock. Before long, the animal, frustrated by its inability to control its environment, would curl up in its cage and
shut down all awareness of the surroundings in a kind of
"learned apathy." To protect itself, its whole system admitted
defeat and shut down rather than tear itself apart by strug-
gling against the constant frustration of its fruitless attempts

to protect its vulnerability to repeated assaults. Even if the helpless animal was later given the option of turning off the shock by pressing a button, it didn't take it. Not only did its awareness shut down, its immune system did too, leaving it vulnerable to disease.

In other words, even though the burden of responsibility for making decisions and responding to threats can be stressful, the body responds dramatically when it cannot exercise any control over a constantly stressful situation, especially if that situation can be anticipated but not changed. The brain's tendency to protect itself by retreating into apathy may also be diagnosed as a symptom of depression. In a depressed state the brain is not eager to take on new experiences; that is, it is not eager to learn.

References

Deinzer, Renate, et al. (2000). Prolonged reduction of salivary immunoglobin A (sIgA) after a major academic exam. International Journal of Psychophysiology 37: 219-32.

Deinzer, Renate, and N. Schüller (1998). Dynamics of stress-related decrease of salivary immunoglobin A (sIgA): relationship to symptoms of the common cold and studying behavior. Behavioral Medicine 23: 161-9.

O'Brien, John T. (1997). The "glucocorticoid cascade" hypothesis in man: prolonged stress may cause permanent brain damage. British Journal of Psychiatry 170: 199-201.

Pedersen, Bente Klarlund, and Laurie Hoffman-Goetz (2000). Exercise and the immune system: regulation, integration, and adaptation. Physiological Reviews 80/3: 1055-81.

Sapolsky, Robert M. (1999). Glucocorticoids, stress, and their adverse neurological effects with relevance to aging. Experimental Gerontology 34/6: 721-32.

MAKE IT MEANINGFUL

The three levels of remembering

The hardest bits of information to store in long-term memory are the arbitrary facts that pop up without any meaningful context — a string of random numbers, for example, or the flurry of names that greet you on your first day at a new job. As an aid to learning and remembering this kind of arbitrary data, a good many memory-aiding, *mnemonic* techniques are based on this principle: *If you want to remember something, attach it to something you already know.* Taking this one step further (and this is key): *The more you know, the easier it will be to remember new things.*

Most of us would probably agree that master-level chess players have good memories. Indeed, one study showed that expert chess players looking at an arrangement of 25 pieces

Filing New Information in Familiar File Folders

One of the secrets to having a good memory is to get into the habit of thinking about new facts and information deeply enough to have them make sense in terms of what you already know. Memory is not like a muscle — you can't automatically make it stronger, or get it to acquire new information effortlessly, just by exercising it. But your memory will improve if you actively engage your mind in reviewing the already-familiar knowledge that the new information relates to, and fitting the new into the context of the old.

This advice applies to long-term memory and not to the short-term, "online" kind known as working memory. If a list of words must be repeated immediately after hearing them — a test of working memory skills relevant to language learning and reading ability — it's just as easy to remember and repeat the list of words in column A as it is to repeat the words in column B:

Column A	Column B
bug	stove
cat	pan
tree	pot
pan	sink
grass	dish
pear	bowl

But if we want to remember the words for more than a few seconds — if we want to *memorize* the list in the usual sense — B is a lot easier to learn since the words are less random. They represent meaningful parts of the familiar, coherent visual image of a kitchen. The same goes for any sequence of words, numbers, or other data. A PIN that matches your youngest child's birth date is much easier to memorize than one composed of four or five completely arbitrary numbers.

from an actual game could memorize the positions of virtually all of them within a period of five seconds. In the same
five seconds, novice players on average remembered the
positions of only about four pieces. That would seem to
clinch the argument that chess masters have better memories
than novices.

But wait a minute. When those same master players were
given five seconds to study a *random* arrangement of pieces
on a board — an arrangement that you'd never see in an
actual game — their memory proved no better than that of
novice players. So it was not any old kind of memory, or
visual memory for objects in general, at which the experts
excelled. It was only memory for a *meaningful arrangement* of
chess pieces that they were so good at.

Levels of processing

Psychologists refer to different approaches to incoming data,
depending on whether you do or don't decide to make them
meaningful (and therefore memorable), as *levels of processing,*
of which there are three:

Shallow processing is the sort used in tests of very short-
term auditory or visual memory, and serves to help you
remember data for a few seconds only.

Phonological processing involves thinking about the sounds
that make up a word. For example, if you want to remember
the company name "Digitex" because your friend tipped you
off that its stock is about to rise sharply, you can make a conscious mental note that the name starts with "D."

Semantic processing involves thinking about the word in
terms of its meaning. For example, you might think about
"Digitex" in terms of an image of an outstretched hand with
a string tied around the index finger ("digit"). You might also
think about the fact that while the "digit" in the name refers

to the computer-software nature of the company's products, the "tex" might refer to the company headquarters location in Texas. And then continue to think about a recent news story about the rise of Austin, Texas as a hi-tech research, development, and business center.

The shallow processing that your working memory's phonological loop and visuospatial sketchpad specialize in will let you remember something for only a few seconds unless you deliberately rehearse it. Phonological processing is

---

WHY VISUAL MNEMONIC TECHNIQUES WORK
The Brain Research

Visual mnemonic techniques for encoding words or names so that they may be recalled later recruit the assistance of brain regions that are separate from the language centers in the left half of the brain. Recent brain imaging studies, using positron emission tomography (PET) and functional magnetic resonance imaging (fMRI), show that the visualization skills used by the working memory's "mind's eye" sketchpad are housed in several regions of the brain, including the parietal cortex, the region around the boundary between the occipital and temporal lobes, and the frontal cortex. Many of the specific visual skills draw more heavily on the right side of the brain than the left side. The multiple encoding of information in several connected cortical networks — not just language regions but also visual ones — gives you more angles from which to approach the knowledge you're trying to access, increasing the chances of successful recall.

a bit better, but even if you do remember that the company name begins with "D," there are so many other possible names that begin with that letter that you might not recall the right one. Semantic processing is the best, because it gives you so many meaningful images and associations to help you work back to the exact name you're looking for. So the deeper you go in the levels, the more likely it is that you'll be able to recall the company's name later.

How to use deep processing to your advantage

Deep processing works for many kinds of learning. If you want to learn a new word, it frequently helps to break the word down into meaningful parts. For example, to remember the meaning of *taciturn* ("inclined to silence; not liking to speak") you might think about it as being partially made up of the more common word *tacit,* meaning "unspoken."

Or, perhaps you've never quite managed to remember the difference between *libel* and *slander.* If you think about the fact that *libel* appears to contain the same word-root found in *library,* that will make it easier to remember that *libel* means "making false statements harmful to a person's reputation" *in writing,* while *slander* refers to making those kinds of statements *orally.*

A variation on this theme works for spelling. Which is correct? "Tyranny" or "tyrrany"? "Miniscule" or "minuscule"? According to those who keep track of such things, these are two of the 50 most commonly misspelled words in the English language. If you remind yourself that a *tyrant* (with a single "r") is responsible for "tyranny," and that the word "minus" (not the prefix "mini") is part of "minuscule," you'll spell them correctly every time. As with remembering word meanings, it doesn't really matter whether the deconstruction is "right" or not. Many people misspell the word *separate* as "seperate." If you're one of them, tell yourself that "there's *a rat* in *separate*." Chances are you'll never misspell the word again.

Reference

Belger, A., et al. (1998). Dissociation of mnemonic and perceptual processes during spatial and nonspatial working memory using fMRI. Human Brain Mapping 6/1: 14-32.

BRAIN NUTRITION

**What foods help you do your best work
at different times of day**

There's an Arab proverb that goes something like this: *Invite all your friends to dinner, and a few of your friends to lunch, but eat breakfast alone.* In other words, at dinner you can share your food as generously as you like, but make sure you get enough to eat for breakfast.

Of course, you don't have to cast your anthropological net very wide to find this kind of advice. We've all been scolded by our mothers for skipping breakfast, and we've all heard that breakfast is the most important meal of the day. But is it true?

In many controlled studies that have evaluated the traditional motherly wisdom, skipping breakfast translates into poorer performance on tests of memory, attention, information processing speed, and reaction time. Breakfast also tends to improve both mood and motivation, although it has no significant effect on IQ. In other words, it has its strongest impact on the skills that need to be functioning well in order to learn effectively.

Why breakfast beats lunch for building brain power

For the kind of performance required in school and most work settings, the morning meal is more important than the other two meals. In fact, lunch tends to have a *detrimental* effect on learning and memory, according to the same sorts of studies that have found breakfast to benefit learning-related skills. Performance on tests of memory, attention, information-processing speed, and reaction time has been found to be better before lunch than afterwards. A midday meal also tends to make test subjects sleepier and less motivated to work.

Why would breakfast and lunch have such different effects? A meal after waking up literally breaks a fast, typically a nine- to 12-hour one. So it makes sense that the body needs to replenish fuel and nutrients that the energy-hungry brain requires to function.

The argument for taking a nap

The body's internal circadian rhythm also affects mental alertness. Even living in a cave with no way of telling what the sun is doing or what time it is, there are two times in a 24-hour cycle when body temperature drops the most and sleep most naturally occurs. One corresponds to the time around the middle of most people's nighttime sleep period, and the other occurs about ten hours later, corresponding to mid-afternoon. The body most naturally falls into a pattern of one long sleep period, an equally long period of being awake, and then another shorter sleep period — that is, a nap. Independently of diet, humans are most prone to sleepiness around those

Vitamins and the Brain

Most of the vitamins that have been reported to have possible brain-protecting benefits are *antioxidants*. Antioxidants are substances that protect cells from *oxygen free radicals*, which are a highly reactive form of oxygen molecule with an unpaired electron. The brain burns a great amount of oxygen. It also contains a lot of polyunsaturated fatty acids; in fact, fat makes up two-thirds of the brain. Polyunsaturated fatty acids are especially prone to damage by oxygen free radicals. So brain cells are particularly susceptible to oxidative stress, and, logically, would benefit from antioxidants.

Vitamin E

Vitamin E is the antioxidant that has been given the most credit for protecting the brain from the effects of aging, and possibly even lowering the risk of Alzheimer's. (Vitamin C is another antioxidant that some studies in the past found to have a potentially beneficial role in protecting brain cells from free radicals. Recent studies have thrown its effectiveness into question.) Although study results have been mixed, some have shown that people with higher blood levels of vitamin E perform better on memory tests, that a history of higher dietary levels of vitamin E correlates with better cognitive performance later in life, and even that vitamin E supplements can slow the progression of Alzheimer's. Good sources of vitamin E are vegetable oils.

A different theory about the brain-protective role of vitamin E focuses on the vitamin's ability to protect against cardiovascular disease. Vitamin E can prevent the oxidation of low-density lipoprotein (LDL), the so-called "bad" type of cholesterol, which might otherwise get deposited on the walls of arteries, leading to strokes.

Vitamin B

Vitamin B isn't an antioxidant, but several studies have shown that people with low blood levels of vitamin B, or poor dietary sources of vitamin B, score low on tests of memory and abstract reasoning. Actually, there are many B vitamins, of which the most frequently mentioned in connection with brain maintenance are B_6, B_{12}, and folic acid. Good sources of folic acid are leafy greens, citrus, and whole grains. Meat and fish are good sources of the other B vitamins.

Raising blood concentrations of B vitamins, especially folic acid, acts to lower the levels of *homocysteine*, an amino acid that may increase the risk for cardiovascular disease. Some studies have even shown a correlation between elevated homocysteine levels and Alzheimer's.

Citations

Miller, Joshua W. (2000). Vitamin E and memory: Is it vascular protection? Nutrition Reviews 58/4: 109-11.

Perkins, A.J., et al. (1999). Association of antioxidants with memory in a multiethnic elderly sample using the Third National Health and Nutrition Examination Survey. American Journal of Epidemiology 150: 37-44.

Snowdon, David A., et al. (1997). Brain infarction and the clinical expression of Alzheimer's disease: the Nun Study. Journal of the American Medical Association 277

times. The body's cycle encourages a nap after lunch during what is sometimes called the "post-lunch dip."

The post-lunch dip might not be a problem in cultures that permit siestas or afternoon naps. But in the United States, unless you're on vacation, retired, self-employed or unemployed, siestas are rarely an option. Usually, you just have to try to stay awake. It's no coincidence that it's during the post-lunch dip, when attention and alertness are at their lowest, that most workplace accidents occur.

Punching the time clock in the brain's chemical factory
One reason the brain responds differently to breakfast and lunch is that the brain synthesizes crucial chemicals from food in different ways according to the body's circadian rhythm. For example, eating carbohydrates can raise brain levels of *serotonin*, a neurotransmitter conducive to calmness. That would be fine at some times of day, but not around lunchtime, when the body's internal cycle is approaching its low-energy point.

Here are some other important food-derived brain nutrients, and how they can affect you at different times of the day:

Glucose is an energy source that all the cells of the body, including brain cells, need to have in good supply in order to do their work. The body readily produces glucose from carbohydrates (the *starch* in potatoes or pasta, for example, is composed of many glucose molecules strung together). Measures of blood glucose generally correlate with performance on memory tests. Glucose concentrations in the blood must remain within a certain range in order for the brain to function normally. If they drop too low, people feel mentally confused or, in extreme cases, even pass out.

Protein is formed from compounds called *amino acids*, which are also essential for effective brain function. The brain

Fish: Good Brain Food — And a
Cure for Schizophrenia?

We've all heard the quaint characterization of fish as "brain food." How fish got this reputation is anyone's guess, but it might be because the protein in fish provides amino acids necessary for synthesizing chemicals brain cells use to communicate. Recent work has also led to theories that the kind of fat found in fish has protective effects on the brain and other body systems. Some of this research has drawn a connection between low levels of fish oil and mood disorders, including depression, bipolar disorder (manic-depressive cycles), and even schizophrenia.

Omega-3 polyunsaturates

Even though we're used to hearing that we should reduce the amount of fat in our diet, the real story is a little more complicated. Cholesterol and saturated fat, found in eggs, butter, and well-marbled steaks, can contribute to heart and cardiovascular disease if consumed to excess. But unsaturated fats, such as the monounsaturates in olive oil or the polyunsaturates in canola oil and fish oil, are a different story. Omega-3 fatty acids, one of the types of polyunsaturated fats, are used to make the cell membranes throughout the body, including heart and brain. Omega-3 is one of the essential fatty acids, meaning that the body can't manufacture it from other sources so it must be eaten directly. Absent enough omega-3, the body will use other, less desirable fats for building cell membranes, resulting in impaired nerve conduction and communication between cells. In particular, some research indicates that insufficient omega-3 interferes with the function of the *monoamines,* which are the neurotransmitters such as serotonin, dopamine, and norepinephrine that play an important role in regulating mood, among other things.

Some cultures, of course, already have diet high in omega-3 fatty acids. Most do not. In fact, estimates of the proportion of omega-3 in the diet of our Paleolithic forebears indicate that the typical modern human's diet has only a fraction of the ratio of omega-3, relative to other fatty acids, that our ancestors ingested. So many different kinds of studies point to the possible role of omega-3 in lowering risk of stroke, heart disease, and mood disorders that many doctors and nutritionists now recommend getting more of it. Recent studies have tested, with positive results, the effectiveness of fish oil supplements to control bipolar disorder and depression.

Fish oil, schizophrenia and the origins of humans
There's even a theory that links dietary fatty acids such as omega-3 and schizophrenia. Some preliminary studies have shown a high success rate treating schizophrenia with, of all things, fish oil.

Some research also suggests that, while the genus *Homo* experienced a dramatic growth in brain size about two million years ago, that brain growth was followed by a long period of cultural stagnation. Between 50,000 and 100,000 years ago, there was a cultural explosion that saw the beginnings of art, music, religion, and warfare. According to genetic evidence, all humans share a common ancestor who lived about 100,000 years ago, suggesting that one small group of Homo sapiens possessed some advantage so decisive that it allowed them and their descendants to replace all other hominids over the entire globe. What might that advantage have been? Some have suggested a language gene. Others propose a genetic mutation that changed the biochemistry of fat in our brains. This mutation resulted in high creativity, strong religiosity, and compelling leadership qualities. It also resulted in mood disorders, psychosis, and psychopathy. In short, it was a genius gene or a schizophrenia gene, or the two may be essentially the same thing. Families with schizophrenia (including the families of Einstein, Joyce, and Jung) also tend to have more than their share of high achievers, creative thinkers, and geniuses. The dietary change since Paleolithic times resulted in this predisposition to schizophrenia leading more often to the full expression of the disease.

This gene theory, while taken seriously by some evolutionary theorists, doesn't explain why so few people (a little under one percent) actually develop schizophrenia, even with a low-omega-3 diet. In the meantime, eat your fish.

Citations

Bruinsma, Kristen A., and Douglas L. Taren (2000). Dieting, essential fatty acid intake, and depression. Nutrition Reviews 58/4: 98-108.

Horrobin, David F. (1999). Lipid metabolism, human evolution and schizophrenia. Prostaglandins, Leukotrienes, and Essential Fatty Acids 60/5-6: 431-7.

needs many types of amino acids to synthesize *neurotransmitters*, the chemicals that brain cells use to communicate with each other. The amino acid *tyrosine* is essential for the production of the neurotransmitters *dopamine, norepinephrine*, and *epinephrine*, a particularly important class of brain chemicals for mood, alertness, and focus.

A meal of nothing but carbohydrates — plain pasta, for example, or bread — would provide glucose fuel for brain cells and boost brain levels of serotonin. But other neurotransmitters, including those conducive to alertness and proper memory function, would drop. Eating carbohydrate-rich "comfort" foods may be appropriate in the evening, but not during times of the day when it is necessary to learn and study. So generally, unless it's close to bedtime, meals with protein to balance carbohydrates are a better bet for cognitive performance.

A neurotransmitter for memory

The glucose from carbohydrates also plays a more specific role in helping memory because it is essential to the production of *acetylcholine*, often referred to as the "memory" neurotransmitter. The brain creates this chemical by combining the amino acid *choline* with the "enzyme activator" *acetyl-CoA* ("acetyl-Coenzyme-A"). Choline can come from a variety of protein sources, especially eggs, liver, and soybeans, but the main source of acetyl-CoA is glucose. Without enough glucose, the brain's acetylcholine levels will be too low for proper memory function. Therefore, maintaining a good supply of glucose not only fuels brain cells but also raises the levels of a specific neurotransmitter needed for a sharp memory.

Of course, different people may respond differently to the same meal, and different body types respond differently to carbohydrates, so everyone needs to monitor their own brain and body response to food to find what works best. People who are highly anxious, and who score high in neuroticism and low on extroversion in personality tests, tend to experience less sluggishness after lunch than other people. For them, a big midday meal may actually have the beneficial effect of helping to feel calmer. For most people, however, the best bet for lunch is an easy-to-digest meal with a balance of protein and carbohydrates. A large or high-fat meal is hard to digest, and draws nutrition-bearing blood from the brain. In fact, from midday to late afternoon, the brain will function better on several smaller snacks than one big lunch.

References

Benton, David, and Pearl Y. Parker (1998). Breakfast, blood glucose, and cognition. American Journal of Clinical Nutrition 67 (Suppl.): 772S-8S.

Donohoe, Rachael T., and David Benton (2000). Glucose tolerance predicts performance on tests of memory and cognition. Physiology & Behavior 71/3-4: 395-401.

Kanarek, Robin (1997). Psychological effects of snacks and altered meal frequency. British Journal of Nutrition 77 (Suppl. 1): S105-S120.

CAFFEINE

In moderation, a smart drug

Coffee, tea, cola drinks — caffeine comes in a host of appealing forms. Many professional writers claim that a cup of nice strong coffee not only helps get the flow of ideas going but will also cure writer's block. Countless employers know that a bottomless coffee pot improves the productivity of employees assigned to boring and repetitive tasks. And research backs both claims. Several tests that measure word fluency, writing expansiveness, and free association show that caffeine does indeed help with creative tasks (see box, p. 176). Other studies confirm that caffeine improves performance on highly practiced, repetitive tasks that require simple decisions and fast reactions, such as driving a car, sorting mail, or inputting text at a computer terminal. Small wonder caffeine is claimed to be the most widely-used psychoactive drug in the world.

Given all this, it might be reasonable to assume that caffeine's ability to stimulate and arouse would apply to learning

Caffeine Can Make Unfamiliar Tasks Harder, But Routine Ones Easier: The Embedded Figures Test

In this multiple-choice test, only one of the designs in the right-hand columns contains the figure in the left. Which one? On a task like this, caffeine can worsen performance initially, but improve performance after the task becomes more familiar. See p. 177 for solution.

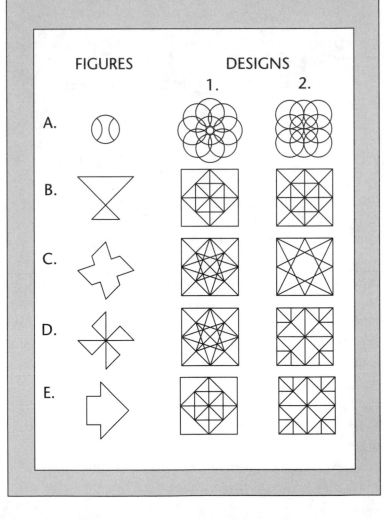

and memory tasks as well, and in fact many textbooks will tell you so.

And, several studies have shown that caffeine helps in learning new information, perhaps by improving attention and reaction time, as well as mood and motivation. Part of the reason for caffeine's motivating impact is that it interacts with the same dopamine brain systems that give cocaine and amphetamines their pleasurable effect. But while caffeine can make it easier to learn and perform, it can also *worsen* your performance, depending on what it is you're trying to do.

Sorting the wheat from the chaff

It has been shown that as tasks become more complex, caffeine won't help performance and it might even hurt for the simple reason that it can interfere with concentration. Also, caffeine can make it harder to pick out the important data, ignoring what's irrelevant. Hence, it may interfere with the ability to keep track of information on an ongoing basis and use it to solve complex problems. These are all components of *working memory* (see *Using Your Mind's Ear*), which is important for both the performance of trickier tasks and learning new problem-solving techniques. As the working memory load gets heavier, the effect of caffeine changes from good to bad.

In one experiment, for example, some subjects were given caffeine and others were not. They were all told to memorize a set of two to four letters, and to press a button every time they saw those letters flashed on a screen. EEG brain activity recordings showed a distinct activation pattern every time any of the subjects saw the memorized letters. The subjects who had ingested caffeine, however, showed the same brain activation pattern when *other* letters were flashed. In other words, their brain found it hard to ignore the irrelevant, distracting stimuli and focus just on the relevant data.

Wide awake but not paying attention

Other studies have confirmed that caffeine may impede *voluntary attention* — a deliberate focus on certain data — while raising *involuntary attention* — the distraction of attention by irrelevant stimuli. This can be especially harmful if you're unfamiliar with the task at hand, although caffeine can be helpful in the beginning by speeding reaction time. If the task is fairly simple and doesn't increase in complexity, the more times the task is repeated and practiced the more coffee will help performance. In effect, it helps to keep you from getting bored. But if the task becomes more complex, the quicker caffeine-induced reaction time is offset by a loss of focus through distraction, and the initially improved performance will get worse.

Here's another example of caffeine's varying effects on the performance of simple and complex tasks. Caffeine can improve performance on a "digits forward" test, where the tester reads a series of numbers out loud (say, 3-8-7-9-5) and the testee must repeat them back. However, on a "digits backward" test, in which the respondent must repeat the numbers in reverse order — a task that places a heavier burden on working memory — caffeine tends to make performance worse.

For a real-world example, consider another study performed on office managers in a workplace setting. When the managers were given quantities of coffee 400 mg. in excess of their usual daily consumption (the equivalent of about four extra cups of coffee), their reaction time improved, which helped them perform better on simple tasks that required simple, rapid responses. But as the tasks became more complex, the managers showed poorer *utilization of opportunity* — a much more important predictor of managerial success — and their performance declined. "Utilization of opportunity" means using information on an ongoing basis to inform decisions, and

Caffeine Can Help With Simple Tasks, But Make Complex Tasks Harder

Here's an illustration of how caffeine can help or harm performance depending on the complexity of the task. See p. 177 for the solution.

(1) Simple task

Go through this grid of letters as quickly as you can, counting all the P's you can find in one minute.

(2) Complex task

Allow two minutes to complete this task. Go through the grid counting every R, W, C, and N. What is the combined total number of all four letters?

On the more complex task, caffeine makes it harder to focus on the relevant data only.

```
S D G O M E N T P W L
D O U T A Z X C F R G
G R Q W I N G D K T R
H N B V C F E O I P H G
Y P D S W A F X Z C T R
E E G H U I O P L K H G
B V N M V C E D X Z S
W Q A D F E F G T H Y
U J I K L O P M N B H Y
G T G V F R F C D E S W
X Z A Q W S D E F G Y H
B U I O P D M P W I A M J
```

requires monitoring and organizing actions that happen one after another. For this important type of executive thinking, simple response speed becomes less useful, and may in fact harm performance by resulting in poorly thought-out decisions.

Caffeine: The Ideal Writer's Drug?

Subjects on caffeine are quicker to come up with a way to complete sentences like these:

> If Max hadn't asked Mary to wear pants to the wedding, ...

> When a large dog came galloping into the women's rest-room, ...

> The problem with using leeches to cure epilepsy is ...

Caffeine tends to help people come up with longer answers to questions like these:

> What problems can you foresee with letting people vote over the Internet?

> Why do you think the US and Canada are prosperous countries with high per capita incomes, while other countries in the Americas are relatively poor?

Subjects on caffeine are quicker to come up with appropriate words or phrases to complete sentences such as these:

> The mailman put the letter into the _____.
> Sam forgot to put his keys in his _____.

Solution for p. 172
Figures A, C and E are in Column 1; Figures B and D are in Column 2

Solution for p. 175
There are seven P's and a total of 23 for the letters R, W, C and N

References

Rogers, Peter J., and Claire Dernoncourt (1998). Regular caffeine consumption: a balance of adverse and beneficial effects for mood and psychomotor performance. Pharmacology, Biochemistry, and Behavior 59/4: 1039-45.

Smith, Andrew P., Rachel Clark, and John Gallagher (1999). Breakfast cereal and caffeinated coffee: effects on working memory, attention, mood, and cardiovascular function. Physiology & Behavior 67/1: 9-17.

Streufert, Siegfried, et al. (1997). Excess coffee consumption in simulated complex work settings: detriment or facilitation of performance? Journal of Applied Psychology 82/5: 774-82.

van der Stelt, Odin, and Jan Snel (1993). Effects of caffeine on human information processing. In: Caffeine, Coffee, and Health, pp. 291-316. Raven Press: New York.

Brain Exercise: Feed Your Learning Addiction

This is a Number Lock puzzle which uses the digits 1 through 9. There are no zeros, and a digit may be used more than once in a combination. Where it seems that more than one combination is possible, look for additional clues in interlocking numbers, as in a crossword puzzle. Par is 5 minutes. See p. 184 for solution.

Across
1. A square; the sum of its digits equals its root
3. The reverse of 1 across
4. The sum of its digits is 8
6. An odd number; the first and second digits are equal to the third
7. An even number; the second and third digits are equal to the first
8. Square of a prime number
9. These two digits added together equal the prime number in 8 across

Down
2. An odd number; the digits increase by twos
3. A palindrome; the digits increase by threes, then decrease by threes
5. As easy as ABC

Hint: Palindromes are the same backward and forward. A prime number is divisible only by itself and one. Examples are 2, 3, 23.

LEARNING ADDICTION

The brain's reward for learning new skills

The natural state of the human brain is a learning state. In fact, it has built-in mechanisms to reward the learning of new skills. The German word *Funktionslust*, which translates loosely as "joy in doing," describes the feeling any living organism gets from doing something it's built to do — and doing it well. For cats, it may be stalking and catching a mouse. For bees, it may be homing in on the sight and smell of a pollen-filled flower. For humans, it's learning something new and solving problems.

Evidence that activity in the left side of the brain acts to support a positive outlook on life

Prefrontal cortex (the very front of the brain's neuron-saturated surface) handles many functions, among them language, planning ahead, and controlling emotion-driven responses. Not coincidentally, perhaps, regions of the left prefrontal cortex are activated by tasks that recruit problem-solving skills. Exercises that particularly involve the left side of the brain include verbal puzzles (crosswords, Scrabble, and other language games) and number-manipulation puzzles. It appears that activities like these, whether performed for work or leisure, may stimulate or "prime" adjacent or overlapping regions of the brain linked to good mood. Of course, the "feel-good" centers of the brain make no distinction between vocational or avocational applications. The activity itself stimulates a sense of well-being, which may or may not explain symptoms of apparently addictive behavior demonstrated by crossword puzzle mavens and workaholics alike.

Different tasks for different sides of the brain

Neuroscientists have also discovered that the two sides of the prefrontal cortex may be specialized for different emotions. For decades, neurologists have observed that their patients developed different kinds of emotional disorders depending on which side of their prefrontal cortex was damaged by injury or disease. Damage to the left side was linked to depression, while damage to the right side was linked to manic happiness. Based on those kinds of observation, they posited a right-hemisphere specialization for sadness and fear, and a left-hemisphere specialization for happiness and eager enthusiasm.

Recent brain imaging studies have confirmed that activity in the left side of the prefrontal cortex correlates with positive emotions. Other research, using modern brain scanning technology, indicates that people with symptoms of depression show less activity in the left side of their prefrontal cortex than other people do.

Dopamine — a chemical that helps neurons communicate and creates a positive mood

Another link between mental exercise and mood lies in the neurotransmitter chemicals generated by the *limbic system*, an ancient collection of alerting and action-provoking organs located below the more recently-evolved cortex. When the brain encounters novelty, studies of both laboratory animals and humans show increased levels in the *amygdala* of a neurotransmitter called *dopamine*. The amygdala is one of the limbic sub-systems equipped to alert the brain to new data.

Dopamine imparts a sense of well-being and, therefore, provides a reward for whatever triggers its production. Thus it seems to be involved in the early stages of learning, when the environment confronts the brain with a novel situation deserving of attention.

Dopamine levels also rise in the prefrontal cortex while the brain applies itself to working memory tasks that require holding onto data long enough to manipulate it to solve a problem, or to evaluate new data in terms of its possible role in achieving a preconceived goal. In a recent study, researchers found that elevated dopamine levels coincide with a person's learning curve. A sharp spike accompanies a rapid, steep curve, while more prolonged dopamine elevation occurs with a longer, slower learning period.

High dopamine levels seem to be sustained as long as a learning task remains new and challenging — that is, as long as you're still learning. Once you've learned a skill and acted it out so many times that it becomes routine and predictable, your brain no longer provides a reward for performing it. That may be why so many people feel the need to resort to stimulants such as caffeine (see *Caffeine*) to sustain their motivation and attention when they have to perform familiar, repetitive routines.

The link between addictive substances and the brain's natural reward system

It is possible that a brain that is denied the stimulation it needs to activate its own reward systems may look for rewards in other ways. On one level, that may be what's happening

How Nicotine Affects Learning and Memory

One way researchers try to figure out how to combat Alzheimer's is by studying large groups of people over many years of their life in so-called *longitudinal* or *epidemiological* studies. They look at many details of how those people live — what they eat, whether they drink alcohol, what kind of job they have, and so on — together with whether or not they end up developing Alzheimer's later in life. Then, they look for patterns. For example, did a higher percentage of teetotalers get Alzheimer's compared to modest drinkers? If so, maybe alcohol has some kind of protective effect. And so on.

One surprising finding to come out of these studies is that smokers appear to be less likely to develop Alzheimer's than non-smokers. Why might that be? (No, not because they die younger. Age is one of the variables the researchers control for. Nice try, though.)

A lot of laboratory research done over the last five years or so points to specific ways that nicotine is beneficial to the brain. Nicotine injections improve working memory in lab rats given the task of figuring out how to find food in a maze. The rats also show improvements in long-term memory — they remember better from one day to the next what they have already figured out.

Experiments have shown that there are several routes by which nicotine can have these learning- and memory-enhancing effects on the brain. First, nicotine raises adrenaline levels, which in turn stimulates a release of glucose into the bloodstream. The adrenaline makes the brain more alert, and the glucose provides fuel for brain cells. Nicotine also suppresses the release of insulin from the pancreas, which further raises blood sugar levels. And, of course, nicotine raises levels of the neurotransmitter *dopamine* — a "pleasure" chemical naturally produced in the brain that is also raised by such drugs as cocaine and heroin — which improves mood and motivation.

More important, nicotine has some specific memory-improving effects that make it different from other addictive drugs and potentially more useful for combating Alzheimer's. It binds to receptor sites in the brain systems crucial for learning and remembering — in particular, sites on neurons in the *cholinergic* system, which interacts with the "memory" neurotransmitter *acetylcholine*. (Other studies have shown that acetylcholine levels tend to be low in the brains of Alzheimer's patients, and that neurons in the cholinergic system are damaged by the disease.) Then, too, nicotine raises levels of *glutamate* neurotransmitter molecules, which are also crucial for proper memory function.

Another area where nicotine's effect on the brain appears to play a role is in male impotence. University of California, Urvine researchers Tammy Tengs and Nathaniel Osgood recently reviewed published literature on impotence and concluded that whereas 28 percent of all U.S. men smoked, among those who were impotent, 40 percent were smokers.

Researchers in labs around the world are hard at work engineering a nicotine substitute that will have the beneficial effects on memory without nicotine's detrimental effects on other parts of the brain and body, including the brain areas that underlie addiction.

when intellectual or emotional deprivation leads to drug and alcohol abuse. Some experimental evidence shows that success in solving mental puzzles boosts not only dopamine levels but levels of the hormone testosterone, an effect which, subjectively, feels good. Though elevated testosterone levels do not necessarily lead to violent behavior, violent behavior does raise testosterone levels. In that light, it is tempting to speculate that when boys and young men become violent, they may be seeking the kind of testosterone rush that an intellectually unfulfilling environment denies them.

The kinds of reward systems that reinforce survival-related behavior, whether violent or peaceful, always involve brain-chemical molecules. One of the reasons people become addicted to drugs is that those drugs contain molecules that mimic the structure of molecules in the brain's own reward system. Nicotine, cocaine, alcohol, and heroin all raise dopamine levels. So does engaging in literal and metaphorical puzzles that require your brain to handle new data and propose novel solutions. Solving problems and learning new things let you feel good while doing something good for your brain. It's perfectly legal, and, at least for now, tax-free.

Solution for exercise, p. 178

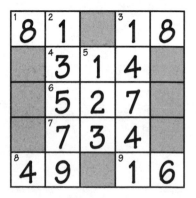

References

Abbott, Alison (2001). Into the mind of a killer. Nature 410: 296-8.

Barinaga, Marcia (2001). How cannabinoids work in the brain. Science 291: 2530-1.

Fried, Itzhak, et al. (2001). Increased dopamine release in the human amygdala during performance of cognitive tasks. Nature Neuroscience 4/2: 201-6.

Levin, Edward D., and Roger W. Russell (1992). Nicotinic-muscarinic interactions in cognitive function. In: Neurotransmitter Interactions and Cognitive Functions (ed. by E.D. Levin et al.), pp. 183-95. Boston: Berkhauser.

Suri, R.E., and W. Schultz (1999). A neural network model with dopamine-like reinforcement signal that learns a spatial delayed response task. Neuroscience 91/3: 871-90.

Umegaki, H., et al. (2001). Involvement of dopamine D2 receptors in complex maze learning and acetylcholine release in ventral hippocampus of rats. Neuroscience 103/1: 27-33.

Wilson, R.I., and R.A. Nicoll (2001). Endogenous cannabinoids mediate retrograde signalling at hippocampal synapses. Nature 410/6828: 588-92.

THE SLIGHTED SENSE

How smells influence memory

It's well known that smell and memory are intimately linked. Of course, we've all heard about Proust's *madeleine* experience. As the narrator dips a madeleine cookie into a cup of lime-blossom tea near the beginning of the monumental *Remembrance of Things Past,* the fragrance takes him instantly, and overwhelmingly, back to his boyhood and then into the long chain of remembrances that make up the rest of the 3,300-page story. But you don't have to be a writer to know that odors can trigger memories. We've probably all had the kind of Proustian experience of an odor triggering an involuntary memory so vivid that it's almost as if we were literally reliving an experience long past.

Our sense of smell is no mere aesthetic luxury. Researchers have discovered a compelling clue to the importance of smell not just to animals, but to humans as well. The smell center of the brain, known as the *olfactory bulb,* is almost the only brain region that's been proven to have its cells regenerate throughout the life of its owner. In other words, our brain's smell center seems to have a special status relative to most other parts of the brain, having its neurons freely replenished even into old age, much the way a shark keeps growing new teeth when any are lost. So a reasonable assumption would be that there's something important about our ability to detect odors.

In all animals, this evolutionarily ancient sense is important for many survival-related skills: detecting food, warning of danger, and identifying a sexually receptive mate. Indeed, people who suffer from *anosmia* — an inability to smell — stand a particular risk of injury, sickness, or death due to the fact that their brain's olfactory center can't warn them of danger, such as the smell of gas or fire, or the odor of rotten food.

In the brain, our olfactory system has a more direct connection to memory and emotion than any other sense. Our emotional center, the amygdala, and memory center, the hippocampus, are parts of our brain's evolutionarily ancient limbic system. The intimate interconnections among these brain regions account for the close relationship between smell, memory, and emotion.

Describe that smell

Connections between the olfactory system and language centers, by contrast, are weak and indirect. Try to describe the way freshly-ground coffee beans smell, or the heady reek of overripe cheese. Without simply referring to other similar smells ("dirty socks," "fishy"), or terms from other sense domains ("sharp," "sweet"), it's remarkably difficult.

The fact that our smell vocabulary is so poor shouldn't be taken to mean that smell is unimportant. Smell, rather, is a sense that's undiluted and immediate, hard to analyze and articulate but nevertheless pervasive and powerful. One way to ensure that an experience or a piece of knowledge becomes entrenched in long-term memory is to imbue it with emotion (see *Learning the Easy Way*). That happens naturally with what are sometimes called *flashbulb memories:* the memory of an emotionally-charged experience such as hearing the news of the assassination of a political leader or the death of a friend. In such cases, the emotional component causes the brain to bypass the usual requirement of practice and repetition for long-term storage.

Some mnemonic, or memory-aiding, techniques exploit the emotional dimension. There's a common salesperson's trick of remembering a person's name by thinking of an object that can serve as a reminder (for example, the flames of a fire for someone with the name "Burns"), and then visu-

Evidence For a Sixth Sense:
Pheromones and the Vomeronasal Organ

One of the ways that animals communicate is through *pheromones* — airborne chemicals secreted by one animal and detected by another of the same species. Pheromones influence the sexual, parental, or social behavior of the animal that senses them. For example, androsterone, a hormone produced by boars and exuded in their breath, automatically triggers the assumption of the mating stance in a sow. Obviously, perfume and cologne manufacturers would love to identify compounds with similar effects on humans. But many researchers have claimed that humans have lost the receptors needed for the brain to receive any pheromone-conveyed messages from our senses.

There's an organ that seems to be specialized for the detection of pheromones in animals. In humans, this organ, the vomeronasal organ (VNO), is connected to the nasal passage by a small opening about an inch behind the nostrils. It's so inconspicuous that it wasn't even discovered until the 18th century, and for a long time after that the human VNO was thought to be a vestigial organ whose function had been lost during evolution. So it made sense that pheromones could no longer play a role in human behavior.

More recent evidence shows that the VNO is intact and functioning in humans, and that it probably does indeed serve to send pheromone-carried signals to the brain. It turns out that pheromones are likely responsible for the fact that women who live together often develop synchronized menstrual cycles. One pheromone is produced before ovulation, and shortens the menstrual cycle of the woman who is exposed to it. The other is produced during ovulation, and lengthens the cycle. In a widely-publicized experiment, researchers took small quantities of sweat from women's armpits, where the pheromones are released, and dabbed it under the noses of ten other women. Within three months, those women were menstruating at the same time as the women who had "donated" the sweat.

There's also evidence that women will respond differently to male pheromones depending on whether they're at a fertile stage of their menstrual cycle. Women rate the male pheromone androsterone (yes, the boar pheromone is also secreted by men) as more pleasant-smelling near ovulation, when they're fertile, than at the beginning or end of their cycle. And androsterone may be influencing the behavior of women whether or not they're aware of it. In one experiment, researchers sprayed the pheromone onto a seat in a dentist's waiting room, and observed that a disproportionate number of women, as opposed to men, chose that seat.

Some of the most fascinating evidence for the influence of smell on human sexual behavior comes from other investigations into the smell preferences of women. Women favor the smell of men whose genetic profile complements their own in a way that would result in healthier offspring. Another recent study ties in with evidence that women prefer "symmetrical" men to men with more asymmetrical faces or bodies. There is speculation that asymmetry may be a marker for more significant imperfections that might compromise a man's longevity, fecundity, and health. Believe it or not, women seem to be able to identify the symmetry of a man through scent alone. In this study, when presented with T-shirts to sniff, women near the peak fertility phase of their cycle preferred the scent of T-shirts that had been worn by symmetrical men. During other phases of their cycle, or if on the pill, women showed no preference.

ally associating that image with a salient feature of their face (bushy eyebrows going up in flames). If you add an emotional component (screams of pain, say), the image naturally tends to become more firmly entrenched in your memory, making the technique even more effective.

What we smell can affect our behavior

So emotion can be used to help you remember. What about smell?

Some experiments suggest ways that odors might be deliberately used to manipulate memory, and influence learning. One study exposed a group of children to a specific smell while they struggled in vain to solve a puzzle that, in fact, had no possible solution. When the experimenters exposed those children to that same smell during a later problem-solving task, they performed worse than children who hadn't been exposed to the smell. The odor had served to trigger an expectation of failure, an expectation that was fulfilled regardless of whether the conscious problem-solving regions of the children's brains would have been capable of succeeding in finding a solution.

Other studies have explored the use of smells as a cue to

memory, as in the flood of recollections cascading over Proust upon smelling his *madeleine*. In one experiment, subjects were shown emotion-arousing pictures while exposed to certain smells, a different smell for each picture. The smells helped to cue recall of the pictures, as did visual, verbal, tactile, and musical stimuli that were also presented along with the pictures the first time around. The smell stimuli, though, were superior to all the others in their ability to trigger a re-experience of the *emotions* originally evoked by the pictures.

Our brain responds to smells we can't smell

These sorts of experiments show that smell can influence our brain, and our behavior, in ways we might not even be aware of. It is, in fact, well documented that air-borne chemicals influence our behavior without our being aware of smelling anything (see box, p. 189). Researchers have recently obtained brain-scan images showing that certain structures, including the amygdala, hippocampus, and thalamus, become activated in response to an airborne compound at such a low concentration that the subjects have no conscious awareness of it.

And there are other indications that smells often inhabit a world at the edge of, or beyond, our conscious awareness. For one thing, not only are smells hard to describe, they are notoriously difficult to attach a verbal label to in other ways as well. We often have the experience of recognizing that a certain smell is familiar, without being able to identify the object that the smell corresponds to. If you *see* the object, on the other hand, you'll have no such difficulty identifying and labeling it. This "tip-of-the-nose" phenomenon may show that there are different brain systems for recognizing smells as familiar (or dangerous, etc.), and for identifying them in a more explicit, verbal, conscious manner, in terms of the names for the objects they're emanating from. In fact, researchers have determined that the conscious identification of odor develops slowly in childhood, peaks in young adulthood, and declines in old age, independently of the ability to recognize an odor as familiar, or the ability to differentiate odors.

Alzheimer's and the sense of smell

So it's normal for children and older adults to have more difficulty attaching a name to an odor than it is for young adults. Some recent research has shown that there are other changes in older adults that are not so normal, and that in fact may be signs of early dementia. In scratch-and-sniff tests, older people with the greatest loss of olfactory acuity seem to be at particular risk for developing Alzheimer's. The risk seems to be especially strong, according to one study, if the person is unaware of any decline in smell-discrimination ability.

There are many other possible reasons for a decline in, or even a total loss of, the sense of smell. But among the subset of olfactorily-impaired older people with Alzheimer's, the connection between the two problems may be very simple. In addition to the olfactory bulb, the other region of the brain that researchers have very recently discovered benefits from the regeneration of neurons is the hippocampus — a memory center closely connected with the olfactory center, and often impaired in Alzheimer's. So it's possible that Alzheimer's and an unusual decline in smelling ability may both involve a loss of the brain's ability to regenerate neurons.

References

Burns, Alistair (2000). Might olfactory dysfunction be a marker of early Alzheimer's disease? Lancet 355: 84-5.

Cutler, Winnifred B., Erika Friedmann, and Norma L. McCoy (1998). Pheromonal influences on sociosexual behavior in men. Archives of Sexual Behavior 27/1: 1-13.

Devanand, D.P., et al. (2000). Olfactory deficits in patients with mild cognitive impairment predict Alzheimer's disease at follow-up. American Journal of Psychiatry 157/9: 1399-1405.

Eichenbaum, Howard (1998). Using olfaction to study memory. Annals of the New York Academy of Sciences 855: 657-69.

Gangenstadt, Steven W., and Randy Thornhill (1998). Menstrual cycle variation in women's preferences for the scent of symmetrical men. Proceedings of the Royal Society of London (B) 265: 927-33.

Gheusi, Gilles (2000). Importance of newly generated neurons in the adult olfactory bulb for odor discrimination. Proceedings of the National Academy of Sciences USA 97/4: 1823-8.

Herz, Rachel S. (2000). Verbal coding in olfactory versus nonolfactory cognition. Memory and Cognition 28/6: 957-64.

Herz, Rachel S. (1998). Are odors the best cues to memory? Annals of the New York Academy of Sciences 855: 670-4.

Koenig, Olivier, Ghislaine Bourron, and Jean-Pierre Royet (2000). Evidence for separate perceptive and semantic memories for odours: a priming experiment. Chemical Senses 25: 703-8.

Lehrner, Johann P., et al. (1999). Different forms of human odor memory: a developmental study. Neuroscience Letters 272: 17-20.

McClintock, Martha K (1998). On the nature of mammalian and human pheromones. Annals of the New York Academy of Sciences 855: 390-2.

Monti-Bloch, Louis, Clive Jennings-White, and David L. Berliner (1998). The human vomeronasal system. Annals of the New York Academy of Sciences 855: 373-89.

Qureshy, Ahmad, et al. (2000). Functional mapping of human brain in olfactory processing: a PET study. Journal Physiology 84/3: 1656-66.

Sobel, Noam, et al. (1999). Blind smell: brain activation induced by an undetected air-borne chemical. Brain 122: 209-17.

DREAMS AT WORK

The crucial role sleep plays in learning

We humans spend a third of our lives in sleep, if we let ourselves. Many of us imagine that sleep is a waste of time, and that we could be more productive if we slept less and worked more. Among some college students and upwardly-mobile young urban professionals, it's almost dishonorable to admit to getting eight hours of sleep a night — as if that would be an admission of weakness, laziness, or self-indulgence.

The thing that's actually detrimental to productivity, though, is *lack* of sleep. A growing body of research is converging on an understanding of adequate sleep as absolutely essential for acquiring new knowledge and learning new skills.

It's not just *some* sleep that's required for optimal transfer of new experiences into long-term memory, according to the most recent studies, but a good eight hours a night. Sleep researchers have also come up with evidence for exactly which stages of sleep are important for which aspects of learning. And their studies even suggest some interesting theories about the reasons we dream.

Sleep, dreams, and learning new skills

One of the earliest pieces of evidence for the role of sleep in learning new skills emerged in the 1970s in the lab of Vincent Bloch of the University of Paris. Bloch observed that when rats were trained in a maze-running task, their proportion of REM sleep increased. REM, or rapid eye movement, is the phase of sleep when we do most of our dreaming. Other researchers showed that depriving people of REM sleep — by waking them up each time an EEG reading showed their brain entering the theta-wave-dominated REM state — made it harder for them to recall events from the previous day.

A very recent experiment, taking advantage of sophisticated technology unavailable during the earlier studies, has shown that, indeed, during REM sleep the brain's neurons fire in the same patterns as in learning tasks performed during the day. So it seems that dreaming might involve a kind of reenactment of daytime learning experiences to somehow entrench them better in our repertoire of knowledge, and that disrupting this process might prevent the storage of that new knowledge in the brain.

Maze-running tasks, which Bloch observed to trigger an increase in REM sleep in lab rats, involve a kind of learning known as *declarative,* a category that includes knowledge and memories we're consciously aware of. In the case of the rats' maze-running skills, the specific kind of learning is called

Sleep, Aging, and Cognitive Decline

The research reported here shows that you won't learn effectively if you don't get a good night's sleep the night after you start trying to learn something new. What's the effect of skipping sleep the night *before* you try to learn something?

The most obvious effects of sleep deprivation are on "higher" thinking skills such as the kind of problem-solving handled by working memory (WM). These are the same sorts of frontal-lobe skills that tend to decline with age. In one recent study, the performance of young sleep-deprived adults on WM tasks was about the same as that of non-sleep-deprived 60-year-olds.

We all know it's harder to get a good night's sleep as you get older. Might this fact account for the deterioration of frontal-lobe-based WM skills among the elderly?

Some researchers think so. University of Chicago sleep researcher Eve Van Cauter has determined that, for men, slow-wave (SW) sleep reaches its peak in adolescence and then declines steadily until, by age 50, most men have very little SW sleep at all. She has also determined that it's during SW sleep that the brain secretes Human Growth Hormone (HGH), which helps maintain brain cells. So by middle age, the brain is secreting less of this important neuron-protecting hormone. At the same time, increasing age appears to bring with it a rise in levels of stress hormones. These higher levels of stress hormones, combined with reduced levels of HGH, may lead to brain deterioration. For women, nightly SW sleep seems to hold steady until menopause, although their

HGH levels seem to be less dependent on that part of the sleep cycle.

A goal of sleep researchers is to develop sleeping pills that promote SW sleep, and thus — perhaps — slow down the aging of the brain.

Here are examples of the kind of task that becomes harder if you're sleep-deprived, or if you're older:

Frontal-lobe thinking test #1

For each noun in the list, supply as many appropriate verbs as you can think of. Example: APPLE: *bite, eat, chew, munch, polish.* Limit yourself to one minute for each word.

> KNIFE
> SHOE
> CUP
> GAME
> MOVIE THEATER

Norms

> Young adult (19-27): 30 verbs.
> Middle-aged adult (55-64): 22 verbs.
> Older adult (66-85): 16 verbs.
> Young sleep-deprived adult: 22 verbs.

(Based on Harrison, Horne, and Rothwell 2000)

Frontal-lobe thinking test #2

For each incomplete sentence, there's an obvious word you can use to finish it. For example, if you're given the incomplete sentence, "The letter was mailed without a(n) —," the obvious word to complete it is *stamp.* So you'd have to complete it with a different word — for example, *care,* or *envelope.*

Captain Bligh wanted to stay with the sinking
—. *(ship)*

They went as far as they —. *(could)*

The old house will be torn —. *(down)*

Most cats see very well at —. *(night)*

It's hard to admit when you're —. *(wrong)*

Marilyn was glad the affair was —. *(over)*

Her job was easy most of the —. *(time)*

When you go to bed turn off the —. *(light(s))*

The game was called off when it started to —.
(rain)

The dispute was settled by a third —. *(party)*

(Based on Bloom and Fischler 1980)

episodic — resting on a memory of having been in a certain place, doing a certain thing, at a certain time. Another kind of declarative memory is called *semantic* — memory for facts and conscious knowledge, such as who the Prime Minister of Great Britain is or when World War I ended.

Different stages of sleep are important for different kinds of learning

In a 1994 *Science* article, two University of Arizona researchers presented evidence for the role of another phase of sleep in learning. Shortly after we fall asleep, our brains normally enter a stage of "slow-wave" (SW) sleep marked by low-frequency rhythms called delta waves. It's during SW sleep that the hippocampus, a structure in the brain involved in creating declarative memories, is active, as it replays recordings of the day's experiences. This period of SW sleep is also punctuated by high-frequency bursts from the hippocampus to the cortex. What seems to be happening is that the hippocampus is sending information to the cortex, so that the memories can be stored or "consolidated" in the cortex permanently. It's during this stage of SW sleep, in other words, that the communication from hippocampus to cortex takes place that results in the formation of stable long-term memories. So even though REM sleep might be required for strengthening that knowledge once it's transferred to the cortex, the SW sleep is first required to transfer the information from the hippocampus.

In another article published in the same issue of *Science,* a group of Israeli researchers showed that disrupting REM sleep also has the effect of preventing people from learning different kinds of skills as well. The skills studied in their experiment involved a kind of knowledge that psychologists refer to as *procedural* — the sort of "how-to" abilities, like riding a bike or hitting a tennis ball, that become automatic with practice. The conventional wisdom had been that practice alone was enough to entrench this kind of skill in long-term memory. What the Israeli researchers showed was that, in fact, people are better at new procedural skills the day *after* practicing them — but *only* if they get their REM sleep.

Another very recent study has shown that the learning of new skills and knowledge doesn't just improve after one night of sleep, but continues to improve for several days after that, as long as you get enough sleep each night. And if you skip the first night's sleep, you'll never make it up: Even if you get good sleep the next few nights, you can't use that "recovery" sleep to perform the memory consolidation that should have started the first night.

How much sleep do you need?

The upshot is that both SW sleep and REM sleep are necessary for learning. During SW sleep, which we get soon after we fall asleep, the hippocampus plays back certain experiences from the previous day and transfers them in bursts to the cortex. This phase of sleep seems to be particularly important for acquiring declarative knowledge, such as remembering facts and events.

During REM sleep, the cortex reenacts those experiences and strengthens the connections between neurons in various sites in the cortex that encode the memory. Since the most crucial, concentrated bout of REM occurs after about six hours of sleep, you'll miss out on the learning-promoting REM period if you only let yourself sleep for, say, six hours. REM sleep seems to be important for both declarative learning and for nondeclarative learning, such as acquiring new procedural "muscle-memory" skills. In fact, many kinds of learning involve both declarative and nondeclarative components, so both SW and REM sleep are important for learning most new tasks.

REM sleep is crucial not just for procedural skills and for making permanent memories of conscious knowledge of facts and events, but for other types of nondeclarative knowledge as well. Those other kinds of nondeclarative knowledge include most of the learning that proceeds on an unconscious level, influencing our behavior on an ongoing basis whether we realize it or not (see *Learning Without Knowing It*). That may be one reason dreams often seem bizarre, from a waking perspective. In dreams, we're reviewing and rehearsing not just consciously accessible memories, knowledge, and skills, but also memories housed in regions of the brain that are normally relatively inaccessible to our conscious minds.

References

Bloom, Paul A., and Ira Fischler (1980). Completion norms for 329 sentence contexts. Memory and Cognition 8/6: 631-42.

Harrison, Yvonne, James A. Horne, and Anna Rothwell (2000). Prefrontal neuropsychological effects of sleep deprivation in young adults — a model for healthy aging? Sleep 23/8: 1067-73.

Karni, Avi, et. al. (1994). Dependence on REM sleep of overnight improvement of a perceptual skill. Science 265: 679-82.

Louie, Kenway, and Matthew A. Wilson (2001). Temporally structured replay of awake hippocampal ensemble activity during Rapid Eye Movement sleep. Neuron 29: 145-56.

Plihal, Werner, and Jan Born (1999). Effects of early and late nocturnal sleep on priming and spatial memory. Psychophysiology 36: 571-82.

Sejnowski, Terrence J., and Alain Destexhe (2000). Why do we sleep? Brain Research 886: 208-23.

Stickgold, Robert, et al. (2000). Visual discrimination task improvement: a multi-step process occurring during sleep. Journal of Cognitive Neuroscience 12/2: 246-54.

Stickgold, Robert, LaTanya James, and J. Allan Hobson (2000). Visual discrimination learning requires sleep after training. Nature Neuroscience 3/12: 1237-8.

Van Cauter, Eve (2000). Slow wave sleep and release of growth hormone. Journal of the American Medical Association 284/21: 2717-8.

Wilson, Matthew A., and Bruce L. McNaughton (1994). Reactivation of hippocampal ensemble memories during sleep. Science 265: 676-9.

FALSE TESTIMONY

Memory for events is highly suggestible

If you ever asked a couple celebrating their golden anniversary about an event that occurred during their youthful courtship, you'd discover how two people's recollections of a shared experience can differ. If you ever heard two grown-up sisters argue over the correct version of a scene from their childhood, you'd realize that strength of conviction doesn't necessarily translate into accurate recall. Even though psychologists have known for a long time that memory is anything but a verbatim record of the past, it's still difficult to comprehend why eyewitness reports of the same event can differ so drastically. After all, it's as plain to see as the nose or mustache on your face!

One reason is that different people are likely to view a scene differently in the first place. Two people may bring two different sets of expectations to the task of observation — in other words, we often see what we expect to see. Take a look at

> *Let's have a*
> *cup of eoffee!*
>
> ---
>
> *There's no such*
> *thing as a*
> *a free lunch.*

the words in the top half of the box above. How many *e*'s are
there? How many *c*'s? What's in the lower half? Are you sure?
Look again. Our brains will automatically fill in gaps or alter
details to match our expectations without our knowing it.

Why memories and revisionist history books have a lot in common

Let's take it a step further and imagine that it's possible for
two people to bring the same expectations to an event that
they witness together. Will they have identical memories days,
months, or years later?

The answer is no, because their recollections will not just
be influenced by their expectations, but also by what happens
after the fact. Memories change over time, with new experiences unconsciously woven into the original fabric, until, ulti-
mately, it becomes impossible to tell original fact from subsequent embellishment.

One of the best-known researchers into the malleability of
memory is Elizabeth Loftus of the University of Washington.
She has spent many years gathering evidence that human
memories are in a continuous state of flux, with new experiences altering and even overwriting previous impressions on

an ongoing basis. Much of her work has shown how easy it is for misinformation to be inadvertently planted in the minds of eyewitnesses to a crime, thus altering their recollections of crucial details. Among other things, Loftus's expert testimony has been used in court cases in which a parent or caretaker has been accused of molesting a child. Young children are even more susceptible to faulty recollections than adults because their brain's frontal lobes have not developed fully. That is the area that processes the "who," "what," "when," and "where" of past events (called "source memory" judgements). Since children tend to be highly responsive to the perceived desires of well-meaning adults, the images and thoughts that come into their minds when social workers or police officers are talking to them can easily become inextricably mixed with their original memories.

Loftus's research has led to restrictions on the ways police officers may question an eyewitness to a crime, particularly about the identification of the individuals involved. A detective will naturally favor a confident identification over an uncertain one. If a witness unconsciously picks up on this, rather than say, "Well, it *could* be the guy, but I'm not sure," the response might be, "Yes, officer, I'm *sure* that's the man!" The positive rapport between cop and witness may make them both feel better, and may yield a more winnable case for the prosecution, but it won't necessarily lead to the conviction of the actual perpetrator.

Two memories rather than one?

The tendency for memories to become revised or altered by subsequent experience is a fact that no psychologist would dispute. Psychologists do have different opinions, though, about whether an original, "pristine" memory might continue to exist in some recess or other of the brain. If it does, maybe that original memory could still be accessed with the right technique. Some researchers believe that two versions of a memory may coexist in the brain, one original and one revised, and "battle it out" for dominance during retrieval.

Loftus, on the other hand, believes otherwise. She once designed a simple experiment in which people were asked to watch a scene in which someone was reading a yellow book. If they were later asked, "Did you see the person reading the *blue* book?" their original memory tended to be revised in response to the question and they claimed to recall seeing a person reading a blue book. If an original, accurate memory continued to coexist alongside the altered one, she reasoned, that version should come to the fore if the witness was

---

FALSE MEMORIES
The Brain Remembers What It Expected to Find

Read through this list of words, then cover the list and write down as many of the words as you can recall:

bed, slumber, dream, drowsy, pillow,
tired, nap, yawn, doze, snore

Did you write down the word *sleep*? That word wasn't on the list, but most people falsely recall that it was. Harvard memory researcher Daniel Schacter has found that, after subjects hear this list read aloud, a PET scan reveals a difference between true and false memories: The auditory cortex lights up when the subject recalls the actually-read words, but not when the word *sleep* is falsely recollected.

Note that, in this case, the false memory doesn't overwrite the original memory, but augments it. Other brain-imaging studies have failed to identify any difference in the brain at all between accurate memories and false, altered versions.

pressed to guess what *other* color the book might have been. In fact, three times as many subjects in her experiment guessed the color next to blue on the spectrum — green — than guessed yellow. The most straightforward interpretation of this result is that a substantial majority of the subjects had

What You See Depends on What You Expect to See

Man or rat? It depends...

(After Bugelski and Alampay 1961)

completely replaced their original memory with a revised version in response to the questioning of the experimenter.

A drug that can erase a memory

Some very recent research supports Loftus's view. Two New York University researchers have found evidence that every time a memory is brought to consciousness, the brain disassembles it and then manufactures new proteins to rebuild it in long-term memory. This suggests that the mere act of accessing a memory opens a window of vulnerability during which the memory is not only rebuilt, but possibly reorganized to integrate new information. Conscious recollection may even make the memory vulnerable to erasure, if drugs that block the production of proteins are administered during that window of vulnerability and, therefore, block the reassembly of the memory itself.

The NYU researchers in fact did just that, injecting into the brain of lab rats an antibiotic that prevented new proteins from being created. When they injected that drug within a few hours of the memory being accessed by the rats, the rats lost the memory — in this case a Pavlovian fear-conditioning-type memory which associated a sound with an electric shock.

In the real world, these new findings may lend themselves to the treatment of traumatic memories — a human-sized version of the lab rats' electric shock traumas. If the protein-blocking drug were administered to the traumatized patient just after the memory was accessed, the memory would then be blocked from reassembling itself, and in effect be erased from the patient's brain. The patient would have developed a kind of amnesia for the trauma, which might not be a bad thing.

The next steps for researchers will be to determine whether the human brain erases and reconstructs conscious autobiographical memories in the same way as fear-conditioning memories, and whether or not memories that have been stored in the brain for a long time are also reassembled every time they're accessed.

References

Dudai, Yadin (2000). The shaky trace. Nature 406: 686-7.

Loftus, Elizabeth (1979). Eyewitness Testimony. Cambridge: Harvard University Press.

Loftus, Elizabeth, and J.E. Pickrell (1995). The formation of false memories. Psychiatric Annals 25: 720-5.

Nader, Karim, Glenn E. Schafe, and Joseph E. LeDoux (2000). Fear memories require protein synthesis in the amygdala for reconsolidation after retrieval. Nature 406: 722-6.

Practice in the Mind

Visualizing a motor skill sharpens performance

Before stepping up to the plate, home-run hitter Mark McGwire visualizes how he'll swing at each ball the pitcher might throw. An exercise in the power of positive thinking? Maybe. But according to recent brain imaging studies, there's more to it than that. By mentally rehearsing what he'll do in the batter's box, McGwire is engaging the very same brain circuits that are involved when he takes a real swing at an actual pitch. He's not only getting those circuits ready for action, but giving them "offline" practice that can translate into improved performance at the plate.

Motor skills as impressive as hitting a 90-mile-per-hour fast ball, or as banal as eating with a knife and fork, are examples of what psychologists call *procedural skills*. Even though they may benefit at first from explicit verbal instruction ("You put your right hand in and take your left foot out"), these are the kinds of skills that only become perfected when they've been practiced long enough to be committed to "muscle memory." Then, they become part of a repertoire of automatic abilities that seem to function on their own, without need of mental effort or conscious analysis. In fact, thinking too much about what you're doing can actually *interfere* with muscle-memory skills. Professional athletes, for example, are less likely to "choke" at a crucial point in a game than amateurs will.

Of course, muscle memory no more resides in our muscles than does our knowledge of the rules of the game. All kinds of memory, whether conscious or not, are housed in the brain. Most long-term memories are formed when an experience gets translated into structural changes in the brain through repetition and rehearsal. Those new structures strengthen the connections and pathways that link the brain cells that fired during the original experience. When that network of neurons is reactivated, an act of memory unfolds.

This all sounds plausible enough for "intellectual" memories of facts (How high would you have to count to reach a number with an "a" in it?) or events (When that car went through the intersection, was the light red, yellow, or green?). But what about "muscle" memory for motor skills? After all, visualizing hitting a home run in the mind's eye is certainly not the same thing as actually doing it.

Motor skills are "practiced" even while dreaming about doing them

A clue might come from studies of the role that dreaming plays in the process of learning and remembering. According to current views, rapid-eye-movement (REM) "dream" sleep is important for learning both *declarative* knowledge of facts and events as well as *procedural* skills such as hitting a baseball (see *Dreams at Work*). People commonly dream at night about even

mundane activities performed during the day before —
inputting data or painting a closet, for example.

According to brain imaging data, visualizing procedural
skills, whether in dreams or while awake, does in fact activate
not just the visual parts of the cortex, but the motor parts as
well. When McGwire visualizes hitting that baseball, he's
using *all* his ball-hitting brain circuits, from the primary visual cortex, through visual-imagery centers in his parietal cortex, to his brain's primary and secondary motor areas —
everything up to the point when his brain would give his
muscles the command to swing. (If McGwire were to dream
about hitting a home run in his sleep, he actually *would* act it
out if the natural biochemistry of sleep hadn't temporarily
paralyzed him from the neck down.)

But does visualization really help when it comes to real-life
performance? According to many studies, it does. Mental
rehearsal actually strengthens procedural-skill brain circuits
just as physical practice does. That doesn't mean that you
don't have to practice the skill physically in order to get good
at it. But visualization techniques combined with physical
practice can yield faster, better results than physical practice
alone. In this way, you can improve your muscle memory even
when you're not using your muscles at all.

References

Kosslyn, S.M., et al. (1995). Topographical representations of mental
    images in primary visual cortex. Nature 378: 496-8.

Roth, Muriel, et al. (1996). Possible involvement of primary motor
    cortex in mentally simulated movement: a functional magnetic
    resonance imaging study. Neuroreport 7/7: 1280-4.

Yaguez, L., et al. (1998). A mental route to motor learning: improv-
    ing trajectorial kinematics through imagery training.
    Behavioural Brain Research 90: 95-106.

SELF-TEST: **Priming**

Study each of the following words carefully for about five seconds. Then continue with whatever else you've been doing — reading this book, for example — for about an hour. At that point, take a look at the box on p. 218.

assassin

octopus

avocado

mystery

sheriff

climate

Learning Without Knowing It

Why a bit of plagiarism is inevitable

It can be absolutely infuriating when someone steals one of our ideas and then blithely takes credit for it. But wait a minute. Every one of us has been guilty of the same kind of intellectual larceny. In fact, many of our best "original" insights are second-hand, gleaned from a source we've conveniently forgotten.

Is this forgetfulness some kind of self-serving psychological mechanism designed to make us to feel comfortable about stealing other people's ideas? Not quite. "Honest" plagiarism results from the way two features of human memory happen to function.

Conscious and unconscious memory systems

First, the *semantic* memory system that is the reservoir for our conscious knowledge of facts — our mother's maiden name or the capital of Switzerland — is designed to retain information while sloughing off the details of when, where, and under what circumstances we learned it. That accounts for some of our forgetfulness. Second, and more intriguingly, honest plagiarism sometimes results from the fact that we have separate, independent memory systems within our brain, some of which are conscious and others that are unconscious. In other words, when we innocently steal someone else's idea, we may be in effect remembering something without realizing it's a memory.

The first kind of forgetfulness is easy to understand. Most of what we know, or think we know, about the world comes from sources we've long forgotten. When did you learn the meaning of the word *nevertheless*? Who first told you where you were born? How did you come to know that restaurants charge money for the food they serve? It doesn't matter *how* this knowledge came into your semantic memory store; all that's important is that the information is there. So the process of forgetting the circumstances of learning things may just be an efficient mechanism for retaining important knowledge without cluttering up the brain with incidental data.

But the second design feature that can lead to unconscious plagiarism is less obvious, and it has taken researchers a little longer to figure it out. Contrary to the view that memory is a single system with multiple expressions (memory for places, for hitting a tennis ball, for unconscious habits and routines), researchers now posit the existence of separate, unconscious, *implicit* memory systems that shadow our conscious recollection and knowledge. They've also been able to prove that these different systems rely on different neural networks that operate in different parts of the brain.

How "priming" works...

One well-studied kind of implicit memory is something called *priming*. That name is based on the notion that previously-encountered information can "prime" the brain to correctly recall having experienced the task before. This takes place even if the data recalled was originally stored below the level of consciousness. For an example of conscious priming, the exercise on p. 212 asks you to study a list of words then, after an interval of time, look at another list of words with only some of the letters filled in. The priming phenomenon will help fill in the blanks to form words from the earlier list. This works whether or not you explicitly remember ever having seen those words on the first list. According to an experiment by memory researchers, the priming effect is just as strong after a week as after an hour, even though explicit memory of the list of words has long since faded.

Priming, then, is a kind of memory that allows us to recognize things that we may not consciously remember having

seen. But things can become even more bizarre than this.
Imagine the following scenario. A patient with profound
amnesia is introduced to a doctor. The doctor leaves the room,
and ten minutes later the patient is shown pictures of several
faces, including the face of the doctor he's just met. He's asked
if he has ever met any of the people in the pictures, and he
answers no. But when pressed to point out which face he *might*
have seen *if* he had met any of the people, he points to the
picture of the doctor he'd met ten minutes before. (The fill-in-
the-missing-letters exercise on p. 218, by the way, also works
for amnesic patients.)

Implicit memory mechanisms such as priming are quite
likely to influence our behavior on an ongoing basis even
though we're not aware of it. If the amnesic patient described
above is asked to perform a "likeability" judgment about faces
he's shown, he will be most favorably disposed toward the face
of the doctor. So mere exposure to something can make us like
it whether or not we consciously remember it — a fact that
advertising agencies have understood for quite some time.
However, if the doctor had behaved unpleasantly toward him,
the patient will usually judge that face as an unfriendly one.
Similarly, an unpleasant experience can engender a fearful
reaction long after the experience itself has been forgotten, as
people who suffer from phobias will attest.

...even in your sleep

Brain researchers have even learned to identify the difference
between explicit memory and priming-type implicit memory
by looking at recordings of event-related brain potentials
(ERPs) — signals of electrical activity that are detected by elec-
trodes placed on the scalp. In a recent study published in the
journal *Nature,* English and Austrian researchers showed that
the patterns of brain activity are different in explicit and

Differences Between the Neural Bases of Explicit Memory and Priming

Researchers have identified different brain-activity patterns for explicit and implicit priming-type memory. They presented subjects with a list of several dozen words, half of which the subjects were asked to integrate into a sentence. For example, if one of the words was *hammock*, it could be integrated into a sentence such as, "The bank robber fell asleep in a hammock after making his getaway." With the other words on the list, the subjects were simply asked to decide whether the first and last letters of the word were in alphabetical order. (In the case of *hammock*, they are.) The first task, referred to as a *deep processing* task, makes it likely that the subject will remember the word a few minutes later. Generally, if you spend a moment thinking about the meaning of a piece of information, it will be easier to remember than if you don't. The other *shallow processing* task, which has nothing to do with thinking about the meaning of the word,

implicit memory, and involve neural networks in different parts of the brain (see box, above). Conscious recognition is more frontal-lobe-based, while unconscious priming-type memory depends more on the parietal lobes further back in the brain.

It's no coincidence that the phenomenon called *source memory* — remembering when, where, or how you learned something — relies heavily on the frontal lobes as well. This is the kind of memory young children are deficient in due to the slow development of the frontal lobes of the brain (see *The Deceiving Brain*). When newborn babies show that they recog-

doesn't help very much in the conscious memorization process.

Then, the subjects were shown each of the words in turn, one every five seconds, mixed in with other words that weren't on the first list. For each one, the subjects had to decide whether they had seen the word before or not. They tended to remember the words they had "deeply" processed better than the ones they had "shallowly" processed. The subjects had a tendency to miscategorize the shallowly processed words together with the new words as ones they hadn't seen before.

For all the words the subjects *explicitly remembered* having already seen, a region of their frontal cortex showed positive waveforms. But for *all* the previously-seen words — regardless of whether the subject *remembered* having seen them on the first list — a different region of the brain, the parietal cortex, showed positive waveforms. So that region of the brain in effect remembered something that the subject was not *aware* of remembering.

nize something—their mother's voice, for example — their circumstances are similar to that of the amnesiac who has implicit but no explicit memory. Even after conscious, explicit memory begins to develop in the second half of the first year of life, our implicit memory systems continue to function and influence our behavior throughout the rest of our lives, even though we're unaware of it

Conclusion of Priming Test, p. 212

You've waited an hour? OK, now take a look at the words below with missing letters. Fill in the blanks, if you can, to form regular English words. Then, turn the book upside-down and read the comment below the words.

ch _ _ _ _ nk
o _ t _ _ us
_ og _ y _ _ _
_ l _ m _ te

Here are the words you could get by filling in the missing letters: *chipmunk, octopus, bogeyman, climate.* Did you get "octopus" and "climate," and miss the others? Those two were on the list you studied an hour ago. If this worked for you, what happened was that seeing the words on the original list primed your ability to more easily think of those words when you just filled in the missing letters.

THE EXPERIENCED MIND

Maintaining treasured qualities of life

Healthy Aging

Lessons from professors about outsmarting age-related memory loss

Even healthy aging typically brings with it some loss of mental quickness and acuity. Slowness in retrieving names, numbers, and facts is normal; it does not necessarily signify the onset of dementia. To the contrary, a once-familiar name hanging on the tip of the tongue most likely is *not* an early symptom of Alzheimer's; it's merely a sign of normal aging. Nevertheless, some older people remain mentally sharper than other healthy older people. Recent research into these differences provides a growing body of evidence that a mentally active lifestyle can help sustain cognitive abilities and perhaps even forestall dementia. Not all memory loss is as inevitable as death and taxes!

What is normal age-related memory loss?

With the aging brain, as with the body, slowing of reaction time seems to be normal and inevitable. Older people normally perform less well than younger ones under time pressure. They also have a harder time juggling simultaneous tasks. An older driver, for example, will typically have more difficulty carrying on a cell phone conversation while concentrating on the road and will typically react more slowly if an accident results. (On the other hand, the older driver might be wise enough to avoid this situation in the first place.)

The longer time required to process information combined with the challenge of coordinating more than one mental task may explain why healthy older people have difficulty recalling the details of a story or a newspaper article. Reading a piece of text requires simultaneous recollection of what has just been read as well as processing the next part of the text. Because processing of information requires more time, the memory traces of the first piece may begin to fade before the next piece is fully processed.

Slowdown of working memory skills

Many of the memory skills that tend to decline with age fall under the category of *working memory*. Working memory tasks often require coordinating two things at once or separating relevant from irrelevant data. These sorts of skills depend on the brain's frontal lobes, which tend to lose some of their efficiency after early adulthood.

For example, think about what it's like to focus on what somebody's saying to you in a crowded, noisy restaurant. From all the noise around you, you have to create a separation between foreground and background, and attend to just one voice. The level of concentration you need to do this requires some effort but is nevertheless manageable. Now, push the envelope a little and imagine attending to two voices at once. Psychologists try to evaluate this kind of real-world task in the lab in the form of *dual task performance* tests or *divided attention tasks*. For example, the subject may wear a headset with one series of numbers coming into the left headphone and a different series coming into the right. Then, the subject has to repeat the two series, without mixing up one sequence with the other. This task is difficult for anyone, more so for anyone over the age of 30, and increasingly difficult with each passing decade (see box, p. 225).

Dementia is not part of the normal aging process

While some loss of mental prowess is a normal part of aging, the risk of suffering dementia varies. Some differences in the cognitive impact of aging are in our genes, but studies of large groups of people with different lifestyles suggest a relationship between level of education and occupation and risk of dementia late in life. For example, an influential French

A Test of Working Memory Skills

Here's a task designed to test two components of working memory — online processing and short-term memory storage. Ideally, have someone read these sentences aloud to you, slowly and clearly. For each sentence, judge whether it makes sense or not. Some do, some don't. At the same time, remember the word at the end of each sentence that serves as a short-hand summary of the sentence's theme.

- Novels are accounts of someone's reality, even if that reality exists in nothing but a world of fantasy. STORY
- A landlord is like the dictator of a land of his own making: he tells his mothers what to do, and they have no choice but to obey. RENT
- When I was young, I would watch my aunt each November planting bulbs in her pockets. GARDEN
- College is supposed to be a place where you learn few skills, except the skill of knowing how to learn. STUDY
- Most young people these days have never learned the value of the kind of sacrifice our softballs had to make. DUTY
- A trip to the outback can be fun, as long as you stay out of the sun, don't drink too much beer, and avoid getting kicked by a kangaroo. AUSTRALIA
- The trouble with magnums is that they're too big for one, but not big enough for two. WINE
- Churchill's wife had a nickname for him that many a biographer has whittled. BULLDOG

Forgotten any of the words yet? To do well on this test, you have to coordinate two cognitive skills: analyzing the meaning of each sentence for semantic incongruities and maintaining a memory of an increasingly long list of words. Older people tend to score lower than younger people on this kind of test.

study has shown that the risk of dementia among laborers in Bordeaux is two to three times greater than among professionals. Education level, too, correlates inversely with likelihood of developing Alzheimer's in many studies. While these findings help explain group differences, they do not go very far in helping individuals improve their chances of avoiding dementia in old age.

Lifestyle can make a difference

Research provides evidence that controllable lifestyle and environmental factors can play a critical role in sustaining cognitive abilities and even, perhaps, in forestalling dementia. In a series of experiments that began in labs at the University of California, Berkeley, in the 1960s, researchers showed that rats raised in an enriched environment — with lots of playthings, playmates, and new things to learn — had larger brains and were smarter than rats raised in an empty cage. The size and quality of the individual brain cells of the rats raised in the enriched environment were superior to those of the impoverished rats. Their dendrites were larger with more developed series of branches; they had more synapses — contact points between brain cells — more learning pathways, and higher intelligence.

While these results may seem obvious, the same experiments also showed that when rats raised in an impoverished environment were moved into an enriched environment late in life, they grew bigger brains and became smarter. Even at an advanced age, the brains of these rats were still flexible enough to respond dramatically to a new lifestyle and environment.

Do these findings apply to people? It's hard to tell for sure, since researchers can't experimentally manipulate the environment of a person in the same way they can with a rat.

How Well You Remember Depends On What You Already Know

Other things being equal, the more you know, the easier it is to remember new things that you can integrate into your pre-existing knowledge base. So, for example, if a researcher were to compare an 80-year-old gardener's memory for the details of the passage below with that of a 20-year-old non-gardener, the 80-year-old would likely perform better.

My mother always enjoyed gardening. For her, winter was a time of deep depression. Each spring, her spirits would rise as she replenished the soil with compost and added new plants to the flower bed. White alyssum and blue lobelia would go on the front border, marking the edge of the bed with a Lilliputian hedgelet of vividly-colored bursts of cloud and azure. Behind the border, she would add plants of medium height, such as dahlias, ranunculus, and snapdragons, which looked to my child's eye, gazing on the garden those spring mornings through my bedroom window, like so much joyous multi-colored birthday confetti. When digging this center strip of the flower bed, she would always take care not to disturb the tulip and daffodil bulbs she had planted the previous autumn, and which were just beginning to poke their pale green noses up from the thawing ground. Rising like giants behind them were the tallest plants forming an almost-solid backdrop against the stucco wall between our yard and the neighbor's. Foxglove, bearded iris, and hollyhock loomed there, stately and vain, so gaudily bizarre in their finery that one almost felt them to be foreign interlopers from the Orient or perhaps from Mars.

Continued

Now, without looking back, try to answer these questions:

1. List one flower from the front border of the bed, one from the medium-height center strip, and one tall one from the rear — in that order.

2. What was the color of the lobelia?

3. According to the passage, would you expect tulips to be very low, medium, or tall?

4. If the narrator's mother had wanted to plant statice, a plant of medium height, which other plant would she probably have put it next to: lobelia, iris, or ranunculus?

5. Of these three, which did the narrator seem to think was the gaudiest? Foxglove, ranunculus, snapdragon.

Answers

1. **Front:** alyssum or lobelia. Center: snapdragon, ranunculus, or dahlia (tulip or daffodil OK too). Rear: Foxglove, hollyhock, or bearded iris.
2. Blue.
3. Medium.
4. Ranunculus.
5. Foxglove.

Key

0-1 right: Remind me not to let you take care of my house plants while I'm on vacation.

2-3 right: You seem to know the difference between a wisteria and a weed.

4-5 right: Either you're a gardener, or you have a mind like a steel trap.

However, several studies have found that frequency and diversity of intellectual and physical activities outside of work throughout adulthood appear to have a protective effect against dementia in humans. In the most recent of these studies, the authors found intellectual activities to be the most important factor, with high diversity and frequency of such activities as studying a foreign language or playing bridge translating into the lowest likelihood of developing Alzheimer's. In contrast, the risk of developing dementia was 250 percent higher among people who were relatively inactive, physically and mentally.

Why intellectual activity makes a difference

Why do intellectual stimulation and activity make a difference? One possibility is that intellectually active individuals build up a reserve of brain cells that can be drawn upon later in life should the need arise. Then, even if advanced age brings with it some structural deterioration of the brain, extra neurons and neuronal pathways are available to compensate. Another possibility is that engaging in varied and stimulating activities actually helps brain cells maintain themselves, or even helps to develop new brain cells. Very recent experiments on adult rats have shown that some enriched environmental factors — mental and physical stimulation — can double the rate of *neurogenesis*, or the production of new neurons, in the *hippocampus*, a brain structure crucial to learning and memory (see *Rebuilding Brain Cells*). For humans as well as for rats, good evidence exists that mental stimulation encourages the brain to maintain itself through its own self-support and regeneration mechanisms, partly by boosting levels of growth hormones and brain-cell nutrients.

Further evidence that some of the age-related declines we consider normal are not necessarily inevitable comes from another Berkeley study comparing the mental abilities of older professors with those of younger professors and other people of a variety of ages who were not professors. The mental abilities tested were reaction time, paired-associate learning (the memorization of arbitrary pairs such as the name that goes with a face), working memory, and prose recall. Among the group of non-professors, the younger subjects performed significantly better than the older ones in all these areas. That fits the general and expected pattern.

Among the professors, on the other hand, age didn't consistently correlate with performance. The skills in which the older professors retained youthful ability involved more complex conceptualization and the integration of new information with prior knowledge. On tests of mere speed or arbitrary memorization, on the other hand, the older professors showed typical age-related declines.

The older professors may have maintained some of their learning and memory skills at youthful levels because they continued to grapple with conceptually challenging material. For inherently meaningless information, on the other hand, such as remembering the name that goes with a face, the older professors had no such advantage; they would have had to use the same mnemonic crutches that older people in general have to use (see *Making Memories*).

This study is consistent with others that have found, for example, that older adults who score high in tests of vocabulary and verbal skill perform just as well as younger people on tests of prose recall, even when the young people they are compared with also have high vocabulary test scores. When older people with lower vocabulary scores are compared with equivalently low-scoring younger people, those older people score significantly lower in prose recall tests. So high verbal

Real-Life Working Memory Tests

An objection that some memory researchers have voiced to many memory tests is that they are highly artificial. How often, after all, does anyone have to remember and repeat back a random list of unrelated words? The risk of using tests like that is that you may end up testing nothing more than a person's ability to perform well on artificial tests. So some psychologists have looked for what they call "ecologically valid" tests, that is, ones that include some of the kinds of tasks that people actually perform in real life.

If working memory is supposed to be something we use in everyday language, then tests of everyday language comprehension should be one way to gauge working memory ability. For example, tests of *inferential reasoning* measure your ability to use the ongoing discourse to fill in gaps and supply missing information. They can be used as tests of working memory assuming that it's your working memory that helps you keep track of the flow of information and use it to solve the puzzle, so to speak, of inferring something that isn't explicitly stated. For example, if a story mentions that "a camper carelessly neglected to put out the fire when he left camp in the morning," and then continues to describe how "his death in the forest fire was poetic justice," the normal inference would be that the campfire caused the forest fire.

Results of natural-language tests confirm that working memory tends to decline with age. Here's an example of another kind of natural-language test of working memory.

Continued

Logical reasoning

Natural-language tests of logic may seem more like reasoning tests than memory tests. But to solve problems like these, you have to be able to hold and manipulate information in your mind in order to judge the conclusion. And it's even harder to do if the sentences are spoken rather than written, especially for older people.

For each of the following, assuming that the premise is true, judge whether the conclusion is true or false. See p. 232 for the answers.

1. *Premise:* If George MacDonald was lying when he said he was at the racetrack all day Saturday, he could have been the murderer. When the police checked his story, they found he had never been to the racetrack at all.
   Conclusion: George MacDonald could have been the murderer.

2. *Premise:* If Jesse played badly in the playoff game he would lose his place on the team. After the game, the coach told him he would stay on the team.
   Conclusion: Jesse had not played badly in the game.

3. *Premise:* Taking the whole family on vacation to Europe is very expensive. Leonard took his wife and kids to Italy for two weeks and it cost him a lot of money. Harry's family vacation was also expensive.
   Conclusion: Harry must have taken his family to Europe on their vacation.

4. *Premise:* If you're good at polo, croquet is boring. April's brother tried to teach her to play polo but she was terrible.
   Conclusion: April must not find croquet boring.

5. *Premise:* Meg's memory is worse than Sarah's, and Joe's memory isn't better than Meg's.
   Conclusion: Joe's memory is better than Sarah's.

ability may have a protective effect on memory or may compensate for age-related declines in processing speed. For real-life tasks such as reading or following a conversation, raw memory alone isn't necessarily the most important thing (see box, p. 229).

What you know and do can help you age successfully
Even intellectually active older adults do less well than younger people on tests of sheer mental speed and association, but studies such as those summarized above provide increasing evidence that engaging in intellectually stimulating activity over a lifetime has a positive effect on complex cognitive abilities in old age and may also reduce the risk of dementia. Challenging games, volunteer service, hobbies, participation in a reading group — all of these can keep the brain and mind healthy despite advancing years.

Answers to Questions, p. 230
1. True 2. True 3. False 4. False 5. False.

References

Brébion, G., M.-F. Ehrlich, and H. Tardieu (1995). Working memory in older subjects: dealing with ongoing and stored information in language comprehension. Psychological Research 58: 225-32.

Dartigues, J.F., et al. (1992). Occupation during life and memory performance in nondemented French elderly community residents. Neurology 42: 1697-1701.

Friedland, Robert P., et al. (2001). Patients with Alzheimer's disease have reduced activities in midlife compared with healthy control-group members. Proceedings of the National Academy of Sciences USA. 98/6: 3440-5.

Gould, Elizabeth, et al. (1999). Learning enhances adult neurogenesis in the hippocampal formation. Nature Neuroscience 2/3: 260-5.

Hartley, Joellen T. (1986). Reader and text variables as determinants of discourse memory in adulthood. Psychology and Aging 1/2: 150-58.

Luszcz, M.A., and J. Bryan (1999). Toward understanding age-related memory loss in late adulthood. Gerontology 45: 2-9.

Rosenzweig, Mark R., and Edward L. Bennett (1996). Psychology of plasticity: effects of training and experience on brain and behavior. Behavioural Brain Research 78: 57-65.

Salthouse, T.A. (1996). The processing-speed theory of adult age differences in cognition. Psychological Review 10: 403-28.

Shimamura, Arthur P., et al. (1995). Memory and cognitive abilities in university professors: evidence for successful aging. Psychological Science 6/5: 271-7.

Stern, Yaakov, et al. (1994). Influence of education and occupation on Alzheimer's disease. Journal of the American Medical Association 217/13: 1004-10.

THE TRICK TO REMEMBERING NAMES

"That's OK, I don't remember yours either"

"What's the name of that actor in that movie about mobsters in L.A., you know, the one with lots of short vignettes strung together, kind of in the style of that movie Nashville, *in fact, they may even have been directed by the same person, you know, the actor who was in* Saturday Night Fever?"

What is it about names that makes them so hard to remember? Here are a few clues. The name of the movie *Nashville* is easy to remember because the movie is set in and, in many ways, is about Nashville. *Saturday Night Fever* is easy to remember because, again, the title has an obvious connection to the theme of the movie. If that weren't enough, it's hard to think of the movie without thinking of its soundtrack, especially that theme song which goes by the same name. And what was the name of that movie about mobsters? Oh yes, *Pulp Fiction*, harder to remember because its connection to the plot is less obvious.

The actor in *Saturday Night Fever* was John Travolta, of course, and Robert Altman directed *Nashville,* facts that you either know or don't, because there is nothing intrinsic in either name that links it to the right film or the profession of its bearer. Movie titles typically have something to do with the content of the movie, but personal names do not foretell character.

Names are arbitrary, and in that sense, meaningless. That's the main reason why they are so hard to remember. Any given person might as well be named John as Robert. Because there's no intrinsic connection between a person's name and anything else about that person — face, job, or hometown — it provides no clues to recollection. Context and meaning help memory work. On the other hand, things that are intrinsically random, meaningless, or arbitrary are hard to remember.

While remembering names is not easy at any age, it becomes increasingly challenging as we grow older. What person over 50 has not forgotten a familiar name and thought, "Oh, no, Alzheimer's!" Oh, no, just a normal result of aging.

Still, some people at any age are better at remembering names than others, and the techniques they employ to give meaning to names are available to anyone. These techniques take advantage of two important features of memory. In order to remember something, *rehearse it* and *make it meaningful*.

Take politicians, for example, who seem to remember everyone they've ever met. Are they naturally gifted with an

Why Are Faces Easier to Remember Than Names?

We've all felt the embarrassment of forgetting the name of someone who greets us by ours. "Don't take offense," we say, "I know your face, but I'm just no good at remembering names."

In fact, almost everyone is better at remembering faces than names. Even though matching a name to a face may seem like a single skill, we use opposite sides of our brain for the two different parts of the task. Recognizing faces is a right-brain skill while the left brain takes over in linking names to faces. People with right-brain damage may be unable to recognize familiar faces, or even match two different photographs of the same face. Left-brain damage may result in a specific inability to think of the name to go with a face, even if the face is perfectly familiar.

Like many other left-brain language skills, memorizing names requires conscious effort. Like many other right-brain skills, facial recognition seems to come naturally. It's a gift that requires so little effort, and that works so well, that adults tend to take it for granted. Facial recognition is a skill that develops gradually in childhood. Children under about seven years of age rely primarily on a piecemeal strategy of processing specific features to remember and recognize a face. That's why they're easy to fool. Something as simple as a pair of eyeglasses might make an otherwise familiar face seem unfamiliar, or an unfamiliar face seem familiar if they know someone else who wears the same kind of glasses. By about age ten, children develop a *configurational strategy* of analyzing the spatial relations among the component features of the face, rather than just the individual features themselves. While a six-year-old sees just the eyes, nose, mouth, and ears, a ten-year-old sees the entire gestalt of the face.

Like most skills you take for granted, you can better appreciate your configurational face-processing skill if you lose it. No, we're not talking about brain damage here. Most people are surprised to learn that their adult ability to recognize and analyze a face as a gestalt is dependent on seeing the face in its normal orientation — that is, right-side up. Familiar faces are much harder to recognize if we see them upside down. Not only that, but a bizarrely distorted face can look completely normal if it is inverted. Why? When we view a face out of its familiar orientation, we can no longer analyze it as a gestalt. We are, in effect, thrown back on a six-year-old's strategy of focusing just on the specific features.

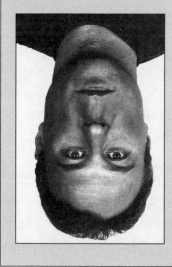 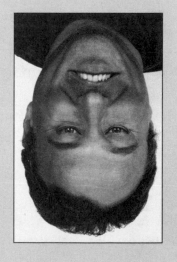

excellent memory for names? No, they put a lot of effort into learning and remembering names because their jobs depend on it. Watch a political candidate work a room. The candidate will look each prospective voter in the eye, repeat the voter's name in response to the introduction, make a comment on it ("Katzenellenbogen? What an interesting name. It means 'cat's elbow' in German, doesn't it? I knew a Katzenellenbogen once, in Des Moines. A relation, perhaps?"), and repeat the name again as many times in the ensuing conversation as possible without sounding foolish, while asking questions about the voter's hobbies and children. In addition to making each and every prospective voter feel good, these techniques will help the candidate remember their names and greet them personally when they meet again. (If all goes well, the voters will also remember the candidate's name because name recollection is a key to being elected.)

Even for those of us who are not running for office, remembering people's names can be important. People feel that if you've forgotten their name, you've forgotten them, as if their name and their identity were one and the same. They take it personally, and you feel embarrassed. If you remember their name, on the other hand, they feel flattered and they like you better. That's human nature.

The first step in remembering someone's name is paying attention to it and finding ways to give it meaning. When you are introduced to someone, pay attention to the name of your new acquaintance, say it out loud as often as you can, without sounding silly, think about whom else you might know with the same name. That's all part of the process of making sure you register the name in the first place, and it's the beginning of a process of turning an arbitrary fact into a meaningful one.

The trick of focusing on the other person instead of on yourself also tends to reduce your self-consciousness and nervousness, which might otherwise interfere with the process of committing the name to memory (see *Stress*). That's also a good point to remember when you see someone whose name you know you should know. Because anxiety interferes with recall, relax and it's more likely to come to you.

To make a name more meaningful and memorable, scan the face of your new acquaintance for any interesting or unusual features. It may be a receding hairline, or long earlobes, or nice big white teeth. Next — and this is the challenging part — make a connection between the name and that feature. If it's the first name Andy you want to remember, and Andy has a receding hairline, modify his name to "Sandy" and picture his forehead as a beach and his hairline as the edge of the water at ebb tide. Whatever works for you is fine, as long as the feature you choose is noticeable enough that you'll remember that that's your cue the next time you see the person. Just be careful not to make Andy uncomfortable by staring at his receding hairline, and don't slip up and call him Sandy by mistake.

Any emotional content you can bring into your strategy helps, too, since emotion helps to make things more memorable (see *Learning the Easy Way*). If John Travolta did not appeal to you in his *Saturday Night Fever* and *Grease* days, you might transform his last name into *revolting* (sorry, John). Sometimes, you'll even do this unconsciously, as Freud was well aware. As the joke goes, "The problem with Freud's theory of the role the subconscious plays in slips of the tongue is that it's not testicle — oops, *testable*."

Another simpler, and less risky, trick is to think of someone else you know by the same name, as our exemplary political candidate did when he remembered the other Katzenellenbogen he knew in Des Moines. If it's Andy's name you want to remember, think of another Andy you know personally or an Andy you know from the news, a movie, a favorite book. If you like comic strips, maybe Andy Capp will do. Once you conjure up that association while making a new acquaintance, you will be surprised how readily and dependably you will recall it and, with it, the name.

Of course, the more times you run into each other, the less you'll need the mnemonic trick to help you recall the new acquaintance's name. Sooner or later, you'll be able to use this now-familiar person as a reference point when meeting a new person with the same name. Eventually you may even find yourself saying, while staring at a full head of hair before you, "Funny, you don't *look like* an Andy."

References

Gorno Tempini, M.L., et al. (1998). The neural systems sustaining face and proper-name processing. Brain 121: 2103-18.

Reinkemeier, Mechthild, et al. (1997). Differential impairments in recalling people's names: a case study in search of neuroanatomical correlates. Neuropsychologia 35/5: 677-84.

MAKING MEMORIES

Techniques for getting around an imperfect memory

Sheer memory power declines with age, and mental gymnastics will not prevent or reverse this process. Objective memory tests have repeatedly documented declining speed in processing, coordinating, and retrieving information in normal healthy older adults. That does not, however, condemn older people to constantly forgetting names, losing their glasses, and missing important appointments. The use of simple organizing techniques can compensate for the loss of memory power.

Mental exercise helps but has its limits

Learning new skills and acquiring new knowledge will help link newly-generated brain cells and help keep the *hippocampus*, a part of the brain that plays an important role in learning and memory, in good working order (see *Rebuilding Brain Cells*). Practicing a skill will help fix it in the part of the brain that supports it. Focusing on and repeating a particular item of information will embed it in long-term memory (see *Focus on Focus*). But no matter how hard you try to memorize a random sequence of numbers, your limit is likely to be seven. Practice will not increase capacity to remember arbitrary information such as this.

Memory-aiding, or *mnemonic*, techniques designed to invest arbitrary facts and details with meaning (see *Make It Meaningful*) are far more effective ways of improving recall than trying to build up memory as if it were a muscle. In a way, that's like using a dolly to move a piano instead of trying to lift and carry it by brute force alone.

To stay fit, learn from the example of the young and fit

A good toolbox of techniques can improve practical memory at any age, but especially if basic memory power has declined due to age. Several studies have shown that people, regardless of age, who report that they use mnemonic strategies for memorizing such things as telephone numbers actually have a better ability to remember them. And yet, according to self-reports, older adults tend to use fewer memory strategies than college-age young adults.

What kind of memory strategies might these be? The simplest kind include keeping an appointment book, writing reminder notes, making lists of things to do, planning each day's schedule in advance, and consistently keeping things in a prominent place where they can't be missed.

Making plans requires focusing on the activity to be planned, and organizing details is a way of investing them with meaning. Most of the habits of a good student — taking notes, identifying prominent themes in course material, and the like — are essentially ones of organization as well. These planning and organizing techniques help to ease the burden on a less-than-perfect memory. If those planning and organizing techniques become automatic and habitual, they will result in better memory in a practical sense.

Try a colorful technique proven to work with older adults

Most mnemonic techniques — even consciously-learned ones such as translating numbers into words that are easy to remember — have a component of organizing data in such a way that it's easy to remember. Some techniques may be especially well suited to the needs of older people. The following technique, for example, takes advantage of the fact that the perception of visually distinctive cues does not weaken with age. The region of the brain responsible for detecting and processing visual stimuli remains, in most cases, just as strong at age 80 as it was 50 years earlier.

How Do Actors Memorize so Many Lines, so Quickly?

Most of us haven't had to memorize two solid hours' worth of text since the time we acted in our high school's annual play. There are some people, though, who have to perform that kind of memorization feat on a regular basis throughout their adult lives. Typically, they may have two or three weeks to memorize over two hours of dialogue, and they have to memorize it well enough that they won't embarrass themselves in front of an audience. How do they do it?

Professional actors don't just memorize the lines of a play in rote-like fashion. What they do as they read and re-read the script is to try to get inside the minds of the characters, inferring the attitudes, emotions, and motivations behind the words. This kind of active, meaning-infusing engagement with the material to be memorized, a process known as *elaboration,* can make anything easier to remember. Once they rehearse the script a few times on this maximally meaningful level, they don't have to devote themselves to a line-by-line memorization.

We've all seen those plastic picnic plates with internal portion dividers. They're cheap, available at most discount stores and supermarkets, and come in a variety of bright colors. Pick out the most garish, ugly color you can find, one that clashes most with the decor of your home. Place the plate in a prominent location in the kitchen or dining room, wherever it is you eat every day. Take those items you own that you have a tendency to lose or forget — keys, glasses, bills, medications — and put them on the plate. Whenever you make an appointment or commit to a task — having dinner with a friend, feeding your daughter's cat while she's on vacation — write that down on a yellow Post-it note and stick the note onto the edge of the plate.

In an experiment testing the effectiveness of this technique, the number of "instances of forgetting" among groups of older people fell dramatically, from a weekly average of over eight to fewer than three. The plate technique proved much more effective than using a pocket-sized notebook to keep track of appointments and the locations of easily-forgotten items. In addition to the normal mnemonic advantage of organizing activities and consistently putting items in the same place, this technique took advantage of the fact that, even though some kinds of memory might weaken in old age, the perception of visually distinctive cues does not. Because the plate was so visually distinctive, it served as a constant reminder of the location of the items and the time, place, and nature of the chores.

References

Gabrieli, John D. E. (1996). Memory systems analyses of mnemonic disorders in aging and age-related diseases. Proceedings of the National Academy of Sciences USA 93: 13534-40.

Hill, R.D., et al. (1997). Effectiveness of the number-consonant mnemonic for retention of numeric material in community-dwelling older adults. Experimental Aging Research 23: 275-86.

Sharps, Matthew J., and Jana L. Price-Sharps (1996). Visual memory support: an effective mnemonic device for older adults. The Gerontologist 36/5: 706-8

INFLUENCE OF STRESS ON MOOD AND HEALTH

**How moods influence the health of your
brain and body**

Historically, Western medical science has advanced by severing a part of the body from the whole and studying it in isolation. (The word *science* has the same root as *scissors;* the meaning they share is one of cutting something into pieces.) Today, at the frontiers of discovery, research scientists are focusing on the interaction among the parts. For example, mood and the immune system, until recently viewed as entirely separate entities, are now recognized as interacting parts of a larger system, and a new branch of medicine called *psychoneuroimmunology* has emerged in acknowledgment of that fact. Linkages between mood and intellectual faculties such as memory are now becoming evident as well.

How moods influence immunity

Health care workers have long recognized that an optimistic attitude helps patients recover from illness. Recent research confirms that observation. For example, studies of H.I.V. positive men show an association between optimism and later symptom onset and longer survival time.

What explains this relationship between optimism and disease resistance? On a practical level, optimists may cope better with disease by, for example, taking a more active role in following doctors' orders. However, mood seems to have a more direct effect on the immune system as well. In a variety of studies, an attitude of optimism correlates with higher blood counts of lymphocyte immune cells, such as natural killer (NK) and helper T-cells. Depression, by contrast, is associated with lower levels of those cells, leaving the body more vulnerable to infections and disease.

Stress is another psychological state that affects the immune system. In our high-stress society, the connection between stress and vulnerability to viral infections such as colds is widely recognized. For example, cold and flu rates increase among students during exam periods. Why? The answer can be found in the blood. Medical students have been shown to have lower levels of lymphocyte immune system cells during exams than during less stressful times. Not all students are equally affected, however. First-year law students who score high on measures of optimism maintain higher lymphocyte counts.

Having a positive outlook on life can help an older person overcome age-related weakening of the immune system. Older adults who have a strong *sense of coherence* (SOC) — that is, a sense of confidence in the manageability, controllability, and meaningfulness of their environment — have been found to have better health, and stronger NK cell activity than others of the same age. One recent study measured SOC among 30 healthy older adults who were being relocated to a new housing situation. Moving can be stressful for anyone, but those with the strongest SOC had the least drop in their immune system cell count.

Depression and stress affect learning and memory

The symptoms of depression can resemble those of Alzheimer's and other dementias. Inattentiveness, disorientation, forgetfulness, and mental lethargy are common symptoms of both. For that reason, one of the first things a health care professional will do in investigating a possible Alzheimer's diagnosis is to determine whether depression is the cause of the symptoms. If it is, the cognitive impairment can be treated with lifestyle changes or medication.

However, the relationship between depression and dementia is more complex than mere resemblance. Some brain-scan studies have revealed that people suffering from clinical depression or stress disorders such as post-traumatic stress have a smaller than normal *hippocampus*, a part of the brain's limbic system that plays a critical role in memory. Research also provides evidence that depression results in some atrophy of the *prefrontal cortex*, a prime problem-solving locus of the brain with connections to emotional centers. In other words, stress and depression as well as Alzheimer's appear to have the ability to shrink some parts of the brain involved in learning and memory by destroying brain cell dendrites and perhaps even killing the brain cells themselves. Very recently, researchers have also discovered that both depression and stress have the ability to impede *neurogenesis*, the replenishment of brain cells in the hippocampus (see *Rebuilding Brain Cells*).

How stress attacks the body and the brain

A prime culprit in the violence visited by stress on immunity and cognition is the class of stress hormones known as *glucocorticoids* (see *Stress*). In the short run and in moderation, stress hormones are useful. During physical exertion, gluco-corticoids work together with *catecholamines* (a class of neuro-transmitters including epinephrine, a.k.a. adrenaline) to mobilize and replenish energy stores for the body and brain. They also act together to help the brain form an instant memory of unexpected events that trigger a stress response, and they help move immune cells to parts of the body where they are needed to fight an infection. These are useful adaptations to life in the wild, providing a surge of energy when a predator is encountered, imprinting a memory of the threatening event as a reminder to keep a distance the next time a predator appears, and providing first aid for a wound.

Like many things, stress hormones are good only in moderation. In the long run, elevated glucocorticoid levels harm both the body and the brain. Chronic stress, with chronically elevated stress hormone levels, can bring about changes in both the brain and the immune system of a young person that are similar to the manifestations which are quite common with advanced age.

Managing stress and depression as we age

Stress hormone levels tend to rise with age, and older bodies tend to be slower and less efficient at shutting off the stress response. Managing stress levels, therefore, becomes especially important as we age.

Stress can be managed through a healthy lifestyle, including physical exercise, which independently aids neurogenesis. For people who are naturally *reactive*, responding with high anxiety to social situations and frequently suffering from low self-esteem, cognitive therapy and antidepressants have been shown to be effective. In addition, research shows that antidepressants promote the growth of new brain cells in the hippocampus (see *Rebuilding Brain Cells*). The hormone estrogen also appears to have a protective role against stress-induced atrophy of the hippocampus, providing another reason for women, perhaps especially those with reactive temperaments, to consider estrogen replacement therapy after menopause.

What Women Know About Healthy Ways of Responding to Stress

The basic physiology of the human stress response is the same for men and women (see *Stress*). Stress triggers the sympathetic nervous system to release the stress hormones *cortisol* and *adrenaline*. Extra blood flows to the brain, muscles, and heart, and blood glucose levels jump. The brain becomes hyperalert to a possible threat, and the body is ready to fight hard or run fast.

In some ways, though, men and women appear to respond differently to threats and stressors. According to a group of researchers at the University of California at Los

Angeles (UCLA), *fight-or-flight* characterizes the male response to stress while women typically react with a *tend-and-befriend* response. And, while men tend to isolate themselves from others, women are more likely to turn to relatives or friends (especially female ones) for help and are more adept at rallying social support in times of stress. By seeking social support, women increase the chances of solving the problem that caused the stress in the first place. The tend-and-befriend response may even contribute to the longer life expectancy of women.

Women's tend-and-befriend stress response cuts across cultures and is even displayed by females of other species. It may be an adaptive response to lower social status and to the burden of child rearing.

When a threat rears its head, stress hormones such as cortisol and adrenaline as well as oxytocin are released. Oxytocin lowers cortisol levels, lessens the fight-or-flight fear response, and promotes relaxation. It has also been found to promote *affiliative* behavior such as grooming and mother-infant bonding.

Both males and females release oxytocin in response to stress, but, in other animal species, females release more of it than males. Oxytocin is modulated by the female hormone, estrogen, and inhibited by male androgen hormones such as testosterone. So, in our species, too, women may produce more of it than men.

Researchers into biological differences between the sexes often point out that, just as biology influences behavior, behavior influences biology as well. Even though biological differences may lie at the core of sex differences in ways of coping with stress, those differences are probably maintained and maybe even accentuated by social conditioning.

Male-female differences in response to a threat are presumably the result of natural selection and, therefore, must have been advantageous to both sexes, but circumstances have changed since evolution pushed men's and women's automatic stress responses in different directions. Females don't just have a stronger oxytocin response to stress, resulting in *tend-and-befriend* behavior; their grooming and touching, in turn, raise oxytocin and lower cortisol levels, further reducing stress. Among men, too, affectionate physical contact has been shown to lower stress levels while social isolation contributes to depression in both sexes and may well make it harder to solve the problems that cause stress in the first place.

In an era when stress itself can be life-threatening — by undermining the body's defense system and reducing the brain's capacity to learn and solve problems — men might benefit from learning to respond to stress as women naturally do.

Citations

Taylor, Shelley E., et al. (2000). Biobehavioral responses to stress in females: tend-and-befriend, not fight-or-flight. Psychological Review 107/3: 411-29.

Uvnas-Moberg, K. (1999). Physiological and endocrine effects of social contact. In C.S. Carter, I.I. Lederhendler, and B. Kirkpatrick (Eds.), The Integrative Neurobiology of Affiliation, pp. 245-62. Cambridge, MA: MIT Press.

References

Gould, Elizabeth, et al. (2000). Regulation of hippocampal neurogenesis in adulthood. Biological Psychiatry 48/8: 715-20.

Lutgendorf, Susan K., et al. (1999). Sense of coherence moderates the relationship between life stress and natural killer cell activity in healthy older adults. Psychology and Aging 14/4: 552-63.

Malberg, Jessica E., et al. (2000). Chronic antidepressant treatment increases neurogenesis in adult rat hippocampus. The Journal of Neuroscience 20/24: 9104-10.

McEwen, Bruce S. (2000). The neurobiology of stress: from serendipity to clinical relevance. Brain Research 886: 172-89.

Segerstrom, Suzanne C., et al. (1998). Optimism is associated with mood, coping, and immune change in response to stress. Journal of Personality and Social Psychology 74/6: 1646-55.

HUMOR THERAPY

When laughter becomes dead serious

Honest, mirthful laughter feels good. It relieves tension, lowers stress, and counteracts depression. Doctors have taken laughter seriously enough to have created a new branch of medicine, known as *gelotology*. Humor and laughter are therapeutic in many ways, probably more ways than even gelotologists know about, and you don't need a doctor's prescription in order to benefit from them.

Laughter helps get stale air out of the lungs and raises blood oxygen levels. It promotes the movement of immune cells throughout the body. It increases the production of the brain neurotransmitters *dopamine*, *epinephrine*, and *norepinephrine*, aiding alertness and memory. The stress-relieving effect of humor may also enhance learning and memory by countering the adverse impact of stress on the capacity to regenerate neurons in the hippocampus, an important memory center in the brain (see *Rebuilding Brain Cells*).

Losing a sense of humor isn't funny

An impaired sense of humor can actually be a sign of brain damage. People who have an injury to their right hemisphere often find it hard to "get" a verbal joke, although they may have no trouble with simpler, slapstick humor. The reason seems to be that various kinds of humor involve different kinds of cognitive processing in different regions of the brain, and one of those regions may be damaged while the others are spared.

Get It?

Humor depends on several cognitive sub-processes housed in different parts of the brain. For someone with right-hemisphere damage, it may be impossible to pick the one humorous punch line out of the four choices at the end of this joke. Someone with damage to the prefrontal cortex might be able to identify the option that's supposed to be funny, without actually finding it to be funny.

The neighborhood borrower approached Mr. Smith on Sunday afternoon and inquired, "Say Smith, are you using your lawnmower this afternoon?"

"Yes, I am," replied Smith warily.

The neighbor said,

(a) "You know, the grass is greener on the other side."

(b) "Do you think I could use it when you're done?"

(c) "Fine, then you won't be needing your golf clubs. I'll just borrow them."

(d) "Gee, if only I had enough money, I could buy my own."

In order to appreciate subtle verbal humor, brain imaging studies show that specific regions of the brain's prefrontal cortex and right hemisphere must be working properly. Otherwise, what might be funny to others appears to be a nonsensical incongruity, a *non sequitur*, an uninteresting and pointless story, or a downright lie.

Consider this Groucho Marx joke. Groucho is boarding an ocean liner, and a steward is helping him with his baggage. Groucho asks the steward, "Excuse me, my good man, do you have change for a hundred-dollar bill?" The steward eagerly replies in the affirmative. Groucho then says, "Oh, good, then you won't need this quarter I was going to give you as a tip."

If you don't think the joke is funny, that doesn't mean that you have brain damage, but you can imagine what someone with damage to the "humor" centers might think. On the face of it, the conversation between Groucho and the steward is just an unremarkable exchange, with a logic to each of Groucho's comments. After all, it does make sense that, if the steward already has something approaching $100 in small bills, he wouldn't be much interested in a two-bit tip. The humor derives from the divergence between the steward's expectations and what Groucho has in mind. People who study such things (yes, there are humor experts, and there's even a serious academic journal devoted to the topic) report that humor often involves an incongruity of some sort.

Why do patients with right-brain damage fail to "get" a joke like this while they have no problem seeing the humor in slapstick? Some aspects of conversational competence lie in the right temporal lobe, directly opposite the left hemisphere's language centers. The right hemisphere appears to excel at parallel-processing, big-picture kind of thinking while the left specializes in serial processing and in a more linear kind of logic.

These differences in information processing style may explain the humor deficit of right-hemisphere patients. They may lack the ability to hold multiple meanings or interpretations in their minds at once, including the kinds of juxtaposition in meaning that make Groucho's exchange with the ship steward humorous and that are the key to recognizing and enjoying puns, intended or otherwise.

The ability to hold multiple interpretations in mind is the kind of skill attributed to working memory, a short-term online memory system in the brain used for many everyday tasks. Working memory helps process and make sense of structurally ambiguous syntax, such as the sentence, "The horse raced past the barn fell." Understanding this sentence requires re-parsing it in line with an interpretation not anticipated the first time through (see *Mindlessness*). "Getting" jokes, too, often requires revision of an initial interpretation once the punch line is delivered, or once the punch line has sunk in. (Consider this example: Why did the golfer need a new pair of pants? Give up? Because he got a hole in one.)

Some of the brain systems underlying working memory also happen to be ones that function differently in the brain of someone with autism. Autistics characteristically suffer from what is sometimes called a deficient theory of mind (see *The Eyes Have It*), which limits their ability to judge the intentions or anticipate the needs of others. In effect, they have a hard time projecting their own mind into that of another person, and seeing things from someone else's perspective. Autistics tend to be bad liars because, in order to deceive someone, they need to have a clear understanding of what the other person knows or doesn't know.

Autistics also tend to have a difficult time understanding jokes. Often for them, what to another person would be a funny punch line simply seems to be a lie because they do not know whether the speaker intends to deceive or to amuse. Children under the age of about six, whose theory of mind has not yet reached maturity, often have the same problem and may find jokes upsetting.

Keeping a sense of humor makes sense

Fortunately, most of us do not have to cope with severe brain damage, and we'll reach old age with our sense of humor

Locating the Brain's Funny Bone

Understanding that a joke is a joke — seeing the juxtaposition, and realizing that it is meant to be humorous — is not the same as actually finding it funny. One recent brain-imaging study has offered evidence for narrowing down the part of the brain responsible for the *affective response*, the perception of the joke as funny, and for the subjective feeling that often expresses itself in mirthful laughter, to the right prefrontal cortex. Another study has moved the locus a little to the left, to the middle of the prefrontal cortex. That makes sense given that the prefrontal cortex is not just responsible for working memory tasks, but also has strong connections to the limbic system that make it an important part of the brain for processing emotion.

Getting a joke involves many brain regions, including other parts of the right hemisphere. But, because for a joke laughter is the big pay-off, the prefrontal cortex may be the most important humor-processing region of the brain.

intact. Laughter, then, doesn't just help us put the foibles of old age in perspective. By fighting off depression and reducing stress, it can help protect our brains and bodies against the ravages of age and disease. So sharpen your wits on word play, slapstick, stand-up comics, or the funny papers, whatever tickles your funny bone, and share the joke with your friends, young and old. Your sense of humor does not require a doctor's prescription, and it will pay dividends as long as you live.

References

Brownell, Hiram H., et al. (1983). Surprise but not coherence: sensitivity to verbal humor in right-hemisphere patients. Brain and Language 18: 20-27.

Fry, William F., Jr. (1992). The physiologic effects of humor, mirth, and laughter. Journal of the American Medical Association 267/13: 1857-8.

Goel, Vinod, and Raymond J. Dolan (2001). The functional anatomy of humor: segregating cognitive and affective components. Nature Neuroscience 4/3: 237-8.

Shammi, P., and D.T. Stuss (1999). Humour appreciation: a role of the right frontal lobe. Brain 122: 657-66.

PERFORMING MUSIC

A mind-saving hobby for aging brains

Both music and language have been with our species for at least tens of thousands of years. There are even 53-thousand-year-old Neanderthal bear-bone flutes dating from before the time *Homo sapiens* was the only hominid species to exist on the planet. It's even possible that music predates language.

A memory for musical melodies is something humans bring with them into the world. After all, lullabies are *not* like green peas — an infant doesn't have to be forced to like them. Infants can learn to recognize melodies well before they start to talk. Believe it or not, they can also recognize when a note is played out of tune.

Does musical talent come from a special part of the brain?

As any grandchild could tell you, music has the power to turn on many different systems in the body. It can influence heart rate, blood pressure, mood, even IQ test performance (see *Music*). There is no single, discrete music center in the brain. What isn't yet clear is whether any brain structures specialize *only* in music. Current research reveals that all of the many structures thus far identified are also used to process other sensory and analytical tasks.

For example, regions of the right hemisphere's *auditory cortex* (the area near the ears where sound is processed) are used for processing pitch, melody, harmony, and rhythm. Those regions are also used to hear and respond to the rhythms and intonations of spoken language. Patients who have suffered a stroke on the right side of the brain may lose not only their musical ability but also their ability to modulate the pitch and pacing of their voice in a normal manner when they speak.

It's been reported that the more sophisticated the musical training and knowledge, the more of the musician's left hemisphere is used in cooperation with the right. The *planum temporale,* an area of the brain's surface over the ears, seems to be especially important. On the left side of the brain, this area is consistently larger in the brains of professional musicians (largest of all in the brains of musicians with absolute pitch), but even it is also part of non-musical systems, used in language processing, for example.

The unexpected, in both speech and music, alerts the same area of the brain to figure out what's going down

Some very recent brain-imaging experiments by German neuroscientists have shown that, even for people with absolutely no musical training, language areas in the left half of the brain are used for the analysis of sequences of chords. The researchers played various chord sequences to people who neither played nor read music. One musical sequence was made up of conventional chords in the key of C major, while another was a mixed series that anyone would perceive as being out of key. For the in-key chords, the part of the brain that processes all sounds became active, just as would happen with incoming speech sounds. For the out-of-key sequence, the left-hemisphere language center known as Broca's area lit up, along with a corresponding region in the right hemisphere. It is these same brain regions, especially on the left side, that become active in analyzing seeming contradictions or mistakes in spoken language. Thus, the same overlapping regions of the brain pick out complex patterns in both sentences and music. Which one evolved first in the brain and which piggy-backed on it is anybody's guess.

Can just listening to music be good for your brain?
Everyone knows that music can be an aid to learning. Who didn't learn the alphabet song as a child? Memory for musical melodies, along with their accompanying lyrics, can be very long-lived. It's not unusual to remember songs from childhood and adolescence after decades have passed. In fact, sometimes it is hard to get them *out* of your head. For an adult, however, it is impractical to weave data into a melody to learn it, especially if you're the one who has to create the song in the first place.

Some kinds of music have been shown to put the brain into a receptive learning state, which amounts to the same thing as an effective *thinking* state. This is, in fact, the kind of application that has gotten a lot of attention as the "Mozart effect" — the ability of a certain kind of music to boost a specific kind of spatial intelligence, albeit only by a few points and only briefly. A more general research finding is that different kinds of music have different effects on mood, brain, and the ability to learn. No single kind of music works for all kinds of learning under all conditions.

What kind of musical experience does boost learning in later years?

The kind of classical music form exemplified by a Mozart sonata enhances a specific type of intelligence called *spatial-temporal,* which becomes involved in visualizing a sequence of changing patterns in space. That is the kind of work the brain does when it foresees the future effects of alternative chess moves, for example, or predicts what final shape a series of paper folds or cuts will produce. Other kinds of spatial intelligence, such as the type that helps visualize what an existing, three-dimensional object would look like from another perspective, are not boosted at all.

How the calming effect of some music helps memory

The impact of Mozart on the brain isn't merely due to its calming influence. In a comparison group tested by the Mozart researchers, listening passively to a relaxation tape for ten minutes failed to boost spatial-temporal intelligence at all. For some other kinds of thinking, though, part of the beneficial effect of music may indeed be that it can help you to *relax.* Take this common situation as an example: You find yourself dismayed that you cannot come up with the name of an acquaintance. The anxiety this dilemma creates blocks your mind from focusing on the problem because it is too occupied with the social embarrassment you are suffering. The brain needs to be relaxed to open the memory door and find an association (such as his wife's name or where you saw him last) that will lead to the specific name you *know* you know.

The role of music in calming anxiety prevents that distracting emotion from inhibiting a practical kind of thinking ability that people use all the time and that shows the signs of decline with aging. That kind of thinking is called *working*

Classical Music May Calm Epileptic Seizures

Investigations of brain-wave pattern responses to music using Mozart's sonata for two pianos in D major, K448, indicated that listening to this kind of music stimulates temporal and frontal regions of the brain into beta patterns, a kind of brain wave corresponding to an alert waking state. EEG recordings of electrical frequency activity (sometimes called "brain waves") in the brains of epileptics reveal "spikes," often originating in the temporal lobe, that send the rest of the brain into a seizure as they spread. Might music be used to somehow alter an epileptic's brain wave patterns in such a way as to reduce the likelihood of a seizure?

In a creative extension of the "Mozart effect" findings, researchers discovered that Mozart's piano sonata reduced epileptic brain wave patterns in a majority of test subjects. Even two comatose patients had their epileptic brain activity reduced by one half to two thirds.

These changes were only temporary, but it seems that a more intensive listening regimen can have longer-term effects as well. An eight-year-old girl with *Lennox-Gastaut syndrome*, a treatment-resistant form of childhood epilepsy, was played the Mozart sonata every ten minutes while she was awake. By the end of the day, her seizures had fallen from nine during the first four hours to just one during the last four hours. The next day, she continued to benefit from the previous day's Mozart therapy, having only two seizures in just under eight hours.

Citations
Hughes, J.R., et al. (1998). The Mozart effect on epileptiform activity. Clinical Electroencephalography 29: 109-19.

Jenkins, J.S. (2001). The Mozart effect. Journal of the Royal Society of Medicine 94: 170-72.

memory, a short-term, "online" system for accessing, holding on to, and manipulating the kind of data required to perform many everyday tasks. For working memory to function well, it is essential to focus and tune out distracting stimuli.

Mood and cultural background both make a difference

You don't need to be a neuroscientist to know that music can aid in relaxation, or to know that not all kinds of music are equally effective in helping you to relax. Different people, and perhaps different cultures, are likely to benefit from different kinds of music. A recent Turkish study showed that, for native Turks, music played on a *ney* — a type of reed flute commonly used in Turkish music — had the effect of jogging the brain into a calmly competent state resembling that found in focused attention or well-functioning working memory. For those same Turkish subjects, Western music played on a violin had no such effect.

The mood you're already in also can play a part in the interaction between a music-induced relaxation state and your learning state. In one recent study, relaxation techniques aided working memory performance in the morning, but not in the afternoon when the subjects were tired. In other words, relaxation isn't always what you may need. A recent Scottish study, surprisingly, found that playing Britney Spears in the classroom helped grade-school students' test scores. It seems that the upbeat popular music succeeded better than the teacher did in nudging the schoolchildren out of a state of boredom, getting them excited, and thereby helping their attention and motivation.

In general, though, and especially for older people, playing music with lyrics in the background spoils concentration and inhibits learning. Background sounds, especially words, can easily be ignored by younger brains but gains unwanted automatic access to older people's short-term working memory system.

Music as Alzheimer's therapy

Medical researchers and caregivers who work with Alzheimer's patients also have an interest in exploring the therapeutic potential of music. According to a study co-authored by one of the original "Mozart effect" researchers, the specific type of spatial intelligence that improved in children was also boosted in Alzheimer's patients. Another study presented recently at the British Psychological Society's London Conference has offered evidence that music can enhance remote long-term memory in people with mild to moderate dementia. Other studies have found that music can help dementia patients begin to communicate more clearly. The reasons for those improvements may be that music wakes up many parts of the brain and stimulates language and memory skills that tend to slow down slightly with normal aging, and seriously with Alzheimer's.

Two ways music can counteract the effects of aging

People who play music or sing with others stimulate their brains in ways that rebuild mental skills. There are many reasons for this. Participating in a group that is mutually supportive, as music certainly must be, is a kind of social interaction that tends to improve mood as well. Equally important as an incentive to keep going with a mind-engaging, neuron-stimulating challenge like reading and performing music is the evidence of improvement in a skill. That builds self-esteem, which fights depression and encourages older people to venture outside a comfortable, but mentally dulling, routine.

It is interesting to note that some musical abilities appear to survive the devastating loss of memory and verbal skills in the progression from dementia into Alzheimer's. For example, one 82-year-old musician with Alzheimer's was found to have an excellent ability to play piano compositions he had learned previously, even though his memory deterioration left him unable to identify the name of the piece or the composer. That's probably because the skill of playing those compositions was housed in his *procedural* memory system — the "muscle memory" system that also handles such skills as riding a bike — rather than the memory systems for events and words that are most strongly affected by Alzheimer's.

The general public's enthusiastic response to Mozart's promise of a quick fix is fueling more research into music's potential to enhance the brain's receptivity to learning, and to help strengthen and maintain other cognitive skills. There are so many different brain regions activated by listening to music — let alone by playing an instrument or singing in a group — that some kinds of music may well turn out to cross over into other skills than just spatial-temporal reasoning.

Perhaps of greater importance to those who wish to stimulate and maintain their cognitive skills, playing or singing music with others presents challenges to many parts of the brain and, especially in the older brain, may work over time to slow down the natural decay of memory and learning skills. In addition, the social support and pride that come with participating actively in music have a positive effect on self-esteem. In turn, that encourages other kinds of brain-nourishing engagement in life and helps to prevent the depression which so often afflicts the elderly.

References

Arikan, M. Kemal, et al. (1999). Music effects of event-related potentials of humans on the basis of cultural environment. Neuroscience Letters 268: 21-4.

Brotons, M., and S.M. Koger (2000). The impact of music therapy on language functioning in dementia. Journal of Music Therapy 37/3: 183-95.

Chan, Agnes S., et al. (1998). Music training improves verbal memory. Nature 396: 128.

Crystal, Howard A., Ellen Grober, and David Masur (1989). Preservation of musical memory in Alzheimer's disease. Journal of Neurology, Neurosurgery, and Psychiatry 52: 1415-16.

Elbert, Thomas, et al. (1995). Increased cortical representation of the fingers of the left hand in string players. Science 270: 305-7.

Gray, Patricia, et al. (2001). The music of nature and the nature of music. Science 291: 52-4.

Hudetz, Judith A., et al. (2000). Relationship between relaxation by guided imagery and performance of working memory. Psychological Reports 86: 15-20.

Koelsch, Stefan, et al. (2000). Brain indices of musical processing: "nonmusicians" are musical. Journal of Cognitive Neuroscience 12/3: 520-41.

Koger, S.M., and M. Brotons (1999). Is music therapy an effective intervention for dementia? A meta-analytic review of literature. Journal of Music Therapy 36/1: 2-15.

Larkin, Marilynn (2001). Music tunes up memory in dementia patients. The Lancet 357: 47.

Lindsay, W. R., and F. M. Morrison (1996). The effects of behavioral relaxation on cognitive adults with severe intellectual disabilities. Journal of Intellectual Disability Research 40: 285-90.

Maess, Burkhard, et al. (2001). Musical syntax is processed in Broca's area: an MEG study. Nature Neuroscience 4/5: 540-45.

Oohashi, Tsutomu, et al. (2000). Inaudible high-frequency sounds affect brain activity: hypersonic effect. Journal of Neurophysiology 83/6: 3548-58.

Peretz, Isabelle, and Sylvie Hébert (2000). Toward a biological account of music experience. Brain and Cognition 42: 131-4.

Petsche, H., et al. (1997). The possible meaning of the upper and lower alpha frequency ranges for cognitive and creative tasks. International Journal of Psychophysiology 26: 77-97.

Saffran, Jenny R., et al. (2000). Infant memory for musical experiences. Cognition 77: B15-B23.

Tervaniemi, M., et al. (1997). The musical brain: brain waves reveal the neurophysiological basis of musicality in human subjects. Neuroscience Letters 226: 1-4.

Tramo, Mark Jude (2001). Music of the hemispheres. Science 291: 54-6.

Watson, Donna (2001). Pop music boosts the brain. The Scotsman, January 22, 2001, p. 7.

Zentner, M. R., and J. Kagan (1996). Perception of music by infants. Nature 383: 29.

THE BEST BRAIN WORKOUTS

Why Fill-in-the-Blank is better than Multiple-Choice

A memory isn't the representation of a past experience that's been folded neatly into a box and carefully stored somewhere in the brain's cortex. Quite the contrary, each and every memory is the result of a nearly instantaneous retrieval of various pieces of that experience that were stored in scattered parts of the brain.

Scanning the wine list in search of a suitable accompaniment for the evening meal might evoke the memory that some Burgundies are white wines that are made from the Chardonnay grape, then the memory of what a white Burgundy tastes like, and then of sitting with a friend in the town of Dijon drinking a white Burgundy and the recollection of the friend saying that the wine was made from Chardonnay grapes even though it didn't say so on the label, and then the memory of what the label looked like.

In general, the more different parts there are to a piece of knowledge—what type of grape a white Burgundy is made from, for example—the harder it is to forget. But there's absolutely no guarantee that the reassembly of all the memory's different parts will match the original experience. You may remember sitting somewhere in France (what was the name of that town?) drinking a glass of wine (what was it called?) and talking with a friend about something that had to do with the wine you were drinking. Or you'll know, or think you know, that a white Burgundy is made from Chardonnay, but not where you learned it or who told you. Or you'll remember sitting with a friend drinking wine, and remember the fact of having visited Dijon, but you won't put the two together. Or you may remember sitting with your friend at an outdoor café in Dijon, but falsely import into that memory an image of tasting an excellent Champagne, which you didn't, in fact, drink until a week later in the town of Reims.

When a richly-nuanced memory comes back in all its vivid detail, it's easy to think that the entire memory has been stored away in one neat chunk awaiting our beck and call. Even when the memory comes back in fragments, and it's easy to see that the different pieces weren't stored together in one place, it often doesn't seem to matter. After all, one knows the facts, does one not, if just the essential pieces are retrieved? It isn't important to remember the circumstances of learning them— when, and where, and who told us. But sometimes it does make a difference.

The role played by the frontal lobes

Did you remember to take your medicine this morning? You may have a mental image of doing so, but you can't be sure whether that image is a memory of actually taking the pills or just a memory of an image that came to mind when you were telling yourself to remember to take them. Or, you think you remember having heard that a friend is having trouble with her marriage, but can't remember if she told you or whether somebody else did — and, if somebody else did, whether it's for public consumption or should be kept under wraps.

A region of the brain that is extremely important for the memory-reassembly process is the frontal lobes. This is the part of the brain that works especially hard when we make a conscious effort to access a memory, or to access memorized knowledge that is needed to answer a question or solve a problem. If the frontal lobes aren't working efficiently, it will become more difficult to access explicit memories of events or facts such as where you were yesterday afternoon at three o'clock, or the present name of Upper Volta — in the unlikely event that a million dollars awaits your recollection that Burkina Faso is a landlocked African country whose capital is Ouagadougou.

Why remembering the source can be important
There are other kinds of memory retrieval problems that may present themselves if the frontal lobes aren't up to par. A typical one is to remember the fact of having seen or heard something without remembering the source of the memory. Generally speaking, the source of information is difficult to access even under the best of circumstances, since the human brain is designed to retain the gist of things while forgetting the incidental details, such as the context in which they were learned. So if the frontal lobes aren't working at full capacity, the source of the information will be among the first pieces to be left behind during the process of reassembling a frag-mented memory into its multifaceted whole.

The frontal lobes aren't only important for accessing and reassembling the different facets of a memory. They also con-trol the process of creating some of those facets in the first place. And the more multifaceted a memory, the easier it will be to access, because it will have many "entry points" that can potentially lead to and connect up with the others.

Many mnemonic techniques — conscious strategies for encoding a piece of knowledge — take advantage of the fact that a piece of knowledge will be better entrenched in your memory, and easier to access, if it's connected to a number of other pieces of knowledge. In essence, this is what happens in the process of *elaboration,* that is, of making things meaningful in order to remember them better (see box, p. 225). Arbitrary facts by themselves are hard to remember. The difference between someone with a naturally good memory and someone who is more forgetful may lie in how automatically their frontal lobes will "elaborate" an otherwise arbitrary piece of knowledge.

The effects of aging on the frontal lobes

One reason older people have a more difficult time encoding and retrieving memories is that the frontal lobes tend to atrophy somewhat with age, and will thus contribute less automatically to encoding and retrieving information. Working with brain scans, Harvard memory researcher Daniel Schacter has found that when faced with a task of recalling a list of recently-studied words from memory, the right anterior frontal lobe of young adults will show more activity than the same region in an older adult's brain. The age differential shows up during the encoding stage, too. Younger people's brains will more automatically and with less effort undertake the process of elaborative encoding that makes a memory easier to retrieve.

Interestingly, these age differences disappear when young and old people are tested for *recognition* memory rather than memory *retrieval*. Almost everyone finds that recognition is

Source Memory Confusion

Read through this list of words, then cover them up and try to recite them back from memory.

tasty chocolate candy sugar honey frosting dessert
ice cream cherries whipped cream syrup

How did you do? Older people are generally less adept than younger people at remembering the words on a list like this, but just as likely as younger people to falsely recollect and report having seen the words "sweet" or "sundae." It's hard not to think of those words as you read through the list. Did you really read one or both of them, or just think of them while reading the other words? That's source memory confusion.

easier than recall. If you're asked to list as many different fruits as you can in one minute, you'll think of fewer of them than if you're asked to pick out the names of fruits from a miscellaneous collection of words in the same amount of time. If someone asks you to name the capital of Tanzania, you're more likely to get it wrong than if someone asks you, "What's the capital of Tanzania — Berlin, Dar es Salaam, or Cairo?"

Recognition relies less heavily on the frontal lobes than does recall, but the fact that older people's frontal lobes kick in less automatically than younger people's when they're faced with a memorization or recall task doesn't mean that older people are unable to use their frontal lobes effectively for learning and remembering. It just means that it takes more conscious effort. And that's why solving a puzzle you've never seen before, or answering fill-in-the-blank questions as opposed to multiple-choice ones, gives a better workout to the part of the brain that can certainly use the exercise the older it gets.

References

Macklis, Jeffrey D. (2001). New memories from new neurons. Nature 410: 314-16.

Schacter, Daniel L. (1996). Searching for Memory: The Brain, the Mind, and the Past. New York: Basic Books.

TEACHING TO STAY ALIVE

A commitment to listening hard feeds neurons

In experiments that show how an "enriched" environment helps to make rats' brains bigger and smarter (see *Healthy Aging*), two of the three pillars of enrichment are mental exercise and social stimulation. In addition to physical exercise, these two lifestyle factors can play an important and satisfying role in maintaining mental fitness. Indeed, several studies have offered evidence that the more intellectual and social activities one pursues outside of work or during retirement, the less likely one is to get Alzheimer's.

The usual way to reap the health benefits of an active mind is to read, to take courses, and in one way or another be on the receiving end of a classroom experience. But it can also be mentally and socially stimulating to teach *others* something that *you* know. That can be a lot more intellectually demanding than one might imagine.

Understanding the underpinning

There's a saying in academic research that goes: If you can't explain a theory to your mother over breakfast and get her to understand it, then either you don't understand it yourself or else it's just plain wrong. This is another way of saying that in order to position an idea in someone else's frame of reference, it must be paraphrased, and paraphrasing means, by definition, expressing more or less the same idea in different words.

To do this successfully, one must have a full and complete understanding of the idea, inside and out. It's neither practical nor particularly smart to hide behind an effluent stream of high-sounding jargon and pray that persons on the receiving end won't ask any questions. Indeed, unnecessary embellishment is likely to muddy the waters and create a forest of waving hands. Identifying the word *phocine* as being "of the same construct, but manifested under a different lexical alias, as the expression *seal-like*" may sound impressive. "*Phocine* means *seal-like*" may not impress, but it gets the job done more effectively.

Getting a grip on what we *think* we know

One of the good things about having children around is that they won't let us get away with our usual assumptions. Their questions have an uncomfortable way of going straight to the heart of the matter, such as: "What does *that* mean?" or, "What *difference* does it make?" It's worthwhile responding to these questions in a thoughtful way. Taking the time to explain how things work, or why they are the way they are, can help a young child develop critical thinking skills and an interest in figuring things out for himself. It also makes us think about the things that we *thought* we understood, but suddenly find difficult to explain. Where does sand come from? Why is a year divided into twelve months? If the gravitational force of the moon makes the tides move in and out, and we're standing on the beach where the tide is rising, how can the moon be way over there on the ocean's horizon, *away* from the direction in which the water's moving?

Learning a language: the ultimate brain exerciser

Learning a foreign language can exercise the brain in much the same way that putting familiar ideas into different words does. It can also be a humbling experience. If you're studying Japanese, or even German, it takes a while before you stop sounding like a young child, and not a particularly bright one at that.

The same thing applies if you were to sit on the other side of the table and help a foreign pupil learn *your* language. If you volunteer your time as a tutor, it can feel good to be the one considered the expert. But in order to teach your own language, you must first come to a conscious understanding of its underlying rules and structures before trying to explain them to someone else. This is the process in which both mental exercise and the sense of fulfillment come into play.

In one of his most famous speeches, JFK declared *"Ich bin ein Berliner"* to a cheering crowd close by the Berlin Wall. What he undoubtedly meant was something along the lines of, "I'm with you, I understand your situation, and I won't let you down." But what he didn't know, when uttering his word-for-word German translation of "I am a Berliner," was that a very natural German interpretation of his declaration would have been "I am a jelly donut." In German, as in French, one doesn't include the indefinite article when identifying one's profession or regional affiliation. Instead, one would say, "I am software engineer," or "I am New Yorker." But one *would* use the indefinite article when saying, word for word, "That is a pastry." And since one meaning of the word

Berliner is a type of jelly-donut-like pastry, that is what JFK appeared to be asserting himself to be.

Why doesn't German use the indefinite article the same way that English does? You'll get the answer to that question as soon as you answer this one: Why does English use the indefinite article differently from German? What are the English-language rules for knowing when to use "a," and when not to? You know when it sounds right, and when it doesn't, but it's another matter to figure it out in a way that will help a non-native speaker sound fluent. It's not as easy as you'd think. Many a promising career in linguistics has foundered on the rocks of this puzzle. But it's an excellent mental exercise, just as long as the dissertation committee doesn't expect a perfect solution.

References

Hultsch, David F., et al. (1999). Use it or lose it: engaged lifestyle as a buffer of cognitive decline in aging? Psychology and Aging 14/2: 245-63.

Hultsch, David F., Mark Hammer, and Brent J. Small (1993). Age differences in cognitive performance in later life: relationships to self-reported health and activity life style. Journal of Gerontology: Psychological Sciences 48/1: P1-P11.

FULL-BRAIN ENGAGEMENT

How building a family tree puts into practice what the experts preach

The three pillars of enrichment have been mentioned several times in this book, but they are so important to our daily lives that their message bears repeating over and over again.

A broad range of studies has provided irrefutable evidence that an enriched environment helps avoid depression, protects the body's immune system, and helps maintain cognitive function throughout a full lifetime. The three pillars of environmental enrichment are mental, social, and physical activity. And the benefits they provide aren't just a matter of making us feel better.

All three domains — physical, social, and mental — operate on biochemical levels that increase the rate at which the brain regenerates neurons. They also help maximize the biological factors that protect existing brain cells and the communication pathways that connect them. It's a shame these pillars are the ones we tend to neglect as we grow older, even though we're perfectly aware of the downside consequences that a less-engaged lifestyle has on our brain and physical well-being.

It doesn't have to be this way. Nor is there any reason to approach each pillar of enrichment individually. There are many activities that provide both social and intellectual stimulation, such as special-interest clubs, discussion groups, or classes at a community college. One good example of an inexpensive pursuit that works on many levels to stimulate the intellectual and social domains of life is the systematic study of one's ancestral history.

Genealogy: real-life time travel

Whether we know it or not, we've all done some dabbling in genealogy at one time or another — when we learned how our parents met, or laughed over the story of how crazy Great-Aunt Mildred connived to get her fourth husband arrested for vagrancy. We do the same thing when we pass stories about ourselves on to the next generation. People have a natural interest in learning about their ancestors. Genealogy helps sustain that interest by supplying a skeleton for the flesh that family stories provide. It gives us the skills we need to dig up more ancestral information, and helps us organize the mass of material that accumulates as we go along.

Genealogy also provides a wealth of intellectual stimulation, especially if we choose to take advantage of all the resources available to help gather data. It naturally brings us into contact with others who will share our enthusiasm — the relatives we contact to gather data, and the family members we share our findings with. If you really get bitten by the bug, there are other amateur genealogists on similar quests who are delighted to swap stories and strategies in club settings or online chat groups. But beyond all this, and probably most important of all, looking back and reflecting upon the lives of our forebears adds to the sense of the significance of our own life by placing it in a meaningful genealogical context.

Getting started on a trip into the past

The best way to begin building a family tree is to start at the present and work backwards. The simplest genealogy is a male-line family tree: father, grandfather, great-grandfather, and so on, along with the wives and siblings of each. A little more challenging, given the custom of women taking their husbands' names, is to broaden the focus to include female-line ancestors. The tree can be further enlarged by including its collateral branches — aunts, uncles, cousins of various degrees and types. One rewarding (or mortifying) aspect of a collateral tree is that you'll probably unearth a group of hitherto unknown relatives who are very much alive and well. In fact, they might be living right next door.

Work could get quickly out of hand if you don't restrict yourself at the beginning. For a direct-ancestor tree including male and female lines, the number of people increases exponentially with each generation (2-4-8-16-32, etc.). If the spouse's ancestry is included, the numbers are doubled. And if collateral branches are included with in-laws, one could suddenly be dealing with hundreds of relatives within just the last few generations.

Fleshing out the dry facts of history

Names and dates are essential to the family tree, but you'll probably want to assemble more than this. The more flesh that can be added to the bare-bones genealogy — occupations, travels, achievements, etc. — the more interesting the project will become. And for every member of the living family, the history will provide a unique way to learn more about history in general. Discovering that a great-great-grandfather was wounded in the first battle of Bull Run might lead to reading historical accounts of that battle, which could lead to a larger examination of the Civil War, which would in turn make that period in American history much more vivid and significant.

An added bonus of enriching the tree with family history is that it offers the chance for positive impact on the development of young children in the family. According to Harvard psychologist Jerome Kagan (see *Parenting*), family stories, perhaps told around the dinner table, help children to achieve a sense of family pride. This helps reinforce confidence in their own talents and abilities, which can increase their prospects for success later in life. Of course, you might want to wait until they're a little older to tell them the story about Great-Aunt Mildred.

It might be wise to begin with a book that walks you through the steps of compiling a genealogy and investigating family history. A few are recommended below. There are also many free online resources that can easily be found simply by doing a keyword search for "genealogy." Some sites have blank family trees or "pedigrees" that can be downloaded and printed out. In addition, there are good genealogy software programs that will help organize data. And if you still haven't learned much about computers or the Internet, a genealogy project is a good excuse to stop putting it off.

All these resources, print and electronic alike, will provide pointers about sources of genealogical information one might not otherwise think of — tax records, census records, militia muster rolls, and so on. Last, and certainly not least, is the Family History Library of the Church of Latter-Day Saints, which has extensive records of baptisms and marriages that can be freely accessed in any of the church's Family History Centers.

Recommended genealogy reference books

The Complete Idiot's Guide to Genealogy by Christine Rose, et al. (Paperback, 1997). MacMillan.

The Researcher's Guide to American Genealogy (3rd edition) by Val D. Greenwood. (Hardcover, 2000). Genealogical Publishing Company.

Unpuzzling Your Past: A Basic Guide to Genealogy (3rd edition) by Emily Anne Croom. (Paperback, 1995). Betterway.

SELF-TEST: Conceptual Priming

List A	List B
For each item, judge whether it's a natural or man-made object:	For each item, judge whether it has two or three syllables:
lemon	candy
diving board	casserole
magazine	painting
asbestos	swimming pool
zucchini	computer
basketball	window
paper	daisy
gasoline	wristwatch
walnut tree	robin
calendar	ocean
pepper	hubcap
ice cream	needle
garnet	watercress
light bulb	pumpkin
ostrich	pillow

See text, p. 289

It's Usually Not Alzheimer's

Healthy aging versus dementia, and how to tell the difference

A decline in memory is one of the most common complaints of people over 65. This is a group of no small demographic importance: it represents over 12% of the population of the United States and is growing fast. So there's no mystery why more people are worrying about Alzheimer's disease than ever. And since more people are getting older, and since age is the greatest risk factor for the disease, more people are getting Alzheimer's. Here are the statistics: At age 65, only about two out of 100 people have serious mental disabilities that turn out to be Alzheimer's. By age 80, the number increases by a factor of ten, to about 20 people out of 100. Add a decade, and about half of all 90-year-olds have Alzheimer's. This translates into about four million Americans who now have the disease, with the number anticipated to jump to 12 million 20 years from now.

The numbers make it obvious why Alzheimer's is such a serious concern and why memory lapses become more and more frightening the older we get. At age 20 or 30, it might be mildly amusing (unless the house burns down) to forget to turn off a stovetop burner before leaving for work. At age 80, the same kind of forgetfulness will be interpreted in much more ominous terms.

But statistics also show that fears that a memory lapse is a sign of Alzheimer's will usually turn out to be unjustified. And it's not just because older people are thought to be more inclined to jump to the unwarranted conclusion that typical forgetfulness is a sign of dementia. It's also due to the fact that some aspects of memory will normally decline in almost all older people, including people who remain perfectly healthy into old age.

Strategies are certainly OK

In healthy aging, it's quite commonplace to experience some difficulty with certain aspects of memory, and it's not unusual to find oneself devising a strategy, often implicitly, to facilitate the retrieval of information from long-term memory. Trying to arrange a series of recently-experienced events in the order of their occurrence may require organizing a set of clues that will put them in the proper sequence, because just remembering the events themselves won't be enough. Recalling the source of the information, rather than the information itself, will also often take some extra effort and may require a helping hand.

Even trying to think of as many vegetables as possible in 30 seconds may depend on a strategy of some sort, whether it's breaking down the task by running through various colors (green, yellow, red), or going through each letter of the alphabet to cue recollection. And all of these kinds of conscious recall that require a little extra effort will become even more effortful with age. That's because they all rely on the brain's frontal lobes which, just as they develop slowly in infancy, tend to decline in old age.

Recognition versus Recall (Part I)

Read quickly through the descriptions of famous people below, and see if you can come up with their names. Limit yourself to about a minute. Then, turn the page.

- Hollywood director who played Opie on television's *Andy Griffith Show* and Richie Cunningham on *Happy Days*.
- Actor who played Perry Mason on the TV show by the same name.
- Jewish girl who wrote a diary while hiding in an attic in Amsterdam.
- Woman who studies chimpanzees in Africa.
- First American woman in space.
- Greek goddess of wisdom who sprang from the head of Zeus.
- Actress who starred in *A Few Good Men* and *Striptease*.
- Three-time Best Director Academy Award winner for *It's a Wonderful Life* and two other films.
- Founder and spokesman of Wendy's hamburger chain.
- Actress who played opposite Humphrey Bogart in *To Have and Have Not*, and married him a year later.
- Grande Dame of American cooking who starred in TV's *The French Chef*.
- 1995 Best Actress Academy Award winner for her role as Sister Helen Prejean in *Dead Man Walking*.
- Watergate figure who now has his own radio show.
- Founder of CNN, owner of the Atlanta Braves, and Jane Fonda's ex.
- Hatchet-wielding anti-alcohol crusader, circa 1900.

Recognition versus Recall (Part II)

Match up the descriptions below with the names on the opposite page. Is this easier than recalling the names with nothing but the descriptions to go on?

- Hollywood director who played Opie on television's *Andy Griffith Show* and Richie Cunningham on *Happy Days*.
- Actor who played Perry Mason on the TV show by the same name.
- Jewish girl who wrote a diary while hiding in an attic in Amsterdam.
- Woman who studies chimpanzees in Africa.
- First American woman in space.
- Greek goddess of wisdom who sprang from the head of Zeus.
- Actress who starred in *A Few Good Men* and *Striptease*.
- Three-time Best Director Academy Award winner for *It's a Wonderful Life* and two other films.
- Founder and spokesman of Wendy's hamburger chain.
- Actress who played opposite Humphrey Bogart in *To Have and Have Not,* and married him a year later.
- Grande Dame of American cooking who starred in TV's *The French Chef*.
- 1995 Best Actress Academy Award winner for her role as Sister Helen Prejean in *Dead Man Walking*.
- Watergate figure who now has his own radio show.
- Founder of CNN, owner of the Atlanta Braves, and Jane Fonda's ex.
- Hatchet-wielding anti-alcohol crusader, circa 1900.

Lauren Bacall	Carrie Nation
Sally Ride	Ron Howard
Dave Thomas	Jane Goodall
Julia Child	Demi Moore
J. Gordon Liddy	Frank Capra
Anne Frank	Ted Turner
Susan Sarandon	Athena
Raymond Burr	

At all ages, the first task is harder than the second, since recall requires more effort on the part of frontal-lobe-based retrieval skills than simple recognition. As people age, their frontal lobes participate less and less automatically in recall, so more conscious effort has to be made, but recognition skills remain about the same. For people with dementia, both recall and recognition become difficult.

Simple recognition memory, on the other hand (see box, left and above), doesn't depend much on the frontal lobes and remains intact in healthy aging. But — and here's a cautionary note — with Alzheimer's, both recall and recognition suffer.

Conceptual priming—another test for Alzheimer's
Another kind of memory system, known as *conceptual priming,* is unaffected by normal aging, but is impaired by Alzheimer's. Look at the list of words in the "A" column in the box on p. 284. Go through the list item by item, and for each one ask yourself whether the object is a natural or man-made object. Next, go through the "B" list and ask whether each entry has two or three syllables. Then, turn to page 292 and mark all the items in the box you remember seeing on either of the two lists.

Normal Aging versus Dementia

Very early symptoms of progressive dementia, including Alzheimer's, are mild — the sort of forgetfulness common among older people, and even among some middle-aged ones. As the disease progresses, it becomes easily distinguished from simple benign forgetfulness.

	Normal	Dementia
1) Memory loss at work	Occasionally forgetting an assignment, deadline, or colleague's name	Frequent forgetfulness and unexplainable confusion
2) Difficulty with familiar tasks	Occasional distractedness — forgetting to serve a dish that was intended to be included with a meal, for example	Severe forgetfulness — forgetting that you made a meal at all, for example
3) Language impairment	Occasional difficulty finding the right word	Frequent and severe difficulty finding the right word, resulting in speech that does not make sense
4) Disorientation	Occasionally forgetting the day of the week	Becoming lost on the way to the store
5) Judgment problems	Choosing an outfit that turns out to be somewhat warm or cold for the weather — neglecting to bring a sweater to a baseball game on a cool September evening, for example	Dressing blatantly inappropriately — for example, wearing several layers of warm clothing on a hot summer day

	Normal	Alzheimer's
6) Abstract thinking difficulties	Occasional difficulty balancing a checkbook accurately	Inability to perform basic calculations, such as subtracting a check for $40 from a balance of $280
7) Misplacing objects	Misplacing keys or a wallet from time to time	Putting things in inappropriate places — a wallet in the oven, for example
8) Mood or behavior changes	Changes in mood from day to day	Rapid, dramatic mood swings with no apparent cause
9) Personality changes	Moderate personality change with age	Dramatic and disturbing personality change — for example, a traditionally easygoing person becoming hostile or angry
10) Reduced initiative	Temporarily tiring of social obligations or household chores	Permanent loss of interest in many or all social activities or chores

(Source: Alzheimer's Association Web site: www.alz.org)

SELF-TEST: Conceptual Priming

Which of these items were on either of the lists
on page. 284?

needle	ocean
paper	collie
credit card	pelican
orange	candy
walnut tree	daisy
painting	asbestos
diving board	surfboard
ice cream	

For most people, young and old, thinking about words in terms of whether the objects they represent are natural or man-made — which requires thinking about the meaning of each word — results in better recognition than thinking about the words in terms of syllable structure. On the other hand, Alzheimer's patients will have lost the conceptual priming effect — they don't remember the words whose meanings they were supposed to think of any better than the words they merely analyzed in terms of syllable structure.

The loss of conceptual priming in Alzheimer's probably results from damage to parts of the brain that also cause attention, language, and reasoning deficits. That's one of the reasons the symptoms of Alzheimer's are so much worse than the symptoms of normal aging: they occur in many more parts of the brain. Moreover, the parts of the brain typically affected by normal aging are much more severely damaged by Alzheimer's. This seems to be especially true for the hippocampus, a brain structure responsible for explicit recollection of experiences and facts, particularly recollection of events encountered very recently.

However, Alzheimer's doesn't harm all parts of the brain, or every kind of memory skill. The areas of the brain responsible for *procedural* memory — motor-skill learning such as how to ride a bike or hit a tennis ball — are not lost. This sometimes results in bizarre incongruities as, for example, the musician with Alzheimer's who retains an expert ability to play a large repertoire of piano pieces, even though he can't recollect the titles of the works he plays, or the names of the composers.

References

Crystal, Howard A., Ellen Grober, and David Masur (1989). Preservation of musical memory in Alzheimer's disease. Journal of Neurology, Neurosurgery, and Psychiatry 52: 1415-16.

Gabrieli, John D. E. (1996). Memory systems analyses of mnemonic disorders in aging and age-related diseases. Proceedings of the National Academy of Sciences USA 93: 13534-40.

STROKE!

Types, symptoms and a new treatment

A sudden loss of memory or sudden mental confusion may signify any of a number of things. Three important possibilities are *stroke, transient ischemic attack* (TIA), and *transient global amnesia* (TGA). The causes of all three are in some ways similar, but their long-term effects can be drastically different. It's important to be aware of the symptoms of these three types of "brain attack," particularly because a rapid response can make all the difference in helping to minimize the brain damage a stroke can cause.

Stroke: a blood clot or a broken blood vessel

There are essentially two main types of stroke, *ischemic* and *hemorrhagic*. The latter type, which is the less common of the two, results from a hemorrhage or burst blood vessel, leading to a loss of blood supply to part of the brain. Ischemic stroke occurs when a blood clot lodges in an artery, cutting off or severely reducing the blood supply to part of the brain. In either case, blood-deprived brain cells lose their ability to produce energy, and will die in a few minutes. Those cells also release excessive levels of potentially brain-damaging molecules, including calcium, glutamate, and free radicals. Brain cells near the center of the blood-deprived region become endangered and may die as well, although not immediately. Those brain cells, in what is called the *ischemic penumbra,* or "transitional zone," suffer reduced blood flow, but not to the extent of the ones in the stroke area's core. It's this broader penumbra region that is the target of the new anti-stroke drugs.

Stroke symptoms

The box on p. 299 shows the major risk factors for stroke, broken down into ones you can and can't do something about. Even if you're at low risk, you should know the symptoms, if only to identify a stroke in someone else and help that stroke victim get to the hospital immediately. Another box, below, shows the major symptoms you should know about. In the event of a stroke, the best thing to do is to dial 911 rather than drive the patient to the hospital. Even including the time it takes the ambulance to pick up the patient, an ambulance will get to the hospital more quickly than a private car, and emergency room personnel will respond sooner.

On average, men have a higher stroke risk than women, but more women than men die of stroke. Women are much less likely than men to get to a hospital quickly and are, therefore, likely to suffer more severe consequences from a stroke. They're also less likely to benefit from the new anti-stroke drug therapy.

TIA: symptoms and consequences

In addition to knowing the signs of a full-blown stroke, it pays to know how to recognize a "mini-stroke," more for-

---

Stroke Symptoms

Most common
>   Sudden numbness or weakness in the face, arm, or leg, especially just on one side
>
>   Sudden confusion, trouble speaking or understanding what others are saying
>
>   Sudden vision problems in one or both eyes
>
>   Sudden loss of balance, dizziness, or trouble walking
>
>   Sudden severe headache

Less common
>   Sudden nausea, fever, or vomiting
>
>   Brief loss of consciousness

mally known as a *transient ischemic attack* (TIA). The symptoms of a TIA resemble those of a stroke, but last only a few minutes. TIAs result from a temporary reduction of blood supply to part of the brain. Unlike in a full-blown stroke, the blood supply is spontaneously restored to normal quickly enough that no cell death occurs, so there is no permanent damage. But TIAs increase the risk of a major stroke. A recent study published in the *Journal of the American Medical Association* found that about 10 percent of people who experience a TIA have a major stroke within three months, and about half have such a stroke within two days. So it's important to take TIAs seriously, and to get to the hospital quickly if you think you've had one.

Signs and causes of a TGA—temporary memory loss

Similar in some ways to a TIA, but less dangerous, is *transient global amnesia* (TGA). TGA is also believed to be caused by a reduction of blood to part of the brain, specifically to memory structures such as the hippocampus. As with a TIA, there is no permanent damage. Unlike a TIA, however, TGA does not appear to increase the risk of a full-blown stroke.

The first sign of TGA is a sudden amnesia for recent events, and sometimes also for events as far back in time as several years. People with TGA lose a sense of time, because they suddenly can't form new memories and so don't know, for example, where they are, what they were doing when the amnesia started, how long they've had the amnesia, or, if they are taken to a hospital, how long they've been there. Other than memory, cognitive functions are normal. Within a day or two, in most cases, the amnesia passes.

Nobody is quite sure what it is that causes the temporarily reduced blood supply to the brain's memory structures that results in TGA. Some researchers believe that there may be a psychological trigger that produces a brief change in brain metabolism. TGA is most common among people over 50, and can apparently be brought on by physical exertion, emotional stress, sexual intercourse, driving a car, and even swimming in cold water.

Since the symptoms of TGA and TIA can be similar to the untrained observer, anything resembling the description of TGA should be promptly evaluated by a doctor. If it is TGA, there appears to be little reason to worry. Although TGA may recur, it usually doesn't, and it doesn't cause any damage or have any lasting effects.

A three-hour window to administer a new drug, but only for ischemic strokes

Traditionally, medical doctors have viewed a stroke as something they can do little about once it's happened. Even if the stroke patient is rushed immediately to the emergency room, from that point on the standard protocol has been essentially to monitor the patient for further complications.

Within just the last few years, however, several stroke-treatment drugs have been developed, and one has been cleared by the FDA for use in hospitals. That drug, known as *tissue plasminogen activator* (TPA), has been shown to make it 30 percent more likely that a stroke victim will recover with little or no disability. The only hitch is that TPA must be administered within three hours of the first symptoms of the stroke. That's one reason it's so important to know how to recognize stroke symptoms, and to get the victim to the hospital as quickly as possible once those symptoms occur.

How the new TPA drug works and when it doesn't

Drugs that are undergoing FDA trials include ones that counteract the destructive effects of calcium, glutamate, and free radicals. The drug that has already been approved, TPA, works

Stroke Risk Factors

Many factors contribute to the risk of stroke. The more you have, the greater the risk. Some of them are things you can't do anything about, but there are others that you can change or control.

Risk factors you can't change

Age: The older you are, the greater your risk.

Gender: More men suffer strokes than women. But women stroke victims are more likely to die.

Heredity: If a close relative or family member has had a stroke, your risk is increased.

Race: African-Americans have higher rates of stroke than whites, partly because they have a higher risk of high blood pressure, diabetes, and obesity.

Previous stroke or heart attack: If you've already had a stroke, or if you've had a heart attack, your risk of having a stroke is increased.

Risk factors you can change

High blood pressure

Diabetes

Cardiovascular disease

Atrial fibrillation: This heart rhythm disorder, in which the upper chambers (atria) beat extremely fast or quiver instead of beating properly, can create blood clots that can lodge in an artery.

TIAs

Smoking

Physical inactivity and obesity

by breaking up blood clots, thus restoring full blood supply to the endangered cells in the penumbra.

TPA is still new enough that even many medical professionals don't know about it. Only 2 to 3 percent of stroke victims are given the drug, and a significant number of that small group are given it incorrectly. In order to work effectively with minimal risk of side effects, TPA has to be administered within the first three hours of a stroke, as was mentioned above. After that time window has closed, or if TPA is given along with a blood thinner, the drug increases the risk of brain hemorrhage, which would result in more brain damage. As you might guess, TPA should only be used after an ischemic stroke, not a hemorrhagic one, so one of the first things the emergency room personnel should do is perform a brain scan to determine which type has occurred.

References

Johnston, S.C., et al. (2000). Short-term prognosis after emergency department diagnosis of TIA. Journal of the American Medical Association 284/22: 2901-6.

National Stroke Association Website: www.stroke.org.

Pantoni, L., M. Lamassa, and D. Inzitari (2000). Transient global amnesia: a review emphasizing pathogenic aspects. Acta Neurologica Scandinavica 102/5: 275-83.

Rebuilding Brain Cells

How physical and mental exercise improve ability to learn and recall

We've all grown up with the belief that, once you lose brain cells, you can't replace them. Who among us hasn't feared that some of our precious, irreplaceable neurons might die every time we hold our breath, inhale some cigarette smoke, drink a glass of wine, or let our Type A side get the better of us while we're stuck in a traffic jam? It's almost enough to make you afraid to get out of bed in the morning.

Only in the last few years have researchers found clear evidence for *neurogenesis*, the regeneration of brain cells. Now, we know that new brain cells can grow in adult rats, tree shrews, marmosets, macaque monkeys, and it has recently been proven true in humans, too. What you really need to give some thought to, it turns out, is not so much what you can do to avoid killing brain cells as what you can do to produce more new ones, and to help those new brain cells to survive.

The two most important areas for memory and learning

According to these new findings, there are very specific parts of the brain where neurons are most certainly replaced. One is the *hippocampus*. If you're going to have any part of your brain renewed on an ongoing basis, you could hardly choose a better one than the hippocampus, since that's a structure that plays a crucial role in learning and remembering new things. And the latest research also offers evidence that new brain cells might be generated in the *prefrontal cortex*, a locus of working memory and problem-solving skills.

It's probably no coincidence that both of these brain regions, the hippocampus and prefrontal cortex, are ones that decline the most as we age. Along with the gradual structural atrophy of these brain regions come the typical age-related declines in memory and mental acuity. These changes happen to almost everyone to some degree. They're most extreme in people who develop Alzheimer's, the most common cause of age-related dementia.

Why some people show more decline than others

All of this raises some questions. If we're regenerating new brain cells all our lives, why do we lose any of our mental acuity at all? If our hippocampus is constantly being renewed, why does our memory decline? And, perhaps most important, why is it that some people's brains remain healthy no matter how old they get, while others become forgetful and easily confused, and yet others develop Alzheimer's?

The first thing to know is that, even though neurogenesis continues throughout life, it naturally slows down with age. But that doesn't explain why some older people are affected more than others.

The explanation for some of these differences lies in genetics. For the common late-onset form of Alzheimer's which typically strikes after age 65, a certain version of a gene that codes for a protein called *ApoE* raises risk of getting the disease to some degree. But the link between genes and Alzheimer's isn't simple or deterministic: Many people without the risky version of the gene get Alzheimer's, while many people with it don't.

New Neurons, New Memories

Very recent evidence shows that newly-generated neurons may play a more vital role in memory than linking up to old neurons to maintain existing learning-and-memory systems. New neurons may be required for the formation of *new* memories.

In an experiment published in the journal *Nature*, researchers injected rats with a chemical that selectively kills newly-generated brain cells. Those rats were unable to acquire new knowledge in a learning task that took place in the *hippocampus*, a structure where newly-generated neurons appear in adult brains. The rats had no problem with other kinds of memory that don't depend on the hippocampus. So without new brain cells, the rats couldn't form new hippocampus-dependent memories.

For humans, the kinds of memory that depend on the hippocampus include *semantic* — memory for facts — and *episodic* — autobiographical memory for places and events. Alzheimer's interferes with these two types of memory the most.

So there must be other factors involved. Very likely, some are the same as those that have been found to affect the rate of neurogenesis in the brain. Unlike the genetic factor, all these others are ones you can easily do something about.

Making brain cells work lowers their mortality rate

One factor appears to be the degree to which you use the skills that the hippocampus controls. Animals that live in the wild maintain more hippocampal neurons than those in captivity, probably because animals in nature use more hippocampus-dependent skills — for example, finding their way around a complex environment and remembering how to get back home again. For some wild animals, neurogenesis fluctuates with seasonal needs. Black-capped chickadees have more new hippocampal neurons during times of the year when they store and retrieve seeds, an activity that exercises their spatial navigation skills. And lab rats that are challenged to learn new skills have been shown to benefit from twice the rate of neurogenesis as ones that are given nothing new to learn.

Researchers aren't yet sure exactly how mental exercise boosts neurogenesis. What they have figured out is that the doubled rate of neurogenesis results from increased *survival* of newly-generated brain cells, not increased *production*. Given everything else we know about the brain, it makes perfect sense that the regenerated brain cells will survive or not depending on whether you use them. That principle, after all, applies to our brain from the moment we're born — actually, even before birth.

Think of it this way

Every time you challenge yourself to learn something new or solve a puzzle you haven't solved before, you're helping brand-new brain cells to move into position and extend their connecting fibers, called *dendrites* and *axons,* that carry impulses to other cells involved in memory and learning. Being able to help the newly-created neurons to survive and increase connections is a much more encouraging vision than the image of relentless brain-cell death we all grew up with. Is there anything you can do to produce *more* of them in the first place? According to the latest research, there is.

Physical exercise helps to strengthen brain cells

Along with mental exercise, physical exercise boosts neurogenesis, too. Lab rats that are given the opportunity to get plenty of exercise end up with twice as many new neurons — the same increase as produced by mental exercise — as sedentary rats. They also perform better on tests of learning and memory. Physical exercise probably works by a different path from mental exercise, perhaps by raising levels of growth factors, such as BDNF, that maintain and repair brain cells.

Feeling depressed harms brain function

A recent study has offered compelling evidence that antidepressants increase the production of new hippocampal cells. One effect of antidepressants is to raise levels of BDNF, the same growth factor boosted by physical exercise, so that may be at least one route by which antidepressants enhance neurogenesis. Preliminary studies show that *serotonin,* a neurotransmitter elevated by some antidepressants, can stimulate neuro genesis as well. That may be another mechanism for the beneficial effect of antidepressants on neurogenesis.

Presumably, people who would benefit the most from antidepressant-induced stimulation of new brain cells are those who would benefit from antidepressants for the usual reason — that is, those who have low BDNF and serotonin levels as a result of depression.

Slim down to think faster

Another factor that's been shown to raise BDNF levels and increase the survival rate of newly-generated brain cells is reduced calorie intake. Many studies have indicated that rats and mice fed a restricted-calorie diet live longer than ones allowed to eat as much as they want. More recently, there's been evidence that a reduced-calorie diet has brain-protective effects as well, and can counteract the sort of degeneration of hippocampal neurons that occurs with Alzheimer's. That may be one reason why in China and Japan, where daily calorie intake is relatively low, there's only about half the per capita

Some Evidence That Estrogen May Help Prevent Alzheimer's

BDNF isn't the only naturally-produced chemical that boosts the production of brain cells. Estrogen does, too. With female rats, a rise and fall in the rate of neurogenesis has been shown to match fluctuations in estrogen levels during their estrous cycle. If a female rat has its ovaries removed, resulting in a drop in estrogen, the rate of new brain cell production drops, too. If it is then given estrogen supplements, the rate rises again.

These findings match the results of human studies that show estrogen to have a protective effect against dementia, which is one reason women past menopause are sometimes advised to go on estrogen replacement therapy. One recent study showed that women over 65 who have higher levels of natural estrogen are less likely to experience cognitive decline. (Even though their ovaries no longer produce the hormone, estrogen is still converted from hormones produced by the adrenal glands.) So women with low estrogen levels may be at greatest risk for developing dementias such as Alzheimer's, and may stand to benefit the most from estrogen-replacement therapy.

rate of Alzheimer's as in the U.S. and western Europe. A recent study of New York City residents, too, found that those with lowest calorie intake had the lowest incidence of Alzheimer's.

These studies point to some practical ways you can influence the state of your brain. First of all, the "use it or lose it" concept isn't just a catchy slogan, it applies quite literally to the survival of newly-generated brain cells. Second, physical exercise doesn't just improve your mood and make you physically fit. It helps to keep you mentally fit, too. In fact, physical fitness, mental fitness, and mood seem so tightly intertwined that you probably can't affect one without affecting the others.

References

Brown, David R., et al. (1995). Chronic psychological effects of exercise and exercise plus cognitive strategies. Medicine and Science in Sports and Exercise 27/5: 765-75.

Gould, Elizabeth, et al. (2000). Regulation of hippocampal neurogenesis in adulthood. Biological Psychiatry 48/8: 715-20.

Gould, Elizabeth, et al. (1999a). Learning enhances adult neurogenesis in the adult hippocampal formation. Nature Neuroscience 2: 260-5.

Gould, Elizabeth, et al. (1999b). Neurogenesis in the neocortex of adult primates. Science 286: 548.

Hollmann, Wildor, and Heiko K. Strüder (2000). Brain function, mind, mood, nutrition, and physical exercise. Nutrition 16/7-8: 516-19.

Mattson, Mark P. (2000). Neuroprotective signaling and the aging brain: take away my food and let me run. Brain Research 886: 47-53.

Melberg, Jessica E., et al. (2000). Chronic antidepressant treatment increases neurogenesis in adult rat hippocampus. The Journal of Neuroscience 20/24: 9104-10.

Shors, Tracey J., et al. (2001). Neurogenesis in the adult is involved in the formation of trace memories. Nature 410: 372-5.

van Praag, H., G. Kempermann, and F. Gage (1999). Running increases cell proliferation and neurogenesis in the adult mouse dentate gyrus. Nature Neuroscience 2: 266-70.

COMING TREATMENTS

What the labs have discovered and what you can do in the meantime

A recurring theme that emerges from every recent large-scale study of age-related dementia can be boiled down to these few simple words: Mental and social stimulation may have a protective effect against Alzheimer's. Using animal models, researchers have found that mental stimulation doubles the rate of *neurogenesis* — the creation of new neurons — in the part of the brain that's particularly important for learning and remembering new things. And this is a part of the brain that is typically hard hit by Alzheimer's.

In humans, mental and social stimulation may give the brain extra neural pathways to fall back on if and when some brain cells start to become less efficient, or begin to become affected by the tangles and plaques of Alzheimer's. This "functional reserve" or "back-up" theory of Alzheimer's prevention is bolstered by evidence that, among people with equivalent *structural* signs of Alzheimer's, the individuals with higher education have fewer *behavioral* symptoms such as impaired memory and reasoning.

We have now learned that physical activity also boosts neurogenesis, and that keeping both body and mind in shape is a good idea. There are also other incentives to keeping ourselves trim: an enriched environment of social, intellectual, and physical stimulation raises the levels of pleasure-inducing neurotransmitters (see *Learning Addiction*), which translates into a richer, more interesting life.

The fact remains that some people with rich and stimulating lives also develop Alzheimer's. This points to other contributing factors, and the genetic factor is clearly one of them. So, obviously, it would be worthwhile to find methods that work on a genetic or brain-chemistry level to prevent and even cure the disease. How close are we to finding these treatments?

The genetic approach to treating Alzheimer's

There are two major types of Alzheimer's, early-onset and late-onset. Early-onset Alzheimer's has a relatively strong genetic component—about 40 percent of the people who get it have a family history of the disease. Two genes have been identified as contributing to early-onset Alzheimer's. One gene, on chromosome 21, produces a protein called *amyloid precursor protein* (APP). If this gene is defective, the APP it produces can have a peptide called *beta-amyloid* cleaved off, which can then accumulate as plaques in the synapses of brain cells. But early-onset Alzheimer's, which strikes before age 65, is rare. Even though it is the form to which the label Alzheimer's was originally applied, it accounts for only a small fraction of Alzheimer's cases, and is not the type most people worry about.

The late-onset form, which strikes after age 65, is more common. It will affect one person in five at age 80, and one out of every two 90-year-olds. The genetic factor in the cases of late-onset Alzheimer's is relatively weak. There is one gene, though, that does appear to play a role in some instances of late-onset Alzheimer's. This gene, which produces a protein called *apolipoprotein E* (ApoE), has three variants. Everybody inherits one ApoE gene from each parent, so there are six possible combinations. One of the variants, known as e4, confers a high risk of Alzheimer's, especially if inherited from both parents.

Recently, a team of pharmaceutical company researchers developed a vaccine against the beta-amyloid plaques, which they tested on mice bred to have a defect in the gene that produces APP. Normally, this genetic strain of mice develops severe amyloid plaques by the age of 11 months. The vaccine, which consisted of a form of the beta-amyloid protein and triggered the production of beta-amyloid antibodies, not only prevented the development of beta-amyloid plaques in mice that had not yet developed them, but cleared plaques out of the cell synapses of those that had them.

More recently, academic researchers have shown that vaccinating Alzheimer's-prone mice also protects the mice from learning- and memory-related problems. In other words, it doesn't just prevent the structural signs of Alzheimer's in the brains of the mice, it also prevents the behavioral signs that this genetic strain of mice would otherwise invariably develop.

What nobody yet knows for sure is whether the vaccine is safe and effective for humans. Even if it is, nobody knows whether it would work for forms of Alzheimer's other than the early-onset kind that's caused by the defective APP gene. But at this point, it's the best hope we have for an effective treatment of Alzheimer's.

Is stem-cell implantation a viable treatment for Alzheimer's?

Another technique that's being investigated as an Alzheimer's treatment is implanting or injecting stem cells directly into the brain. Stem cells are general-purpose cells that can divide and develop into any of the specialized cells that make up the body. One of the controversial aspects of stem cell research has to do with harvesting the cells from aborted human fetuses. The cells are then coaxed into developing into whatever specialized cell might be needed for the disease that is being treated. An even more direct technique is to extract fetal tissue that has already become specialized to some degree in the right direction — in Alzheimer's research, for example, into progenitor brain cells that secrete neural growth factor. Another promising, and less controversial, source of stem cells is the patient's own body. In addition to sidestepping ethical issues, this technique has the advantage of avoiding rejection of the implants by the recipient's immune system.

Stem cell implants are currently being tested as a way to restore the function of brain systems that are damaged or lost due to neurodegenerative disease or injury. For example, Parkinson's disease causes the brain cells that produce dopamine to die. Fetal cells capable of producing dopamine have been experimentally injected into the brains of Parkinson's patients to replace and take over the function of those that have been lost. The same approach is envisioned for treating Alzheimer's, except that in the case of Alzheimer's it would be replacing cells in the system that produces and responds to the "memory" neurotransmitter *acetylcholine*.

Unfortunately, the most recent news from a carefully controlled human experiment using fetal cell implants for Parkinson's is not good. Most of the patients in the experiment failed to benefit at all from the implants. Worse, in about 15 percent of the patients the implanted cells grew too successfully, resulting in uncontrollable, spasmodic movement. This side effect shows how much still has to be learned about inducing injected cells to develop and connect with existing brain cells in the right way

"Use it or lose it" will always apply

Even when an Alzheimer's cure is available, either in pill form or through surgical cell implants, the importance of using — which is another way of saying "stimulating" or "exercising" — both existing and new brain cells for their intended purpose cannot be overemphasized. In stem-cell implant experiments with animals, when the implants are combined with a program of mental stimulation they stand a better chance of succeeding than do implants without subsequent stimulation.

The same applies to the natural regeneration of brain cells that we know occurs on an ongoing basis even in a mature human brain. Without mental stimulation—without specifically and consciously using the new cells for new learning and memory tasks—far fewer of those cells actually become functional. So, either with or without pharmaceutical or surgical therapy, the "use it or lose it" principle still applies (see *Rebuilding Brain Cells* and *Healthy Aging*).

References

Freed, C.R., et al. (2001). Transplantation of embryonic dopamine neurons for severe Parkinson's disease. New England Journal of Medicine 344/10: 710-19.

Morgan, Dave, et al. (2000). A-beta peptide vaccination prevents memory loss in an animal model of Alzheimer's disease. Nature 408: 982-5.

Schenk, Dale, et al. (1999). Immunization with amyloid-beta attenuates Alzheimer-like pathology in the PDAPP mouse. Nature 400: 173-7.

INDEX

Absolute pitch, 260
Acetyl-CoA, 169
Acetylcholine, 169
  nicotine and, 183
Actors, memorization abilities of, 243
Adrenaline, and stress, 249, 250
Affective response, 257
Aging
  dementia in, 222, 224; frontal lobes in,
  272-274; intellectual activity in, 227-228,
  231; music to counteract, 265-266; normal
  loss of cognitive function in, 221; normal
  memory loss in, 221-222; sleep and, 197;
  slowdown of working memory in, 222;
  tips for successful, 231
Alzheimer's disease, 222, 224
  distinguished from normal memory
  decline, 286, 290-291; early learning and,
  75, 224; education level and, 224; effects
  on brain, 247, 302; estrogen to combat,
  306; future treatments for, 310-312; genetic factors in, 302-303, 310-311; homocysteine and, 164; incidence of, 284; intellectual activity to prevent, 227-228, 231, 309,
  312-313; lifestyle and, 224, 227; music as
  treatment for, 265; nicotine as negative
  factor, 182-183; screening test for, 284,
  289, 292; and sense of smell, 193; socioeconomic status and, 223-224; stem cells as
  treatment for, 311-312; stress and, 147;
  symptoms of, 290-291; types of, 310; vaccine for, 11, 310; Vitamin E as treatment
  for, 163
Amino acids, 165
  functions of, 169
Amnesia
  anterograde, 133; infantile, 65; and priming, 215; transient global, 295, 297-298
Amygdala, 14, 70
  and learning, 181; and memory, 114, 115,
  132; and stress response, 51, 148; training
  of, 135-136
Amyloid precursor protein (APP), 310
Androsterone, 189, 190
Anosmia, 187
Anterograde amnesia, 133
Antidepressants, brain effects of, 248-249, 305
Antioxidants, 163
Apathy, learned, 153-154
ApoE, 302, 310
Attachment theory, 52-53

Attention
  brain role in, 107-110; distraction and,
  110-111, 144-145; effect of caffeine on,
  174, 176; effort and, 144; and learning,
  107; optimizing, 112; research on, 111-
  112; voluntary vs. involuntary, 174;
  Attention deficit-hyperactivity disorder
  (ADHD), 52
Auditory cortex, 260
Autism, 43, 256-257
Autobiographical memory, 63
Axons, 58, 304
  insulation of, 123

Babbling, 28
Babies
  bonding with mother, 30-31; emotional
  needs of, 50; eye contact by, 23-24, 26;
  hearing and sound discrimination by, 31-
  33; information processing of, 37-39; intelligence measurement of, 36-37; language
  acquisition by, 29-33; memory in, 61-62;
  prenatal brain development, 19-21; solipsism of, 56; stress reduction for, 74
Baddeley, Alan, 128
Basal ganglia, and memory, 114
Belladonna, 24
Bloch, Vincent, 196
BNDF, 305
Bonding, mother-baby, 30-31
Brady, Joseph, 153
Brain
  anatomy of, 13, 14, 109; and attention,
  107-110; at birth, 18; chemical makeup of,
  163; connection with eye, 108; development in second year, 58; effect of neglect
  on development of, 48; exercises for, 269-
  274; glossary of terms about, 13-14; gray
  matter development, 58, 59; imaging of,
  10-11; memory storage by, 115; music-
  caused changes in, 82, 84; nutrition for,
  161-170; pharmaceuticals for, 11; perception of the unexpected, 260-261; renewal
  of, 153, 227, 247, 301-307; resilience of,
  49-50; stress response, 51-52, 147-150; vitamins and, 163-164
Breakfast, importance of, 162
Broca's area, 261

Caffeine
  attention effects of, 173, 174; cognitive effects of, 171, 173; creativity effects of, 176; sources of, 171; tests to demonstrate effects of, 172, 175
Carbohydrates, 165, 169
Catecholamines, 248
Ceaucescu, Nicoleau, 48
Central executive, of working memory, 142
Central fissure, 109
Cerebellum, 14
  and memory, 132
Character
  affected by temperament, 73; distinguished from temperament, 68; parenting and, 73
Children
  language learning in, 32-33, 41, 42; neglect of, 48-53; parenting of, 72-76; self-consciousness in, 55-60; stimulation of, 74; visual perception of, 38-39
"Choking," as interference with muscle memory, 210
Cholesterol, 164, 166
Choline, 169
Cholinergic system, 183
Chunking, 119-120
  and short-term memory, 122
Classical conditioning, 137
Cloninger, Robert, 66, 70, 73
Cognitive therapy, for stress and depression, 248
Color, as memory aid, 243
Concentration, self test of, 106
Conceptual priming, 284, 289, 292
Conceptualization, age stability of, 228
Conditioning, 62
  classical, 137; as learning, 114
Constraint-seeking questions, 90-91
Cooley, Tatiana, 149
Corpus callosum, 14, 58
Cortex
  aging effects on, 302; anatomy of, 109; and memory, 132; parietal, 108; prefrontal, 52, 58, 63, 64, 108, 111, 181, 183, 184, 247; and sleep, 200, 201
Cortisol
  effects of, 151; and stress, 148, 249, 250, 251
Cramming, 128
CREB, 129, 130

CREB-2, 129-130
Cytowic, Richard, 83

D4 dopamine receptor gene, 69
Deception, 26
Decision making, focus and, 145-146
Declarative learning, 196
  REM sleep and, 210
Declarative memory, 62, 127
Deep processing, 159-160
Delta waves, 199
Dementia, 222, 224
  distinguished from normal memory decline, 286, 290-291; early learning and, 75, 224; education level and, 224; effects on brain, 247, 302; estrogen to combat, 306; future treatments for, 310-312; genetic factors in, 302-303, 310-311; homocysteine and, 164; incidence of, 284; intellectual activity to prevent, 227-228, 231, 309, 312-313; lifestyle and, 224, 227; music as treatment for, 265; nicotine as negative factor, 182-183; screening test for, 284, 289, 292; and sense of smell, 193; socioeconomic status and, 223-224; stem cells as treatment for, 311-312; stress and, 147; symptoms of, 290-291; types of, 310; vaccine for, 11, 310; Vitamin E as treatment for, 163
Dendrites, 304
Depression
  effects on brain, 247, 305; humor therapy for, 253; management of, 248-249; symptoms of, 179-180
Developmental verbal dyspraxia, 44
Digit span tests, 85
Direct interactions, in parenting, 72-73
Discipline, guidelines for, 58, 60
Distractions, 110-111, 144-145
  avoiding, 112, 262, 264; from caffeine, 173, 174
Dopamine
  activities that raise levels of, 181, 184; and ADHD, 52; drugs that raise levels of, 185; and learning, 181, 184; in stress response, 51; synthesis of, 169; and temperament, 69
Dreaming, 196, 199
During, Matthew, 75
Dyslexia
  and phonological loop, 122, 124; quick test for, 46; treatment of, 123-124

Early-onset Alzheimer's, 310
Einstein, Albert, 168
Elaboration, as memory strategy, 86-87, 243
Embedded figures test, 172
Emotion, 113
  and learning, 114-116; prefrontal cortex and, 180; smell and, 188
Emotional identification, in parenting, 73-74
Enrichment
  components of, 275, 279; and neurogenesis, 223; and vocabulary, 93
Epilepsy, music to counteract, 263
Epinephrine
  synthesis of, 169; and stress, 148
Episodic learning, 199
Episodic memory, 63, 136, 138, 140, 303
Estrogen, 249
  and Alzheimer's, 306; modulation of oxytocin by, 250
Estrogen replacement therapy, 249
Event-related brain potentials (ERPs), 215
Executive functions
  development of, 59; mind's ear and, 118-124; self test of, 22
Explicit memory, 62, 115
  distinguished from priming, 215-217
Eye
  connection to brain, 108; contact by babies, 23-24, 26; pupil dilation, 24

Faces, mental processing of, 235-236
False memories, 61-65, 205, 207
Family stories, in parenting, 76
Fear, 69-70
Fight-or-flight response, 250
First-order belief attribution, 25
Flashbulb memories, 188
Fleming, Ian, 130
Focus
  brain role in, 107-110; distraction and, 110-111, 144-145; effect of caffeine on, 174, 176; effort and, 144; and learning, 107; optimizing, 112; research on, 111-112
Foreign language learning, as brain exercise, 277-278
Free radicals, 163
Frontal lobe, 109
  aging and, 272-274; role in memory, 270-271; role in perception, 271-272

Garden path sentences, 143
Genealogy
  as brain exercise, 280-282; methodology of, 281; as stepping stone, 281-282
Genome, mapping of, 11
Glucocorticoid cascade, 148, 151
Glucocorticoids, in stress response, 51, 53, 248
Glucose, 165
Glutamate, nicotine and, 183
Grammar, development of, 30
Gray matter, 58
  development of, 59
Greek prefixes and roots, 95

Habits, memory and, 139
Habituation, 20-21, 62, 101-104, 137
Harm avoidance, dimension of temperament, 68
Hearing perception, development of, 30-33
Hemorrhagic stroke, 295
Hess, Eckhard, 24
HGH (human growth hormone), 197
Hippocampus, 14
  aging effects on, 302; effects of antidepressants on, 248-249, 305; effects of estrogen on, 249; and memory, 114, 132, 138, 241, 303; neurogenesis in, 227, 301-302, 303-304; and sleep, 199-200; stress effects on, 247; and stress response, 148, 150, 151
Homocysteine, 164
Hooking, 139-140
Humor
  cognitive processes involved in, 254; impairment of, 254-255; maintaining sense of, 257-258; physiology of, 257; therapeutic value of, 253
Hypothalamic-pituitary-adrenal (HPA) axis, 51

Imaging technology, advances in, 10-11
Immediate digit-span test, 120
Immune system, effects of stress on, 151-152, 245-247
Implicit memory, 62, 115, 214
  priming, 134, 214-217, 284, 289, 292
Infantile amnesia, 65
Infants
  bonding with mother, 30-31; emotional needs of, 50; eye contact by, 23-24, 26; hearing and sound discrimination by, 31-33; information processing of, 37-39; intel-

ligence measurement of, 36-37; language acquisition by, 29-33; memory in, 61-62; prenatal brain development, 19-21; solipsism of, 56; stress reduction for, 74
Inferential reasoning, tests of, 25, 27, 229
Information overload, 144-145
Insecure attachment, 52-53
Intelligence
  development of, 35-36; measurement of infant, 36
Involuntary attention, 174
Ischemic penumbra, 295
Ischemic stroke, 295
  treatment for, 298

Joyce, James, 168
Jung, Carl, 168

Kagan, Jerome, 58, 69, 70, 73, 94, 281
Kandel, Eric, 129
Kennedy, John F., 277
Knowledge
  and memory, 88, 225; reconsideration of, 276-277; and understanding, 276
Ky, Katherine, 78

Language learning, 16
  adult, as brain exercise, 277-278; child vs. adult, 32-33; effects of, 74; stages in childhood, 41, 42; stages in infancy, 28-29
Language skills, test of, 46-47
Late-onset Alzheimer's, 310
Lateral fissure, 109
Latin prefixes and roots, 95
Laughter, 253
Learned apathy, 153-154
Learning
  addiction to, 178-185; appropriate pacing of, 34; conditioning as, 114; declarative, 196; episodic, 199; language, 29-33; nondeclarative, 135; organization and, 128; prefrontal cortex and, 181, 184; prenatal, 16-21; sleep and, 195-201; stimulation and, 74, 75; stress as inhibitor of, 247
Learning addiction
  dopamine and, 181, 184; game for, 178; left brain and, 179-181; testosterone and, 184
Left brain
  anatomy of, 14; and attitude, 179-180; information processing by, 256; and remembering names, 235-236; tasks exercising, 181

Lennox-Gastaut syndrome, 263
Levels of processing, 157-160
Limbic system, 14, 114
  and emotions, 180
Limits, setting, 60
Loftus, Elizabeth, 204-207
Logical reasoning, tests of, 230
Long-term memory, 127-131
  formation of, 210
Lying, 26
  distinguished from false memory, 61-65

Medial temporal lobe, and memory, 132, 135
Memory
  acetylcholine and, 169; age-related loss of, 220-231; alteration of, 203-207; autobiographical, 63; chunking and, 119-120, 122; competitions for, 149-150; declarative, 62, 127; development of, 62-63; episodic, 63, 136, 138, 140, 303; erasure of, 207-208; expectations and, 203-204, 206, 207; explicit, 62, 115, 215-217; false, 205, 207; flashbulb, 188; implicit, 62, 115, 214; knowledge and, 88, 225; levels of processing, 157-160; long-term, 127-131, 210; meaningful arrangement and, 155-157; molecular basis of, 129-130; muscle, 139-140, 210; nondeclarative, 135, 201; and organization, 87; physiology of, 114-115, 132, 135-136, 270-271; prenatal development of, 19-20; priming, 134, 212, 214-218; procedural, 127, 138, 139, 140, 200, 201; recency effect, 121; recognition, 62, 272-273; rehearsal and, 121, 127-128; semantic, 136, 138, 140, 213-214, 303; short-term, 122, 127, 129; smell and, 187-193; source, 63, 216, 271-272, 273; storage of, 115; stress as inhibitor of, 148-150, 247; techniques for enhancing, 241-244; tests of, 64, 85, 87, 223, 229-230; types of, 62-63, 133-140; working, 43, 46, 63, 110, 121-122, 142, 222, 223, 229-230, 256, 264
Memory strategies, 85, 286, 289
  elaboration, 86-87; exercise for, 90-91; learning of, 87-88; organization, 86; rehearsal, 86; use of, 89
Mental exercise
  games, 227-228, 231; genealogy, 280-282; importance of, 275, 279; language learning, 277-278; music performance, 81-84, 259-266; and neurogenesis, 309; puzzles, 178-185

Miller, George, 119
Miller, Zell, 78, 79
Mind, theory of, 25, 26, 61
Mindlessness, 141
reducing, 142, 143, 144; upside of, 142-143
Mnemonics, 128
advantages of, 241-242; bases for, 155, 272; for remembering names, 238-239; visual, 98, 158, 188, 191
Monoamines, 167
Monounsaturated fatty acids, 166
Moods, and health, 245-246
Mozart, Wolfgang, 77, 262
Mozart effect
popular conception of, 77, 266; research on, 78-79, 261-262; and spatial-temporal reasoning, 80
Muscle memory, 139-140, 210
Music
as Alzheimer's therapy, 265; brain localization of, 259-260; calming effect of, 262, 264; to counteract aging, 265-266; cultural considerations in, 264-265; effects of listening to, 77-79, 261-262; effects of playing, 81-84, 259-266; reducing seizures, 263; and short-term memory, 145, 262, 264; and spatial-temporal intelligence, 262
Myelin, 58, 123
Myelination, 123

Nabokov, Vladimir, 83
Names, remembering, 233-239
Napping, importance of, 162, 164
Natural-language tests, 229-230
Neglect
case study of, 48; effects of, 49-50; stress caused by, 50-51
Neurogenesis, 153, 301
environmental stimulation and, 227, 303-304; and memory, 303; mental exercise and, 309; physical exercise and, 305; stress effects on, 247
Neurotransmitters
diet and, 167; laughter and production of, 253; synthesis of, 169; and temperament, 69
Nicotine, and memory, 182-183
Non-words test of language skills, 46-47
Nondeclarative memory, 135, 201
Norepinephrine
synthesis of, 169; and stress, 148; and temperament, 69, 70

Novelty seeking, dimension of temperament, 68
Novelty tests, of babies, 37-38
Nutrition, 161-162
brain effects of, 165, 169-170, 305-306; importance of breakfast, 162; naps and, 162, 164; omega-3 fatty acids, 166-168; reduced-calorie diet, 305-306; vitamins, 163-164

Occipital lobe, 109
Olfactory bulb, 187
Omega-3 fatty acids
to combat mental illness, 166-168; sources of, 166-167
Optimism, and health, 245-246
Organization, as memory strategy, 86
Ornstein, Robert, 101
Oxytocin, and stress, 250, 251

Paper Folding test of spatial-temporal reasoning, 79
Parenting
direct interactions, 72-73; effects of, 94; emotional identification, 73-74; family stories, 76; reading, 94; and vocabulary development, 94, 96
Parietal cortex, 108
Parietal lobe, 109
Parkinson's disease, 312
Pavlov, Ivan, 102
Persistence, dimension of temperament, 68
Personality. See Character; Temperament
Pheromones, 189-191
Phonological loop, 46
capacity of, 124; chunking and, 119-120; dysfunctions of, 122, 124; rehearsal and, 121; self test of, 118; and working memory, 121-122
Phonological processing, 157, 159
Phonological-syntactic deficit, 44
Physical exercise
importance of, 275, 279; and neurogenesis, 305
Planning skills, self test of, 22
Planum temporale, and music skill, 260
Polyunsaturated fatty acids, 166
in brain, 163
Pragmatics, defined, 44
Prefrontal cortex, 52
aging effects on, 302; and attention, 108; development of, 58, 64; and emotions,

180; and humor, 254, 255, 257; and learning, 181, 184; and memory, 63; nicotine
and, 183; MRI scans of, 111; stress effects
on, 247
Prenatal brain
learning by, 19; memories formed by, 19-
20; studies of, 20-21
Pride, development of, 58
Priming, 134, 214-215
conceptual, 284, 289, 292; distinguished
from explicit memory, 215-217; neural
bases of, 216-217; self test of, 212
Procedural memory, 127, 138, 140
accessibility of, 139; sleep and, 200, 201
Procedural skills, 209
REM sleep and, 210
Protein, 165
Proust, Marcel, 187, 192
Prozac
effect of, 69; as social force, 11
Psychoneuroimmunology, 245
Psychopathy, 180
Pupil dilation, 24
Putamen, and memory, 132

Rapoport, Judith, 59
Rauscher, Frances, 78
Reaction time, caffeine and, 174
Reading, benefits of, 94
Reagan, Ronald, 210
Recall, vs. recognition, 287-289
Recency effect, 121
Recognition memory, 62, 272-273
vs. recall, 287-289
Rehearsal, as memory strategy, 86, 127-128
REM sleep, 196, 200, 201
and learning, 210-211
Remembering names, 233-234
difficulties with, 235; strategies for, 234,
237-239
Reward dependence, dimension of tempera-
ment, 68
Right brain
and humor, 254, 255; information process-
ing by, 256
Rimski-Korsakov, Nikolai, 83
Role models, 74
Schacter, Daniel, 206, 214, 272
Schizophrenia, dietary control of, 167-168
Sea slug, as subject for habituation studies,
101-103, 137

Second-order belief attribution, 25, 27
Secure attachment, 52, 53
Seizures, music to counteract, 263
Self tests
of concentration, 106; of executive func-
tions, 22; of mind's ear, 118; of priming,
212; Self-awareness; development of, 56;
test of, 57
Self-consciousness
consequences of, 57-58, 60; development
of, 55, 56-57
Semantic memory, 136, 138, 140, 303
characteristics of, 213-214; hooking to
muscle memory, 139-140
Semantic processing, 157-158
Semantic-pragmatic disorder, 44
Sense of coherence (SOC), and health, 246-
247
Serotonin, 165
and neurogenesis, 305; and temperament, 69
Shallow processing, 157
Shame, development of, 58
Shaw, Gordon, 78, 84
Short-term memory, 122, 127
physiology of, 129
sIgA antibody, stress and, 152
Sleep
aging and, 197; attitudes toward, 195;
effects of lack of, 195-196, 198; and learning of new skills, 196, 199; need for, 201;
REM, 196, 200, 201, 210-211; slow-wave,
197-198, 199-200; tests to demonstrate
effects of lack of, 198-199
Smell
Alzheimer's and, 193; and behavior, 191-
192; descriptions of, 188; and emotions,
188; importance of, 187; and memory,
187; and sexuality, 189-191; unconscious
dimension of, 192-193
Social stimulation, importance of, 275, 279
Sound discrimination, evolution of, 31-33
Source memory, 63, 216
confusion in, 273; importance of, 271-272;
music and, 262
Spatial-temporal intelligence, 79, 80
music and, 262
Specific language impairment (SLI), 40-41
example text, 43; genetic aspect of, 42-43;
symptoms of, 44; and working memory,
43-44
Starches, 165

Stem cells
    implantation of, for brain diseases, 311-
    312; regenerative capabilities of, 11
Strange Situations test, 53
Strategizing skills, 64
Stress
    and age-related mental decline, 151; brain
    response to, 51-52, 147-151; caused by
    neglect, 50; and disease, 147, 148, 153-154;
    effects on brain, 247-248; experiments on,
    153; gender-based responses to, 249-251;
    humor therapy for, 253; immune effects of,
    151-152, 245-247; learning inhibition by,
    247; management of, 248-251; memory
    inhibition by, 148-150, 247; physiological
    effects of, 51, 249; reduction of, 53, 74, 152
Striatum, and memory, 132
Stroke
    symptoms of, 295-296; risk factors for,
    299; treatment of, 298, 300; types of, 295
Synesthesia, 83
Syntax, defined, 44

Temperament
    affecting character, 73; childhood vs.
    adult, 70-71; components of, 66-67; envi-
    ronmental influences on, 71; models of,
    66, 67; neurotransmitters and, 69-70; traits
    composing, 68-69
Temporal lobe, 109
    and memory, 132, 135
Tend-and-befriend response, 250
Testosterone, 250
    and learning, 184
Thalamus, 14, 108
Theory of mind, 25, 26, 61
Tissue plasminogen activator (TPA), 298
    mechanism of action of, 298, 300

Tower of Hanoi, 64
Transient global amnesia (TGA), 295
    symptoms of, 297-298
Transient ischemic attack (TIA), 295
    consequences of, 297; symptoms of, 297
Tyrosine, 169

Van Cauter, Eve, 197
Verbal dyspraxia, developmental, 44
Visual 20 Questions, memory enhancement
    game, 90-81
Visual mnemonics, 98
    examples of, 188, 191; mechanism of, 158
Visual perception, development of, 38-39
Visualization, 209-211
Visuospatial sketchpad, 142
Vitamin B complex, importance of, 164
Vitamin E, 163-164
Vitamins, 163-164
Vocabulary
    age stability of, 228; environmental fac-
    tors, 93; genetic factors, 93; Greek-derived,
    95; Latin-derived, 95; parenting and devel-
    opment of, 94, 96; strategies for building,
    97-99; visual mnemonics for, 98
Voluntary attention, 174
Vomeronasal organ, 189

Weiskrantz, Lawrence, 214
Working memory, 63
    age-related slowdown of, 222; central exec-
    utive component of, 142; effect of humor
    on, 256; effect of music on, 264; impor-
    tance of, 110; and information overload,
    144-145; phonological loop component of,
    46, 121-122, 142; sleep and, 197; and SLI,
    43; tests of, 64, 223, 229-230; visuospatial
    sketchpad component of, 142

 Catch a New Brain Wave!

Brainwaves® Books ■ 252 Great Western Road ■ South Yarmouth, MA 02664

Please see page 5 for our other titles. Order them from your
bookseller or at **www.brainwaves.com**
For questions or special orders, call toll-free **1-877-876-2787**